P9-BYU-644

ALSO BY ROB NEYER

Baseball Dynasties: The Greatest Teams of All Time
(with Eddie Epstein)

Feeding the Green Monster

Rob Neyer's Big Book of Baseball Lineups:
A Complete Guide to the Best, Worst, and Most Memorable Players
to Ever Grace the Major Leagues

The Neyer/James Guide to Pitchers:
An Historical Compendium of Pitching, Pitchers, and Pitches
(with Bill James)

ROB NEYER'S

BIG BOOK OF
BASEBALL
BLUNDERS

A COMPLETE GUIDE TO
THE WORST DECISIONS AND STUPIDEST MOMENTS
IN BASEBALL HISTORY

ROB NEYER

A FIRESIDE BOOK
PUBLISHED BY SIMON & SCHUSTER

NEW YORK   LONDON   TORONTO   SYDNEY

FIRESIDE
Rockefeller Center
1230 Avenue of the Americas
New York, NY 10020

Copyright © 2006 by Rob Neyer

All rights reserved,
including the right of reproduction
in whole or in part in any form.

FIRESIDE and colophon are registered trademarks
of Simon & Schuster, Inc.

For information regarding special discounts for bulk purchases,
please contact Simon & Schuster Special Sales at
1-800-456-6798 or business@simonandschuster.com.

Designed by Ruth Lee-Mui

Manufactured in the United States of America

1   3   5   7   9   10   8   6   4   2

Library of Congress Cataloging-in-Publication Data
Neyer, Rob.
Rob Neyer's big book of baseball blunders : a complete guide to the
worst decisions and stupidest moments in baseball history / Rob Neyer.
        p.   cm.
Includes bibliographical references and index.
1. Baseball—United States—History.
I. Title: Big book of baseball blunders.   II. Title.
        GV863.A1N49   2006
796.357'640973—dc22   2006040246

ISBN-13: 978-0-7432-8491-2
ISBN-10: 0-7432-8491-7

This book is for Don Zminda and Geoff Reiss.

THINGS IN THIS BOOK

An Approximate Guide

HELLO, AND GOOD LUCK

"What's a blunder?"

When I told people . . . cab drivers, deliverymen, the produce guy at the grocery store . . . I was writing a book about baseball blunders, that was always what they wanted to know. What's a blunder?

Here's what a blunder isn't: a blunder isn't a physical mistake or an error of judgment in the heat of the moment. In other words, in my book (in *this* book) it's only a blunder if there was premeditation. Bill Buckner did not blunder when he let that ball squirt between his legs; John McNamara did blunder when he let Bill Buckner let that ball squirt between his legs.

So that's one requirement: the blunder must be premeditated. Somebody has to have thought, "Hey, *this* would be a good idea."

Another requirement: a reasonable person might, *at the time*, have made a reasonable case for doing something else. It's impossible to avoid the temptation of hindsight, and I'm not going to ignore a player's on-base percentage simply because his manager had never heard of on-base percentage. But I'll be as fair as I can be.

And thirdly—or rather, ideally, because some of the blunders in this book don't completely meet this test—the blunder must have led to some reasonably ill outcome. You're not going to find much in this book about the St. Louis Browns or the Boston Braves or other similarly woebegotten franchises, because their fortunes were far beyond the reach of just one move, good or bad. In fact, many of the blunders within were committed by *good* teams and *good* managers and *good* general managers. Their blunders are generally the ones that mattered.

Premeditation. Contemporary questionability. Ill effects. That's the perfect blunder. And most of the blunders in this book are, to me at least, perfect. Occasionally I've fudged a bit on the last of those categories, but I think you'll agree with me that, even if the Indians' ten-cent Beer Night did no lasting damage, it was a pretty crummy idea.

Some might argue that it's cruel of me to highlight the failures of my fellow men. After all, haven't they suffered enough? Well, maybe they have. But 1) many of the men featured within these pages are no longer walking this earth, and 2) there's nothing I'm going to write that hasn't been written elsewhere, and with less compassion than I've got in my medium-sized heart.

And again, this book isn't about *mistakes*. Every pitcher grooves the occasional slider, every hitter sometimes misses a hit-me fastball in the middle of the strike zone, and every umpire blows a big call every so often. But there's only so much we can do with those. Yes, Luis Aparicio slipped as he rounded third base in a big game in 1972, and if he hadn't slipped the Red Sox might have wound up in the World Series. Yes, the umpires blew any number of calls during the 2005 World Series, without which the Astros might at least have won a game or two.

But what are we supposed to do with those? I remember reading about an umpire who, when he got a call wrong and knew it, would tell the protesting manager, "Okay, so I missed that one. Now what do we do?"

We can use Luis Aparicio to illustrate a cautionary tale about taking special care when rounding third base, and we can use Don Denkinger to argue for the use of instant replay in important baseball games. But *then* what do we do? We can't really hold Aparicio or Denkinger responsible for what happened—they weren't trying to do what they did—and neither can we really learn much from what happened. All of which is my long-winded way of saying that this book isn't about Luis Aparicio and Don Denkinger or any of the other thousands of players and umpires who have, at some key moment in baseball history, messed up. This book is, for the most part, about managers and general managers and owners who sat down, considered something for at least a moment, and said, "I sure think *this* would be a good idea." Except it wasn't.

A Note about Statistics

For better or worse, this book isn't filled with sophisticated statistical methods. It's not that I don't care about such things. If you've read my work in other places, you know that I do. It's just that I've found that blunt instruments do, for the most part, tell us most of what we want to know.

You will find, in these pages, a few statistical measures that you don't see in your newspaper every day, but they're nothing to get worked up about.

"ERA+" is simply the ratio of the league ERA to the pitcher's ERA (adjusted for the pitcher's home ballpark). An ERA+ of 100 is dead average. Anything above 100 is better than average, anything below 100 is worse than average, and yes it's really that simple. My source for ERA+ (and many of the other statistics in this book) was www.baseball-reference.com. (My other primary source for statistics was www.retrosheet.org, which is only the greatest Web site in the history of the InterWeb.)

Win Shares are somewhat more complicated, but here's what you need to know: Win Shares were invented by Bill James. Win Shares are published in *Total Baseball* and various other books and Web sites. Win Shares represent an effort to sum a player's total value to his team, including hitting, pitching, fielding, and base-stealing. Three Win Shares equals one win (so a player with thirty Win Shares is worth three wins more than a player with twenty-one Win Shares). And why Win Shares? Because Win Shares are the best tool we've got for evaluating the long-term impact of trades, and trades occasionally will come up in the pages that follow.

Sometimes I'll write that a player "batted .300"; that means his batting average was .300. Sometimes I'll write that a player "batted .300/.400/.500"; those numbers are his batting average, his on-base percentage, and his slugging percentage.

And that's about it. I told you, I'm not sophisticated.

A Note about Tables

I can't help myself. I just love 'em. I wrote another book a few years ago, with a title similar to this one, that was essentially three hundred pages of tables. Nobody squawked, because the book wouldn't have worked without tables. This one, though, would've been just fine without them, and if one hundred authors were asked to write a book like this one, ninety-five would make do without any tables (or with many fewer of them).

I like them, though, so I use them. Don't be afraid. They're just more words, except they look like numbers (or maybe the words are numbers, except they look like words; I can't remember).

A Note About the Old Days

You're not going to find much about them here. I tried. I really did. I asked all my friends to suggest long-ago blunders, and I even came up with a few candidates on my own.

In 1890, the players formed their own league. They called it the Players' League. Most of the best players joined up, and I suspect one could make a fairly convincing argument that the National League in 1890, bereft of its stars, wasn't really a "major" league at all. The Players' League competed directly against the National League in seven cities, and attracted more fans in five of them. Both leagues lost a great deal of money, and after the season the Players' League—especially the nonplayers who provided most of the financial backing—blinked first during negotiations with the National. The players would have to wait for another eighty-five years for some measure of justice.

Following the 1899 season, the National League contracted, shedding franchises in Baltimore, Louisville, Washington, and Cleveland. This came near the end of a period in which the magnates practiced something called "syndicate baseball," whereby many owners had financial interests in more than one team. You can, I suspect, see the problem with such an arrangement, and in '99 this was manifested in its illogical extreme, as the Cleveland Spiders won twenty games and lost 134.

Contraction helped foster the nascent American League, which opened play in 1900 with a team in Cleveland, and in 1901 shifted franchises to Baltimore and Washington. That began a sort of war between the leagues, which wound up costing everybody a lot of money. And the National League owners might have saved themselves the headache if they'd kept franchises in Washington and Cleveland, placed new franchises in Detroit and New York, and formed two six-team divisions. (Yes, I know this takes some imagination. Now you see why this doesn't get its own chapter.)

In 1908, Fred Merkle neglected to touch second base in a big game late in the season. This was certainly a blunder—actually, at the time it was called a "boner"—but for the purposes of this book, it wasn't a "blunder" because Merkle didn't think about not touching second base. It was more or less an accepted practice, and he certainly didn't consider the possible ramifications.*

On the last day of the 1910 season, the St. Louis Browns conspired to throw the American League batting title to Nap Lajoie, and away from Ty Cobb. The winner of the title had been promised a shiny new Chalmers "30" automobile, and just about everybody in the American League was pulling for Lajoie. Cobb, apparently with a safe lead in the race, decided to skip the Tigers' last two games. To catch Cobb, Lajoie would need a hit in nearly every at-bat during a doubleheader against the Browns on the season's final day. And thanks to the Browns, that's what Lajoie did.

Browns manager Jack O'Connor told rookie third baseman Red Corriden to play deep when Lajoie batted. Real deep. Lajoie tripled in his first at-bat. In each of his next eight at-bats, though, Lajoie bunted toward third base, and was credited with seven hits and one fielder's choice. (After the fielder's choice, Browns coach Harry Howell sent a note to the official scorer, offering to buy the scorer a new suit if he would change his ruling.)

The results? They're complicated. Lajoie went 8 for 9, but when the figures were computed, Cobb was still ahead by a single point, .385 to .384.†

---

* For more on Merkle, you'll have to wait for my next book: *Rob Neyer's Big Book of Baseball Boners* (and yes, I'll be self-publishing that one).

† In 1981, researchers discovered that Lajoie actually finished one point ahead of Cobb, but two of Cobb's hits had been double-counted. Whether this was done purposefully, to redress the injustice of the season's final day, we'll probably never know.

In the end, though, Chalmers awarded automobiles to both players, O'Connor and Howell were both fired, and Ban Johnson "used his vast influence to ensure that neither man found a job with a team in Organized Baseball."

So yes, there were some blunders there. There were others, I'm sure. Connie Mack's decision to break up his pennant-winning A's after the 1914 World Series certainly looks strange to us, today. But the first blunder that gets the full treatment in this book happened in 1917.

A Note About Our Sad Legacy

Segregation wasn't a blunder.

From 1884 through 1945, every major league and perhaps every minor league in so-called "Organized Baseball" enforced a strict policy that excluded any man who might be considered a "Negro" (in the parlance of the time). And after 1945? For every team, from the Dodgers to the Red Sox, you'll find a story about a team that could have signed Jackie Robinson—or Satchel Paige, or Willie Mays, or some other future Hall of Famer—but didn't, because his skin wasn't the right color.

That's not a blunder. That's a crime. I've left this crime out of the book because of its enormity, and because there's a sameness to the stories. Yes, maybe the Red Sox had a clear look at Jackie Robinson but weren't interested because they were racists. But what about the Athletics and the Yankees and the Browns and all the rest of the teams?

Yes, the Red Sox were particularly slow to integrate. And yes, this probably hurt their chances in the American League during the 1950s and early '60s. The Yankees' general lack of interest in black players probably started showing up on the field in the early '60s, and thus was an instrument in their sudden decline. Serious books have been written about the failures of all the teams, and about the failures of specific teams, to integrate earlier and more effectively. All those books are worth reading, but I didn't believe I could do the topic justice in this particular book.

A Final Word

Enjoy.

WHITE SOX REPLACE HITTER WITH CROOK

Chick is a fighting ball player. He has no friends among the opposing players during a game, and his presence on first base will liven up our infield and keep the other boys battling all the time.

—*Chicago Tribune*, 1917

Let's say you've got Justin Morneau playing first base for your team, but you've got a chance to replace him with Darin Erstad. Do you do it?

Wait, don't answer.

Imagine that Erstad, instead of being the selfless, hustling ballplayer that Angels fans have grown to love so much, is a selfish bastard who will do just about anything for a few extra bucks.

Now do you do it?

Probably not. The Chicago White Sox did, though.

Jack Fournier debuted with the White Sox in 1912, when he was twenty-two. After struggling against major-league pitchers for a couple of seasons, Fournier broke through with a .311 batting average and a .443 slugging percentage that was sixth-best in the American League in 1914 (remember, this was the Dead Ball Era). The next year he slugged .491:

higher than Cobb, higher than Joe Jackson, higher than Speaker . . . higher than everybody. He was twenty-five, and a slugging star.

Fournier slumped terribly in 1916, though. And after just one at-bat—a strikeout—in 1917, the White Sox shipped him to Los Angeles (then a Pacific Coast League town), having given his job at first base to a slick-fielding veteran named Charles Arnold "Chick" Gandil.

Fournier played well in Los Angeles, earning a month with the Yankees in 1918. There was some controversy over who owned the rights to Fournier, and in 1919 he returned to Los Angeles. A few years later, as Fournier was preparing to return to the majors with the Cardinals, *The Sporting News* noted, "Fournier failed to please with the White Sox or the Yankees in the American League. In Chicago they wanted him to live up to the Jiggs Donahue brand on first—and be an outfielder as well. He wasn't consid-

Advance Scouting . . .
Black Sox—Style

Regarding the Black Sox scandal, have you ever wondered what the hell utility infielder Fred McMullin, whose action was limited to two pinch-hitting appearances, did to earn his $5,000 share of the filthy lucre? You may recall that he became a conspirator only because he overheard Chick Gandil and Swede Risberg plotting indiscreetly, and demanded a piece of the action. Once involved, though, he was no mere passive participant. He worked hard at the corruption of the other players needed to assure a successful fix, particularly the all-important Eddie Cicotte. On the field, he singled meaninglessly late in Game 1. His other at-bat, in Game 2, actually meant something, though. The Sox were down only 4–2, with a runner on first and two outs. McMullin ended the game with a groundout. Still, it would seem he cut himself a pretty good deal.

There may have been more. Years ago, I read Warren Brown's *The Chicago White Sox* and discovered that the Sox's advance scout for the World Series was none other than Fred McMullin. And it makes sense: the full-time advance scout as we know him did not exist in 1919; why not send an unneeded veteran player? (A probably unanswerable question: did McMullin lobby for the job, or was it foisted upon him?)

Now, you might reasonably ask, so what? What difference did it make what kind of a scouting report McMullin returned with? Eight players had already decided to

ered 'smart' enough for the White Sox style. In New York they thought he should be a Hal Chase and a Tris Speaker combined."[1]

Were the White Sox smart to replace Fournier in the lineup with Gandil? Here are their Win Shares in each season from 1914—when Fournier was twenty-four, Gandil twenty-seven—through 1920:

	Fournier	Gandil
1914	17	17
1915	28	16
1916	9	12
1917	*15*	16
1918	*15*	10
1919	*18*	13
1920	19	*12*

Those italicized Win Shares for Fournier and Gandil are simply educated guesses at what they would have done, had they spent those seasons in the majors. Fournier's are based mostly on what he actually did with the Los Angeles Angels. In 1917, he batted .305. In 1918, he batted .325 to finish third in the Pacific Coast League batting race and stole thirty-seven bases, then batted .350 in twenty-seven games with the Yankees. In 1919, back in Los Angeles, his .328 batting average was good for sixth in the PCL and he topped the loop with nineteen triples.

In 1920, Fournier joined the St. Louis Cardinals. He didn't show any home-run power—that would come in '21—but he did bat .306, and ranked in the top ten in the National League in both on-base and slugging average.

Gandil didn't play in 1920. He'd have been thirty-three that season, and twelve Win Shares seems like a reasonable estimate of what he might have done. As it happened, that season's actual White Sox first baseman (Shano Collins) did earn a dozen Win Shares. So either way, the Sox would have been better off with Fournier in 1918, in 1919, and in 1920.

I have, of course, been avoiding the 800-pound gorilla in the room.

In 1919, eight Chicago White Sox conspired to throw the World Series. Gandil was, by most accounts, the conspiracy's ringleader.

In *The Great Baseball Mystery: The 1919 World Series*, author Victor Luhrs is about as kind as anybody could be, writing, "Jackson, Felsch, Weaver, and Cicotte did give their best efforts . . ."

Buck Weaver? Sure. That's what everybody tells me. But those other three guys? As I said, Luhrs is exceptionally kind. But about Gandil he writes, "At no point did Gandil and [co-conspirator Swede] Risberg give their best efforts."

Gandil made a small fortune, as did Eddie Cicotte. According to Warren Brown in *The Chicago White Sox*, shortly after the Series ended in Cincinnati's favor, Gandil was seen "with a new automobile, diamonds, and other marks of sudden affluence." He probably pocketed $10,000, though it might have been more.

That winter there were all sorts of whispers and half-hearted investigations, and perhaps Gandil, who wintered on the West Coast, figured he wouldn't gain anything by coming back east in the following spring. Whether because he didn't want to play or because the White Sox didn't want him, Gandil stayed home. And after the scandal broke late in the '20 season, he was officially banned for life from Organized Baseball.

Not many observers made the obvious connection between the White Sox letting Fournier get away and what happened in 1919. Fred Lieb did, though. In 1921 he wrote

> Fournier isn't the smartest player in the business, and throws have to come to him just so at first or he doesn't get them. But the Canadian always is trying and hustling, and has a pretty good idea of his ability as a hitter.

Transcendental Graphics

Jacques Fournier

dump the Series, and that was that. But think for a moment. McMullin was a bit player whose very presence in the conspiracy was strictly an accident. The seven others—five regulars and the club's top two starters—didn't need his help to lose. How could he be sure to get his fair share of the booty? By contributing in every way possible.

What better way to cover yourself and your co-conspirators than to drag your honest teammates down with you? And how best to do that? Maybe by feeding them false information about what to expect from the Cincinnati pitchers. Is there any direct evidence that this happened? No. But a peek at the batting statistics for the Series makes you wonder, because there is no apparent disparity between Clean Sox and Black Sox hitting. Conspiracy leader Gandil batted .233; future Hall of Famer Eddie Collins .226. Risberg was a miserable .080; Nemo Leibold a pitiful .056. Shano Collins contributed an empty .250.

Ray Schalk was the only impressive Clean Sock, checking in at .308. But oddly, even he was topped by two Black Sox: Buck Weaver batted .324 and slugged .500, while Shoeless Joe Jackson (who may have saved his bumbling for the field) batted .375 and slugged .563. What unites Weaver and Jackson? Perhaps the fact that they would have known better than to listen to a Fred McMullin scouting report.—*Mike Kopf*

Had Comiskey retained Fournier instead of engaging Gandil, the Old Roman might have been able to sidestep the great disgrace of his career, the scandal of 1919. Fournier likes to hit and win too well to have been mixed up in such a filthy mess.

Fournier wasn't Canadian—he was born in Michigan and grew up on the Washington coast—but everything else here seems about right. (Fournier really did like to hit; prior to the 1917 season, *The Sporting News* reported that he'd "rigged up a batting device which he believes will put him in the .300 class next season.")[2]

Perhaps it's overly generous to simply assume that Fournier wouldn't have been tempted by the big money the gamblers offered. It's not that he was a bad guy. But a lot of non-bad guys in those days did not have serious qualms about throwing the occasional ballgame if the money was right.

Frankly, we can't know that Fournier wouldn't have been "mixed up in such a filthy mess." But without Gandil, there probably wouldn't have *been* a filthy mess. The details of the scandal remain murky, of course, but the general consensus is that Gandil conceived the conspiracy in the first place.

It's certainly *possible* that if Gandil hadn't been around, somebody else would have figured out a way to throw the World Series. But it's incredibly unlikely. When the White Sox threw over Jack Fournier for Chick Gandil, they cost themselves a few games over the next few seasons because Fournier was much the superior hitter. But what they really lost was the World Series in 1919 and the American League pennant in 1920 (when the scandal broke on September 28, the Sox were only a half-game out of first place, but lost two of their last three games and finished two games behind Cleveland).

And beyond? Who knows. Aside from his outstanding 1915 performance, Fournier's best seasons were 1921 through 1924. And if the scandal hadn't resulted in the dismemberment of the roster . . . well, as I said, who knows? A lot of things would have been different.

---

1. *Sporting News*, Feb. 19, 1920, p. 2.

2. *Sporting News*, Jan. 18, 1917, p. 4.

FRAZEE SELLS RUTH

Nineteen nineteen, their miserable greedy pig of a boss decides to sell Babe Ruth to the Yankees to finance a Broadway musical. And since 1919, the Red Sox have not won a World Series. And the Yankees have won twenty-six.

—Ben, in *Fever Pitch* (2005)

In the space of three years and two days—December 18, 1918, through December 20, 1921—the Red Sox made four significant deals with the Yankees, deals that essentially stocked a Yankees roster that would, beginning in 1921, win three straight American League pennants. We'll save the biggest of the four deals until a little later . . .

July 29, 1919: Red Sox trade Carl Mays (79 Win Shares in the first three seasons following the trade) for Allan Russell (21), Bob McGraw (8), and $40,000.

Mays, one of the top pitchers in the American League, essentially forced a trade by leaving the club. On July 13, Mays suffered some tough breaks in the first two innings of a start in Chicago, and after being stranded on first base, he "stalked off into the clubhouse, showered, took a cab back to the hotel, gathered his belongings, and was on a train

before the game ended." Mays said he would never pitch another game for the Red Sox, and there was every indication that he meant it.[1] Faced with the prospect of receiving absolutely nothing on the field from Mays, Red Sox owner Harry Frazee decided to make the best of the bad situation, and traded Mays to the Yankees.

There was, however, a problem. When Mays walked out, the American League suspended him indefinitely. And according to league rules, a team was prohibited from trading a suspended player (which makes a great deal of sense, as you don't want players jumping to precipitate a trade). American League President Ban Johnson attempted to enforce the rule. The Red Sox and Yankees ignored him, and somehow they got away with it. (There would, however be ramifications.)

December 15, 1920: Red Sox trade Waite Hoyt (66), Wally Schang (46), Harry Harper (4), and

Mike McNally (9) for Del Pratt (48), Muddy Ruel (43), Hank Thormahlen (4), and Sammy Vick (0).

This was a rough one for the Red Sox almost solely because right-hander Waite Hoyt became a star after joining the Yankees. At the time of the deal, Hoyt had just turned twenty-one, and in his action with the Sox he'd gone 10–12 with ERA's higher than the league average. A few years earlier, when Hoyt was only eighteen, he'd pitched an inning for the Giants, but John McGraw was apparently unimpressed and returned him to the minors, no strings attached.

In Hoyt's first season with the Yankees, he won nineteen games. Second season: nineteen. He won twenty-two games in 1927, twenty-three in '28. Eventually Hoyt won 237 games and was (many years later) elected to the Hall of Fame (which was a mistake, but hey nobody's perfect).

The deal didn't work for the Red Sox because Hoyt became a star and "Lefty" Thormahlen became a bust. But Thormahlen, who was a couple of years older than Hoyt, could have become a star, too. In 1919, he'd gone 12–10 with a 2.62 ERA.

When this deal was made, most of the Boston writers figured it was, at worst, an equitable transaction, and one scribe opined, "it almost makes one think that Frazee is getting a conscience payment from the Yankee owners . . . all Boston fans must applaud the move."

December 20, 1921: Red Sox trade Everett Scott (36), Bullet Joe Bush (73), and Sad Sam Jones (53) for Jack Quinn (55), Roger Peckinpaugh (53), Rip Collins (34), and Bill Piercy (17).

Sam Jones was a fine pitcher and would remain one after joining the Yankees. But spitballer Jack Quinn was just as fine, and would pitch (and pitch well) for another eleven seasons . . . even though he was thirty-eight when the Red Sox got him. Trading Bullet Joe Bush did hurt the Red Sox, though it's worth mentioning that he had only a few more seasons of good pitching (after the '24 season, the Yankees wisely included him in a trade to the Browns for Urban Shocker).

Taken together, if you're going to fault the Red Sox for these trades, it can be based mostly on their failure to predict Waite Hoyt's and Joe Bush's futures (which, it should be said, might not have happened if they'd remained with the Red Sox). And those failures didn't break the Red Sox. In 1922 and '23 the Sox finished eighth; in '24 they squeaked into seventh place by half a game. The three deals listed above a) were not all that bad when they were made, b) were not considered particularly uneven by contemporary observers, and c) did not, with the exception of Hoyt and Bush, look all that bad in the long run.

There is an obvious question that must be answered: "But why did the Red Sox trade so many players to the Yankees?" Certainly, it doesn't look good. After the fact, some have concluded that the owners of the Red Sox and Yankees were conspiring to help the New Yorks and hurt the Bostons.

The answer is that Red Sox owner Harry Frazee didn't have many choices. When the Mays trade blew up, Ban Johnson's enmity toward Frazee only grew. The Yankees were on Frazee's side in the ongoing battles against Johnson, as were the White Sox—which, by the way, impacted the Black Sox scandal, but that's a story for another day—with the three teams becoming known as the Insurrectos. Meanwhile, the five other American League franchises backed Johnson, and would have as little to do with the rebels as possible. So Frazee traded with the Yankees because they would take his phone calls.

Now, the big one . . .

On December 26, 1919, Harry Frazee agreed to sell Babe Ruth to the Yankees. The terms were somewhat complicated: the Red Sox would receive $100,000: $25,000 in cash and three $25,000 notes, payable at one-year intervals, at six percent interest. (The owners of the Yankees also loaned Frazee $300,000, with Fenway Park serving as security.) The deal, the largest in baseball history, was contingent upon the Yankees signing Ruth to a new contract. Technically he already was under contract; prior to the 1919 season, Ruth signed a new contract that would pay him $30,000 over three years. But Ruth wanted more, and told the writers he wanted $20,000 for 1920 alone, or he might not play at all.

Rather than recite a list of Ruth's offenses while a member of the Red Sox, I would like to reproduce two passages from the 1920 *Reach Guide*, because I think it goes a long way toward expressing not only editor Francis Richter's feelings, but those of many who followed the game with professional interest . . .

NEW YORK'S JUDGMENT QUESTIONED

We question the judgment of the New York Club in buying another
player who has no respect for his obligations, who is not a team player
in any sense of the word, and who is a constant trouble-maker, according to Mr. Frazee's confession; and that, too, at a price which is out of

all reason. However, leaving the price out of consideration, where will the New York Club come out artistically? With Mays' assistance the New York Club could finish no better than a scant third, while Boston, with Ruth, was lucky to finish fifth. By adding Ruth to its team, the New York simply gains another undesirable and uncontrollable player, adds enormously to its expense account and its salary roll, and gains absolutely nothing except the probability of boosting Ruth's home-run record, which never did and never will win any pennants. This was proven by Boston's experience last year, despite Ruth's home-run record, and also by Detroit's experience, which finished fourth in spite of having five .300 hitters on its team.

JUST A DESPERATE GAMBLE

However, the deal has been made and New York is now the owner of Ruth's more or less remarkable services, and can proceed to capitalize Ruth for all of the publicity that can possibly be secured, and they will need it all, granting that Ruth will come up to expectations in every particular. If he doesn't—and that is very likely to happen with a player of his disposition—the New York Club will sustain a big loss. Just what kind of player Ruth is has been revealed by the magnate who has just sold him. Mr. Frazee is reported as saying: "While Ruth, without question, is the greatest hitter that the game has ever seen, he is likewise one of the most selfish and inconsiderate men that ever wore a base ball uniform. Had he possessed the right disposition, had he been willing to take orders and work for the good of the club, like the other men on the team, I would never have dared let him go. Twice during the past two seasons Babe has jumped the club and revolted. He refused to obey orders of the manager." That puts Ruth in a class with Mays, so far as respect for contract goes, and almost puts him by a class himself as an intractable player. The wonder is that the New York Club would take him on after knowing all this, assuming they did know it. We prefer to believe, however, that the New York Club is just taking one more desperate gamble on pennant honors and World's Series pelf.

Think about it. Ruth had set a new record in 1919 with twenty-nine home runs. Could anybody have guessed, even wildly, that Ruth would nearly double that mark just one year later? Not the editors of the *Spalding Guide*: "Perhaps, and most likely, Ruth will not be so successful in 1920. The pitchers will eye him with more than ordinary caution and they will twist

Babe Ruth

Transcendental Graphics

their fingers into knots to get more curve and still more curve on the ball. They will give one another private little tips."[2]

Ruth was—and for that matter still is, nearly ninety years later—a singular phenomenon. Nobody had any idea what he might do, except everybody knew that he would do something spectacular, that he would be paid a great deal of money for doing it, and that he would frustrate his employers all the while.

Selling Ruth did not, of course, benefit the Red Sox either in the short or the long term. It certainly could have, though. Frazee could have put the cash he received from the Yankees to good use. Ruth could have drunk and eaten himself out of baseball, or he could have contracted a debilitating case of syphilis, or he could have rammed one of his cars into a ravine and broken every bone in his body.

The Babe led a charmed life, though. He remained relatively healthy and incredibly productive for another fifteen years after the Red Sox sold him.

And finally, a few words about the demonization of Harry Frazee. It's often been written that Frazee sold Ruth in order to finance a Broadway production of a silly musical called *No, No, Nanette*. It's often been written that Frazee was a failure not only in baseball but also in his theatrical pursuits, and that he died in 1929 a poor man.

As Glenn Stout has ably demonstrated in various places—including in a long 2005 essay in *Elysian Fields Quarterly*—none of those things written about Frazee are true. Frazee was *not* in financial trouble when he traded Ruth. He simply thought the Yankees were offering a fair price for a player who'd become a huge headache. Frazee did *not* use the Yankees' money to finance *No, No, Nanette*, which wasn't put into production until 1925. Frazee did not die penniless. When Frazee died in 1929, the *New York Times* did report that he was nearly broke . . . but a few days later the *Times* issued a correction (which nobody noticed, of course), and eventually the value of his estate was reported as approximately $1.3 million.

Stout argues that much of the demonization of Frazee was fostered by baseball writer Fred Lieb, an anti-Semite who believed Frazee was Jewish (he wasn't). But whatever the reason for the misconceptions, unless you've read Stout, what you've read about Harry Frazee is mostly wrong.

1. Glenn Stout and Richard A. Johnson, *Red Sox Century: One Hundred Years of Red Sox Baseball* (Boston: Houghton Mifflin, 2000).
2. In Bill James, *The Bill James Historical Baseball Abstract* (New York: Villard Books, 1985).

BIG TRAIN RUNS OUT OF STEAM

In a grave of mud was buried Walter Johnson's ambition to join the select panel of pitchers who have won three victories in one World Series. With mud shackling his ankles and water running down his neck, the grand old man of baseball succumbed to weariness, a sore leg, wretched support and the most miserable weather conditions that ever confronted a pitcher.

—James B. Harrison, *The New York Times* (1925)

In 1924, it finally happened. In Walter Johnson's eighteenth season with the Washington Senators,* the club finally reached the World Series. And though Johnson lost Games 1 and 5 to the Giants, he earned a victory in Game 7 with four scoreless relief innings as the Nats won in the bottom of the twelfth.

Johnson waited eighteen years for his first World Series, but would have to wait just one more year for his second.

In the '24 Series, Johnson lost twice before winning Game 7. In the '25 Series, Johnson would *win* twice before *losing* Game 7.

In the opener, Johnson gave up just one run while racking up ten strikeouts. Afterward, Babe Ruth (or,

rather, Babe Ruth's ghostwriter) wrote, "I have watched Walter Johnson pitch a lot of ball games, but I don't believe I ever saw him when he was better than he was yesterday."

Johnson wasn't as overpowering in Game 4, striking out only two Pirates, but pitched a 4–0 shutout anyway. While running the bases in the third inning, Johnson aggravated an old leg injury. Trainer Mike Martin advised Johnson to retire from the game, but instead Johnson soldiered on after Martin wrapped the leg. (A couple of days later, on the train from Washington to Pittsburgh, Johnson reportedly suffered from a bad cold.)

Stan Coveleski started Game 5 for the Senators, and pitched well before getting knocked out (and losing) in the seventh inning. There was no scheduled day off between Game 5 in Washington and Game 6 in Pittsburgh. Alex Ferguson—who'd

---

* The franchise had officially been renamed "Nationals" in 1905, but most fans never stopped calling them "Senators," though newspaper headline writers appreciated the abbreviation, "Nats."

racked up a 6.18 ERA during the regular season—started Game 6, and like Coveleski he lost despite pitching reasonably well.

No team had ever been down three-one in a best-of-seven World Series and come back to win, but the Pirates were now threatening to do just that.

It had generally been expected that Johnson would pitch Game 7, if necessary. On October 12, the day after his Game 4 victory, Johnson said, "I didn't do any workout today outside of picking up a bat once in a while around the dugout, but I doubt that my sore leg will interfere if I have to go in. It's not so good today, but I think it will be all right."

Game 7 was scheduled for the 14th, but heavy rains caused postponement. As Lee Allen later wrote, "It rained hard all day when the seventh game should have been played, and Washington fans, hearing of the postponement, were deliriously happy with the news; for it meant that Walter Johnson, on whom all hopes were now pinned, would have a third day of blessed rest."

The field was still soaked on the 15th, but Johnson would get no more rest. Game 7 would be played.

The Senators made quick work of Pirates starter Vic Aldridge—working on only two days rest—who struggled terribly with the soggy pitcher's mound. Aldridge faced six hitters, walked three of them, uncorked two wild pitches, and was yanked with the bases loaded. Before reliever Johnny Morrison was able to stop the bleeding, the Senators had a 4–0 lead that must have seemed safe as houses.

Johnson batted in that inning, and it was obvious that his sore leg was bothering him. As *The Washington Post* noted in its pitch-by-pitch account, "Johnson bunted right down the first base line on the first pitch. Morrison waited for the ball to roll foul. It was apparent that the Washington pitcher could run with difficulty."

Then in the bottom of the first, "The Pittsburgh team started a bunting campaign, an easily understood move *with a crippled man in the box.*"

The crippled man shut down the Pirates in the first two innings, but they scored three runs in the third. The Nats scored two of their own in the fourth to forge a 6–3 lead.

In the bottom of the fifth the skies opened—literally and figuratively—as the first two Pirates doubled to plate a run. Johnson recovered, though, dispatching the next three Bucs with relative ease. And heading to the bottom of the seventh—the rain falling harder now—the Senators still owned a 6–4 lead. Second baseman Eddie Moore led off with a pop fly to short left field, which was muffed by shortstop Roger Peckinpaugh—already named American League MVP—for his seventh error of the Series. Max Carey followed with an RBI double, and two batters (and outs) later, Carey scored on Pie Traynor's triple. The inning ended when Traynor was thrown out trying for an inside-the-park homer, but now the game was tied.

With one out in the top of the eighth, Peckinpaugh homered to put the Senators back ahead by one run.

Walter Johnson took the mound in the bottom of the eighth, got two quick outs, and was one strike away from retiring Pirates catcher Earl Smith. But Smith doubled. Next,

> Carson Bigbee . . . hit an ordinary fly ball to right field that would have been an out any other day. This day it sailed through the gloom unseen and over Rice's head for another double, tying the game once again. Moore walked—Johnson's first free pass, surprisingly. Carey hit a routine grounder to short, and Peckinpaugh, instead of going to first for the easy out, played for the force at second. But Bucky Harris, positioned toward first for the left-handed-hitting Carey, had no chance to reach the base in time. In addition, Peckinpaugh's throw was high and only a great leaping grab by Harris kept it from going over his head into right field. It was Peckinpaugh's eighth error of the Series, and the most costly.[1]

Costly because Kiki Cuyler followed with a ground-rule double, scoring Bigbee and Moore with Pittsburgh's eighth and ninth runs of the game. Johnson retired the next batter to finally escape the inning.

In the top of the ninth, Red Oldham—no star, and the fourth Pirates pitcher of the game—retired the Nats in order, and Pittsburgh's unlikely comeback was complete.

The media in those days certainly wasn't as inquisitive as it would become, but Johnson's struggles in the seventh and eighth innings led to a great deal of second-guessing.

Bucky Harris supposedly replied, "I have no apologies or alibis. I went down with my best." A Dallas columnist wrote, "I believe Harris left Johnson in there because he had no one else who could pitch better than Big Barney." Catcher Muddy Ruel opined, a couple of years later, "I contend that Bucky was right in his judgement. We had confidence in Barney and I feel that if any Nationals pitcher could have come through with a victory, Johnson was the man."[2]

Maybe. But I really, really, really doubt it. There's no way of knowing how much Johnson's leg was hurting him; you can find sources saying the injury wasn't a factor at all, and you can find sources saying Johnson was in ter-

Letting Them Play

On October 14, with Pittsburgh's Forbes Field a sodden mess, Commissioner Kenesaw Mountain Landis postponed Game 7 of the 1925 World Series, and Washington Senators president Clark Griffith expressed relief. "World's Series games should be played on merit alone," he said, "and it would not have been a fair test of skill to have the two teams wallowing around in the mud."

So instead they wallowed around in the mud on October 15.

In the 1926 *Spalding's Official Base Ball Guide*, John B. Foster wrote of Game 7, "The field conditions were bad before the game began. To add to that, another drenching rain that fell all afternoon made the playing surface of Forbes Field a quagmire, and for the second time in succession saturated spectators with more water than most of them had encountered in years without protection against it . . . With outfielders invisible from the stands, rain pouring steadily, the field thick with mud like mortar, and the corners of the field blocked from the vision of those in the press box and in the center of the grand stand, the final inning was keenly fought as if the contestants were laboring under an invigorating June sun."

In *The Washington Senators*, Shirley Povich wrote, "Never had a ball game been ordered to proceed under such circumstances."

In *The Pittsburgh Pirates*, Fred Lieb wrote, "By the fifth inning a dark mist hung over the field, and the outfielders looked like

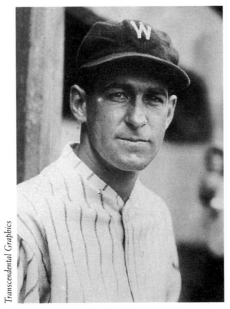

Transcendental Graphics

Bucky Harris

rible pain for nine innings. But considering all the evidence we've got, it's not at all far-fetched to guess that he was in less than perfect condition.

And then there were the conditions. It was raining from the fifth inning on, so Johnson's wool uniform would have been soggy, even heavier than usual. And considering the muddy mound, he'd likely have been throwing with an unnatural motion. Meanwhile, Pirates manager Bill McKechnie employed four pitchers, none for more than four innings.

Did Harris have anybody else who could have pitched? You bet.

◆ Stan Coveleski won twenty games that season; in fact, his record (20–5) and his ERA (2.84) were both better than Johnson's. He'd pitched decently in two Series starts, and had a couple of days to rest since the last one. He did have a sore back, though, at least according to one source.[3]

◆ Dutch Ruether won eighteen games during the regular season, but was shaky in September and hadn't pitched in the World Series at all.

◆ Tom Zachary pitched 218 innings for the Senators in '25, with a solid 3.85 ERA. He'd pitched only once during the Series, a couple of innings in Game 5, three days earlier.

Why had left-handers Ruether and Zachary pitched so little? During the World Series, Washington shortstop Roger Peckinpaugh (or his ghost-writer) wrote in the newspapers, "For some reason or other, Bucky is depending mostly upon his right-handers. I know that the McKechnie crew is said to dote on southpaw flinging . . ."[4]

Southpaws or not, though, either Ruether or Zachary would have been a good choice to start the eighth. Both were starters, of course, but in those days starters were routinely used as relievers, and anyway managers just didn't use good pitchers purely as relievers.

Except Bucky Harris. In 1924, Harris occasionally used a big flamethrower named Fred "Firpo" Marberry as a starter, but Marberry more often worked out of the bullpen. He led the American League with fifteen saves (figured many years later), and in the World Series he played a key role in each of Washington's three victories over the Giants. In 1925, Marberry worked exclusively out of the bullpen—it was the only season in his career in which he didn't start at least once—and again saved fifteen games, while also winning nine and posting a 3.47 ERA.

But Marberry hardly pitched in the '25 Series. In Game 3 he pitched two scoreless innings to preserve a 4–3 lead, and in Game 5 he faced two batters, giving up an RBI single and a fly-out. According to Marberry's entry in *Baseball: The Biographical Encyclopedia*, "Harris was widely criticized for underutilizing Marberry" in the World Series.

Perhaps. But Marberry wasn't right. On the eve of Game 7, the *Washington Post*'s Frank H. Young reported the following:

> Fred Marberry reported to Forbes field this afternoon with his salary wing sorer than ever. The big pitcher has re-strained the elbow first hurt in the Chicago series, on the Nats' final swing through the Western sector, and can not bend it properly. Mike Martin is working strenuously on the arm and hopes—but is not particularly optimistic—that he will have "Firpo" somewhere near ready for tomorrow in case he is needed.[5]

So Harris had the best reliever in the game, but he probably was not available. That's no excuse for not going to Coveleski or Ruether or Zachary, though. The Senators caught a lot of bad breaks in Game 7 (see sidebar), but it simply wasn't reasonable to expect an old and injured Johnson to pitch a complete game after all that he'd already done. Nevertheless, he threw 130 pitches[6] and gave up fifteen hits and nine runs. In the clubhouse after the game, Pirates manager McKechnie said, "Johnson didn't seem to have much stuff out there today and the boys continued their clouting."

President Ban Johnson of the American League sent Bucky Harris a telegram that read, "You put up a game fight. This I admire. Lost the series

ghoulish figures in the general gloom."

Nationals outfielder Goose Goslin would recall, roughly forty years later, "Oh, that was ridiculous. That seventh game of the 1925 World Series was played in a terrific rainstorm. I'm not kidding, it was pouring like mad from the third inning on, and by the seventh inning the fog was so thick I could just about make out what was going on in the infield from out there in the outfield.

"In the bottom of the eighth we were still ahead, 7–6, when Kiki Cuyler hit a ball down the right-field line that they called fair, and that won the game for Pittsburgh. It wasn't fair at all. It was foul by two feet. I know because the ball hit in the mud and *stuck* there. The umpires couldn't see it. It was too dark and foggy."[8]

I've bothered with all these accounts because a general idea of the conditions throughout the day is necessary if we're going to critique Commissioner Landis's decision to play through it all.

Many observers thought that the game should not have started at all. Others thought it should have been stopped after the fifth or sixth, with the Senators ahead by two runs; had that happened, the game would have been "official" and Washington would have been world champs. Others thought it should have been stopped in the seventh or eighth; had that happened, the game would have been declared a tie, with a Game 8 scheduled for the next dry afternoon.

The decision to begin Game 7

rested with Commissioner Kenesaw Mountain Landis, and it's a decision that must have weighed on him heavily.

The Series had already been delayed by a day, and the weather forecast—granted, meteorology was far from an exact science in those days—was far from encouraging: cold and wet for the foreseeable future.

So Landis let the game begin. And once it began, Landis was determined to see nine innings.

In fairness to Bucky Harris and Walter Johnson, it should be noted that the Senators were exceptionally unlucky in Game 7.

Perhaps it was just sour grapes, but everybody on the Washington side was absolutely convinced that 1) Max Carey's pop double in the seventh actually was foul by at least foot, and 2) Johnson should, by all rights, have struck out Kiki Cuyler with the bases loaded in the eighth.

But Carey's "double" led to a couple of runs, and after Cuyler got his reprieve, he too struck a two-run double, this one giving the Pirates the 9–7 lead with which they would finish.

There were also Peckinpaugh's two errors and a couple of cheap Pittsburgh hits. Like most managers who are remembered for screwing up, Harris could have met a happier end with just a touch more luck. But then, that's why you don't screw up; if your margin for error is too small, everybody remembers.

George Brace Collection

Walter Johnson, showing his years.

for sentimental reasons. This should never occur in a World Series."[7] And it shouldn't.

Three years earlier, in the '22 Series, Game 2 was tied 3–3 after ten innings when the umpires declared the game a tie on account of darkness . . . even though it was only 4:46 P.M. and there was roughly forty-five minutes of daylight remaining. It was the umpires' decision but Landis took the heat, and he acted quickly to defuse criticism; shortly after the game, he announced that "the entire receipts of to-day's game shall be turned over to the funds for the benefit of disabled soldiers and to the charities of New York." Just like that, he'd given away $120,000 of the owners' money. And the fans loved him for it.

The owners weren't nearly so thrilled, and there's little doubt that Landis wanted to avoid another choice between public-relations nightmare and angering his paymasters. According to Landis biographer David Pietrusza, "Landis, fearing a repeat of 1922, refused to allow a rainout . . . Landis saw to it that, come hell or high water (particularly high water), play would continue."[9]

The Sporting News opined, "Understandably the distinguished commissioner was urged on all sides to play and 'get it over' and these words are not intended as adverse criticism, yet realizing the importance of the games and how they interested persons throughout the length and breadth of the land, it is a pity that the concluding contest was not played on a dry field and under more ideal weather conditions."[10]

A pity, indeed. And if *The Sporting News* was criticizing the most powerful man in the game, you know they had a pretty good case.

1. Henry W. Thomas, *Walter Johnson: Baseball's Big Train* (Arlington, Va.: Phenom, 1995).

2. Ibid.

3. Paul W. Eaton, *Sporting News*, Oct. 22, 1925, p. 1.

4. Roger Peckinpaugh, "Rain to Help Nats, Peck Asserts," *Washington Post*, Oct. 10, 1925.

5. Frank H. Young, *Washington Post*, Oct. 15, 1925.

6. *The Washington Post*, Oct. 16, 1925, p. 20.

7. Associated Press, "Ban Johnson Criticizes Harris," *Washington Post*, Oct. 16, 1925, p. 17.

8. Lawrence S. Ritter, *The Glory of Their Times* (New York: Macmillan, 1966).

9. David Pietrusza, *Judge and Jury: The Life and Times of Judge Kenesaw Mountain Landis* (South Bend, Ind.: Diamond Communications, 1998).

10. *Sporting News*, Oct. 22, 1925, p. 2.

RUTH WALKS, THEN RUNS

My biggest thrill in baseball was making a simple tag on a runner trying to steal second base. The play was the biggest surprise of my career, and I'd have to say the biggest break any of my teams ever got. It also goes to prove that the World Series is not won—it's lost. The guy I tagged out—and by a mile, too—was Babe Ruth.

—Rogers Hornsby

The most famous play in the 1926 World Series came in the seventh game, when Grover Cleveland Alexander trotted to the mound, with the bases loaded, and struck out Tony Lazzeri to preserve the Cardinals' 3–2 lead.

Some people think Alexander was seriously hungover, if not actually drunk. Some think he was just old and tired (he was thirty-nine, and twenty-four hours earlier he'd gone the distance to win Game 6). I lean heavily toward the latter opinion, but a serious appraisal will have to wait for another book. Some also think that Alexander's strikeout of Lazzeri ended the game and thus the Series. It didn't. That was just the bottom of the seventh. With the Cardinals leading by just one run, Alexander's work was just getting started.

In the eighth, Alexander breezed through the bottom of the order (oddly, Yankees pitcher Herb Pennock was allowed to bat for himself, but baseball was different then). In the ninth, with the score still

3–2, Alexander retired Earle Combs and Mark Koenig on grounders to third baseman Les Bell.

The Yankees weren't quite done yet. Next up was Babe Ruth, who'd already set World Series records with four home runs and ten walks. As Bell later recalled, "It would be nice to say that Alec struck him out to end it, and he nearly did. He nearly did. He took Babe to a full count and then lost him on a low outside pitch that wasn't off by more than an eyelash." By one account, Ruth paused before trotting to first base; by another, Alexander started to walk off the mound, thinking he'd struck Ruth out. Nevertheless, Ruth took his base as the potential tying runner.

Maybe manager Miller Huggins should have sent in a pinch-runner. The Babe wasn't as fat and gimpy as he would later become, but he was thirty-one and certainly not in the trimmest of condition. Then again, do you really want to tie the game, then head into extra innings without the best baseball player on earth? Me neither. So if the Yankees tied the game, it would be Ruth doing the tying.

And next up? Not Lou Gehrig (as many people think). Gehrig didn't move into the No. 4 slot in the lineup until 1927. In '26 the Yankees' cleanup hitter was still Long Bob Meusel. He'd missed a chunk of the season with a broken foot, but in 1925—with Ruth missing much of that season—Meusel had led the American League with thirty-three home runs, and in '26 his .470 slugging percentage was more than respectable. In four plate appearances against Alexander in Game 6, he'd walked, doubled, and tripled (though it should be noted that the double was a Texas Leaguer and the triple was a grounder past third base). And if Meusel somehow reached base? Gehrig, who'd led the American League with eighty-three extra-base hits, lurked on deck. And of course Ruth would be in scoring position.

In *Yankees Century*, Glenn Stout wrote, "Ruth, on first, had made a career of careening between incredible and incorrigible. He now added the inexplicable to his resume."[1]

Alexander later recalled what happened next:

> If Meusel got hold of one it could mean two runs and the series, so I forgot all about Ruth and got ready to work on Meusel. I'll never know why the guy did it but on my first pitch to Meusel, the Babe broke for second. He (or Miller Huggins) probably figured that it would catch us by surprise. I caught the blur of Ruth starting for second as I pitched and then came the whistle of the ball as O'Farrell rifled it to second. I wheeled around and there was one of the grandest sights of my life. Hornsby, his foot anchored on the bag and his gloved hand outstretched was waiting for Ruth to come in. There was the series and my second big thrill of the day. The third came when Judge Landis mailed out the winners' checks for $5,584.51.[2]

Hornsby: "I'll always remember putting the ball on him. He didn't say a word. He didn't even look around or up at me. He just picked himself off the ground and walked away to the dugout and I had lived through the greatest day any man could ask."[3]

Ed Barrow, who'd built the Yankees into a powerhouse since taking over as business manager in 1920, later said, "That's the only dumb play I ever saw Ruth make. With Meusel and Gehrig following him in our batting order, anything still could have happened."[4]

Obviously, Ruth's decision—and there's never been any indication that Huggins had anything to do with it—didn't work out. But did it make sense?

Darby O'Brien's Ill Luck

To this day, the Babe remains the only player who's ended a World Series with a caught stealing.

Sort of. We tend to dismiss 19th-century baseball as if it didn't really exist, but there *were* postseason series pitting the champions of the top leagues—the National League and the inferior American Association—against each other, and the term "World Series" (among others) was even used.

The next-to-last of these N.L.-vs.-A.A. affairs was played in 1889, and featured the New York Giants and the Brooklyn Bridegrooms in a best-of-eleven series. That's just too many games, and only 3,647 paying customers were in the ballpark for the ninth and final game, which ended when Brooklyn's Darby O'Brien tried to steal second base with two outs in the top of the ninth inning. Buck Ewing, renowned as perhaps the finest-fielding catcher of his era, gunned down O'Brien with a throw to second baseman Danny Richardson.

It wasn't a bad idea, though. Stolen bases were a huge part of the game in those days; in the nine games, the Giants and Bridegrooms combined for *fifty-two* steals. This one just didn't work out.

We've got caught-stealing data beginning in 1920; from that season through the end of the '26 season, Ruth stole seventy-two times and was caught seventy-nine times. That's a forty-eight percent success rate, which obviously isn't real good. In '26, Ruth stole eleven bases and was thrown out nine times (in the World Series, he owned the Yankees' only steal, and it came in Game 6 with Alexander on the mound). This wasn't a typical steal attempt, though. Not only was the situation exceptional, but there's evidence suggesting that Ruth wasn't trying to steal on Alexander, but rather on Cardinals catcher Bob O'Farrell. According to John B. Foster in *Spalding's Official Base Ball Guide*, Ruth tried to "catch O'Farrell napping," and other sources support the notion that it was a delayed steal attempt. But if there's one thing about which everyone agrees, it's that the play wasn't close.

Robert Creamer, one of Ruth's biographers, wrote,

> Ruth's decision to steal was discussed for years. It was generally considered a bad play, a dumb play, but some baseball men defended it. There were two outs, not much chance left to develop a rally. A man on second base could score on a single, and the way Alexander was pitching, a single was about all you could hope for. A successful steal at such a startling moment might upset the pitcher, even the veteran Alexander.
>
> But it did not work, and despite his four home runs, a new World Series record, Babe was considered a bit of a goat. He didn't seem to mind. It was a hell of a try, he thought. Strikeouts never embarrassed him, and neither did this.[5]

Ruth himself put things a bit more prosaically: "I wasn't doing any fucking good on first base."[6]

1. Glenn Stout and Richard A. Johnson, *Yankees Century: 100 Years of New York Yankees Baseball* (Boston: Houghton Mifflin, 2004).

2. John P. Carmichael, *My Greatest Day in Baseball* (New York: Grosset & Dunlap, 1951).

3. Ibid.

4. Fred Lieb, *The Story of the World Series* (New York: Putnam, 1965).

5. Robert Creamer, *Babe: The Legend Comes to Life* (New York: Simon & Schuster, 1974).

6. Marshall Smelser, *The Life That Ruth Built: A Biography* (New York: Quadrangle, 1975).

BUCS SEND OFF HALL OF FAMERS

The deal for Cuyler brings an end to varied and sundry trade rumors, in which the outfielder was the central figure. A reported run-in with Manager Bush during the season, opened the difficulty which banished Cuyler from active service with the Pirates . . .

When he failed to break into the World's Series against the Yankees, there was considerable criticism from the fans, but Bush held fast to his disciplinary measures and when a pinch-hitter was needed, it was not Cuyler who was called into play.

—Irving Vaughan, *The Sporting News*

When the Pirates traded Hazen "Kiki" Cuyler (by the way, that's pronounced *ky-ky*, not *kee-kee*) for two nobodies* it was not, as they say, a "baseball deal." This was something else, the sort of deal you don't want to make but feel like you have to.

In the mid 1920s, Cuyler was a big star. In 1925, his greatest season, Cuyler batted .357 with eighteen home runs, drove in 102 runs, and led the National League with 144 runs scored. In the World Series that fall, he drove in six runs as the Pirates beat the Senators in seven games. Cuyler's power dropped off quite a bit in 1926, but again he led his league in scoring.

Big star.

In 1927, with the Pirates fighting for the pennant, Cuyler got benched. Permanently.

The way the story goes, the Pirates were in first place, but sort of scuffling a bit, in the middle of the season. Rookie manager Donie Bush decided to shake up the lineup, shifting Cuyler from his accustomed third slot to second.

Cuyler was not a bad guy. When he died in 1950, his obituary in *The Sporting News* included this: "A model on and off the field—he didn't drink or smoke—Cuyler had only one flaw that kept him from being rated with the leading immortals of the game. He lacked the ruthlessness that might have carried him to great heights and made his record even more brilliant."[1]

Here's Cuyler's side of things:

> During that season, Bush seemed to dislike me for no reason in the world. He ordered me to bat second, instead of third, in the lineup. I said to Bush, "You're the manager and I'll hit any place you say, but I'm not adapted to second place. I am a free swinger

---

* Actually, the Pirates traded Cuyler for Sparky Adams and Pete Scott, a couple of fairly decent players.

Kansas City Here I Come . . .

On April 1, 1928, just a few months after trading Cuyler for so little, the Pirates sold a young shortstop named Joe Cronin to the Kansas City Blues. And a few months later, Kansas City—an independent club in the American Association—sold Cronin to the Washington Senators for $7,500.

Cronin signed up with the Pirates in 1925, when he was eighteen. In '26, he spent half the season with the big club, and half in the Eastern League (where he batted .320 with New Haven). Oddly, he spent the entire 1927 campaign with the Pirates—he even was on the World Series roster—but got into only twelve games all season. And the next spring he was gone.

By unloading Cuyler and Cronin within six months, the Pirates transferred a great deal of talent to other teams and received relatively little in return. Did the loss of both players cost them any pennants? Perhaps one.

In 1932, one of the Pirates' outfield slots was manned by Adam Comorosky, who played 108 games and earned eleven Win Shares. Shortstop was held by rookie Arky Vaughan, who—beginning a Hall of Fame career—picked up twenty-one Win Shares.

Meanwhile, with their new teams, Cuyler (Cubs) earned fifteen Win Shares in 110 games and Cronin (Senators) was brilliant for a third straight season, earning thirty-one Win Shares. So that's thirty-two Win Shares for the two now-Pirates, and forty-six Win

and take a long cut at the ball and, therefore, miss a lot of swings. Neither can I place a hit as a man in that position should be able to do." Well, that didn't do any good. Bush told me to bat second just the same.

Soon after, I was on first and the batter grounded to the infield. Instead of sliding into second base, I went in standing up so that I could interfere with the second baseman and prevent a double play. It happened that on this particular play the second baseman dropped the ball and, if I had slid, I would have been safe.

Because I failed to slide, Bush fined me $50 and benched me. Stories in the newspapers magnified the situation and Bush refused to put me back in the lineup. We won the pennant, but I was left on the bench to watch the Pirates lose four straight games to the Yankees without getting a chance to help stop the massacre.[2]

The game in which Cuyler didn't slide was on August 6. They lost that one, and fell three games behind the first-place Cubs. Not the best time to bench one of your best players, perhaps. But Bush, with the support of owner Barney Dreyfuss, did bench Cuyler, who started just once more, on September 5, and did not so much as pinch-hit or play an inning of defense the rest of the season (including the World Series).

Did benching Cuyler cost the Pirates the pennant? Obviously, it did not. Afterward they went 34–18 and finished in first place, just ahead of the Cardinals and Giants (the Cubs finished well back). Did benching Cuyler cost the Pirates the World Series? Almost certainly not. The '27 Yankees were among the greatest teams ever; the '27 Pirates were not. The Pirates lost four straight. Games 1 and 4 were very close, but 2 and 3 were blowouts. And Cuyler's replacement, Clyde Barnhart, actually led the Pirates in runs batted in (with four).

Did trading Cuyler cost the Pirates any future pennants? Probably not. Cuyler remained a fine player, if less than wonderfully durable, through 1936. In all those years, the Pirates were competitive in only 1932 (four games out) and '33 (five).

On the other hand, the Pirates didn't get much out of infielder Sparky Adams or outfielder Pete Scott. After two seasons, they sold Adams to the Cardinals, for whom he did his best work. Scott was actually a pretty good hitter; he'd batted .314 with the Cubs in '27, and in June of '28 he made the news by hitting five home runs in three games. Not long afterward, though, he "almost dashed out his brains in a collision with the concrete right-field wall at New York's Polo Grounds."[3] That happened on July 26—actually, "an

X-ray revealed he was suffering from a severe dislocation of the atlas verte-brae. His condition was said to be painful but not critical." Critical or not, Scott didn't return to the lineup until early September, and went just 5 for 26 the rest of the way. (Scott's obituary in *The Sporting News* suggested that the neck injury knocked him out of the majors, but the truth is that if you shook a tree in those days, a bunch of .300 hitters would fall out. Scott returned to the minors in 1929, and batted .335 in the Pacific Coast League.)

Then again, there's this pesky sidebar to consider . . .

Shares for the ex-Pirates. Roughly speaking, that's a five-win edge for the ex-Pirates. Pittsburgh finished four games behind the first-place Cubs (who, by the way, would themselves have been without the services of Cuyler). There's no telling exactly how the math would have worked out in real life, of course. But it would have been one hell of a pennant race. And if the Pirates had finished on top, Babe Ruth never would have not Called his Shot.

1. *Sporting News*, Feb. 22, 1950, p. 20.

2. Ibid.

3. Fred Lieb, *The Pittsburgh Pirates: An Informal History* (New York: Putnam, 1948).

TIGERS DISCARD MEAL TICKET

Carl Hubbell was in the Tigers' farm system the same time I was. Carl and I knew each other. Later, of course, he had all those great years with the Giants. Threw that screwball, you know. That was his bread-and-butter pitch. You know what Cobb told him to do with it? "Get rid of that damn pitch." Cobb didn't like him and Detroit released him outright. He wound up with some team in the Texas League, won ten or eleven straight, and John McGraw signed him. I was with Newark at the time. One day we had a day off, so I went up to the Polo Grounds to talk to Hubbell. He told me, "The best thing that ever happened to me was when that son of a bitch released me."

—Tigers pitcher Bill Moore[1]

Without checking, I would guess that a significantly higher percentage of Hall of Fame pitchers than hitters are just sort of given away. Christy Mathewson, Mordecai Brown, Red Ruffing, Fergie Jenkins, Nolan Ryan . . . the list is extensive, there's a story about all of them, and perhaps the best of the giving-away stories is about Carl Hubbell.

The way the story goes—actually, I'll let Bob Broeg tell it . . . "Hubbell's first spring training with a big league club in 1926 was a bitter experience. First, George McBride, a coach for the Tigers, advised him not to throw the screwball and then none other than Ty Cobb himself, still player-manager, cautioned that he could hurt his arm as Hub Pruett had done."[2] (Pruett was a left-handed screwball pitcher of the 1920s who gained a measure of renown for his success against Babe Ruth.)

As the story continues, Hubbell is first sent back to the minors (before getting the chance to pitch even one inning during spring training), and then

forbidden to throw his screwball. Even without the screwball (or so the story goes), Hubbell pitched well (7–7, 3.77 ERA) with Toronto in the International League.

In the spring of '27, Hubbell was again with the Tigers in spring training, but again McBride wasn't all that impressed. So Hubbell was sent all the way down to Decatur in the Class B Illinois-Indiana-Iowa League. Again he pitched well (14–7, 2.53) . . . after which the Tigers released him, the next spring, to Beaumont in the Texas League. Encouraged to throw his screwball, Hubbell thrived with the Exporters, and that summer he joined the Giants—who exported $40,000 to Beaumont, resulting in a quick and substantial profit for that club—and almost immediately became a star.

The general consensus is that Cobb deserves most of the blame for letting Hubbell get away from Detroit. The following passage is taken from Frank Graham's 1952 history of the New York Giants:

George Brace Collection

Carl Hubbell

June of 1928. It is the month in which the Giants acquired one of the greatest pitchers any ball club ever owned and if they didn't precisely get him by chance, chance figured largely in his transition from a discouraged castoff of the Detroit Tigers to a star at the Polo Grounds.

He was Carl Owen Hubbell, born in Carthage, Missouri, reared in Meeker, Oklahoma, and discovered—for the Giants, that is—pitching for the Beaumont club of the Texas League in Houston by a man who should have been in attendance at the Democratic national convention, to which he was a delegate from Illinois. The truant was Dick Kinsella, who saw no point in sitting through a dull afternoon session when he could be at the ball game. He hadn't planned to scout anybody but it was natural that his eye should be caught by this lean southpaw and his interest aroused when he learned this was Hubbell, for although he had never seen Carl, he knew of him.

Although he was only twenty-five, Hubbell had been up twice with the Tigers. The first time, Ty Cobb was the manager; the second time, George Moriarty. Each was convinced he would not succeed in the majors. Later, Hubbell was to say, "I had just about got around to believing them when Kinsella recommended me to Mr. McGraw. I figured they must know something when they both turned me down and it looked to me like the other managers must have figured the same way. I never expected to get up here again."

George Brace Collection

Carl Hubbell's screwball grip

Kinsella wasn't sure the Tigers had released him outright, since Beaumont was a Detroit farm club. Once he had established that there were no strings on the pitcher, he made some discreet inquiries and learned that Cobb believed the screwball, Hubbell's big pitch, would ruin his arm, and that Moriarty, on hearing this, agreed with it. He called McGraw that night.

"I like him, Mac," he said, "but there's one thing you ought to know about. Cobb didn't keep him because he said the boy would throw his arm out with his screwball."

"That's a joke," McGraw said. "When Matty was pitching it, they called it a fadeaway and it never hurt his arm. If there isn't anything wrong with him, I'd like to know more about him."

"I'll follow him around for a while," Kinsella said.

Forsaking the political arena, Dick tucked himself in behind the Beaumont club and made the grand tour of the Texas League. Then he called McGraw again.

"He's got it, John."[3]

It was actually July of 1928 when the Giants purchased Hubbell,[4] and he wound up winning 253 games in only sixteen seasons. And all because Ty Cobb didn't trust a screwball pitcher.

But not so fast. As Cobb says in his autobiography, "This is a very strange charge. Every bit of evidence you could ask to see shows that Hubbell still was the property of the Detroit organization in 1926, when I departed as manager. He did not become a Giant until the winter of 1927" (actually, evidence points to the summer of '28, but reports conflict).

Further, Cobb claimed that one of his last acts as manager was to urge Tigers owner Frank Navin, "Never let Hubbell go. He may be wild and not ready now, but he's going to be one of the best. Any man with his speed who can turn the ball loose below the belt side-arm only needs control to succeed."[5]

That strikes me as the fanciful ramblings of a dying man (which is exactly what Ty Cobb was in 1960, when he dictated his autobiography to Al Stump). But I do think it's unfair to pin the loss of Hubbell on the Peach. When Cobb saw Hubbell in the spring of 1926 he probably *was* wild; in 1925 with Oklahoma City in the Western League, he'd walked 108 batters while striking out only 104 (in 284 innings).[6]

Okay, so the Tigers—whether Cobb, McBride, George Moriarty, or all three of them—blew it. But what did it cost the franchise, really? Hubbell first pitched in the majors on July 26, 1928, and he last pitched in the majors on August 24, 1943 (at which point he was about four years removed from greatness). Did his absence during those fifteen years cost the Tigers any pennants?

From 1928 through '33, the *closest* the Tigers finished to first place was twenty-five games. Then, somewhat miraculously, they jumped the line and won pennants in both 1934 and '35. In 1936, the Yankees took over the American League, absolutely outclassing their competition for four seasons. In 1937 the Tigers won eighty-nine games and finished second, but were still thirteen games out of first place.

The Tigers won a tight pennant race in 1940, edging the Indians by one game and the Yankees by two. And over the next three seasons—all of which concluded with the Yankees in the World Series—the Tigers finished twenty-six, thirty, and twenty games off the pace. After which Carl Hubbell was an ex-pitcher.

Hubbell wouldn't have made a difference in a single pennant race if he'd been pitching for the Tigers. Every time they were close they won, and in every other season they weren't close at all.

Which leaves the three World Series.

In 1935, the Tigers beat the Cubs in a six-game Series, and they could hardly have done better with Hubbell. Both Detroit losses were charged to Schoolboy Rowe, and he posted a 2.57 ERA. Tommy Bridges started twice, and went 2–0 with a 2.50 ERA. Alvin Crowder started once, and beat the Cubs 2–1. Elden Auker started once, and gave up three runs in a game the Tigers eventually won in the eleventh inning.

Giving One Away

Why did Tigers player-manager Mickey Cochrane choose Alvin Crowder to start Game 1 of the 1934 World Series? Well, Crowder had gone 5–1 with a decent ERA after coming to the Tigers in a waiver deal on August 4. But there probably was more to it than that. Shortly after Crowder joined the Tigers, Cochrane selected him—rather than Schoolboy Rowe, his ace—to start against Yankees ace Lefty Gomez in the first game of a doubleheader. When asked why, Cochrane said, "I have never believed it effective to use ace against ace. When it comes to winning games throughout the season the percentage is against it. Why sacrifice an almost certain win for a possible low-score loss?" (The Tigers won that game, 9–5.)

Upon naming Crowder as his Game 1 starter, Cochrane cited Rowe's youth, and years later he suggested the move was inspired by Connie Mack's shocking decision to start sore-armed veteran Howard Ehmke in Game 1 of the 1929 Series.

According to one of Dizzy Dean's biographers, while Crowder was warming up on the field before the first game, Dean strolled over to Cochrane and shouted, "Mickey, the General ain't got nothin. You better go find Schoolboy and get him ready."

Cochrane's reply: "Go to hell, Diz."

Dean beat Crowder and the Tigers, 8–3.

The Tigers lost the 1940 World Series, but arguing that they'd have won with Hubbell is highly problematic. For one thing, he really wasn't all that good in 1940: 11–12 with an ERA close to the league average. And for another, if the Tigers had Hubbell they might not have traded for Bobo Newsom in '39, and without Newsom in '40 there's no way the Tigers win the pennant.

So we're left with only the 1934 Series, which the Tigers lost to the Cardinals in seven games. Here are the four Tigers who started in the '34 Series, along with Hubbell that season:

	W-L	ERA
Schoolboy Rowe	24–8	3.45
Tommy Bridges	22–11	3.67
Elden Auker	15–7	3.42
Alvin Crowder	5–1	4.18
Carl Hubbell	21–12	2.30

Hubbell would have been the ace of the staff, obviously.

In the Series, Rowe and Bridges both pitched well. Auker started Game 3 and pitched reasonably well, though it really didn't matter because the Tigers scored ten runs to rout the Cardinals. In Game 7, though, Auker got knocked out in the third inning. That probably didn't matter, either, because St. Louis's Dizzy Dean pitched a six-hit shutout. Then again, perhaps if Hubbell were a Tiger the Series wouldn't have gone seven games, because he'd have been the ace and taken not only Auker's innings, but probably some of Rowe's or Bridges's, too. He'd also have taken some of Alvin Crowder's; or rather, he'd almost certainly have taken all of them. Because if Carl Hubbell had been a Tiger in 1934, Crowder probably wouldn't have been.

Crowder had been a good pitcher for a number of seasons, but in 1934 he got off to a horrible start with Washington—4–10, 6.79 ERA—and they cut him loose. He pitched better after joining the Tigers, but at best he was the fourth-best pitcher on the staff, and it was a real surprise when he started Game 1 of the World Series (see sidebar). But if the Tigers had Hubbell, they probably wouldn't have grabbed Crowder off waivers in the first place.

Conclusion? Letting Hubbell get away didn't cost the Tigers a single pennant, and in fact his absence might have *gained* them the pennant in 1940. And while not having Hubbell quite possibly cost them the 1934 World Series, it might have gained them the 1935 World Series. Obviously, giving

Hubbell away cost the Tigers a whole lot of regular-season games over the years, which is why this one qualifies as a blunder. But the stuff that really counts, the pennants and the World Series? It probably did not cost the Tigers a thing.

1. Richard Bak, *Cobb Would Have Caught It: The Golden Age of Baseball in Detroit* (Detroit: Wayne State University Press, 1991).
2. Bob Broeg, *Super Stars of Baseball* (St. Louis: Sporting News, 1971).
3. Frank Graham, *The New York Giants* (New York: Putnam, 1952).
4. Joe Vila, *Sporting News,* July 19, 1928, p. 1.
5. Ty Cobb with Al Stump, *My Life in Baseball: The True Record* (Garden City, N.Y.: Doubleday. 1961).
6. John Duxbury and Clifford Kachline, *Baseball Register* (St. Louis: Sporting News, 1967).

MISSED IT BY *THAT* MUCH

(Part 1)

Who has good luck is good.
Who has bad luck is bad.
—Bertolt Brecht, *The Exception and the Rule* (1937)

We praise or blame as one or the other affords more opportunity for exhibiting our power of judgement.
—Friedrich Nietzsche, *All Too Human* (1878)

It always occurs to me, after watching a basketball game decided by one or two points, that the final score was completely noneducational. All it tells me is who won and who lost, but it tells me almost nothing about which team played *better*. Each team is going to have the ball . . . what, seventy-five times in a fast-paced college game? Make one more shot among those seventy-five possessions, and you've turned a one-point loss into a one-point win. One or two points in a basketball game is nothing.

Well, a pennant race is like that. But more.

It's often said that when the season begins, you know you're going to win sixty games and you know you're going to lose sixty games, and it's what you do in the other forty that matters. That's got the virtue of simplicity, but it's also a bit simplistic, because you don't know beforehand which forty games are up for grabs. And of course, a lot more than forty games actually are up for grabs. I would guess that the great majority of games decided by three runs or fewer hinge, at multiple points, on just one at-bat.

This isn't to say that close games, or close pennant races, are all about luck. The better team will win more close games and more pennant races than the worse team. But if you think about it—even leaving aside the mathematics, which make a powerful argument—you'll realize this is true. Just watch your favorite team for a couple of weeks, and count the number of times a game is won or lost because a ground ball snuck through the infield or a pop fly found no-man's land or a line drive was a foot foul rather than a foot fair.

Okay, now multiply by thirteen. That's the part of the iceberg that's above the water, and is dwarfed by all the stuff under the water. Which is to say, one game in the standings is meaningless in every sense but the most important. If one team finishes one game ahead of another, it doesn't mean the players played better, or the coaches coached better, or the manager managed better, or the general manager generaled better, or the owner owned better. Not in a significant way.

Nevertheless, it's impossible to not wonder about what might have been. All of the teams that follow finished their season just one game out of first place, and they could have done just a little better if they'd been just a little smarter . . .

1899 Boston Beaneaters (first place: New York Giants)

This pennant race was a travesty. The end of it, anyway.

As would be the case well into the 20th century, there wasn't any rule stipulating that pennant contenders must play the same number of games. In this case, both Boston and New York won eighty-three National League games, but New York took the flag because they lost forty-three while the Bostons lost forty-five.

Boston's management didn't have a lot of options (that we know about). There weren't any farm systems, of course, and the rosters were tiny; only seventeen men played for the Beaneaters in 1899. The weak link in the lineup was Dick Johnston, a speedy outfielder who batted .228 and posted a .285 on-base percentage that was easily the worst among the club's non-catchers and -pitchers. But while Johnston had always been OBP-deficient, just the season before he'd slugged .472, good for fifth-best in the National League. Maybe Boston should have given up on him during the season—though just twenty-six, he never did rediscover his power—but, again, there just weren't many options for a desperate pennant contender in those days. The Beaners couldn't just reach down and pluck an outfielder from the Western League's Grand Rapids Furnituremakers.

1908 Pittsburgh Pirates and New York Giants (Chicago Cubs)

As I'm sure all of you know, the Giants finished behind the Cubs as the result of a makeup game necessitated by Merkle's Boner. What you might not know is that the Pirates also finished just one game behind the Cubs. And if you'll permit a slight disgression, here's all you need to know about the National League from 1903 through 1912:

Cubs
Giants
Pirates

Those three clubs accounted for all ten pennants in those years, and in fact they accounted for first, second, and third place in each of those years except 1904, when the Pirates finished one game out of third place (which was held by the Reds).

Or, looking at it from the other end of the standings, for a decade running there were four National League teams—Brooklyn, Boston, Philadelphia, and St. Louis—that never, not even once, managed to finish higher than fourth. And people today talk about competitive balance . . .

In any case, 1908 was the peak of the Pirates', Giants', and Cubs' collective hegemony, as all three clubs won either ninety-eight (Pirates and Giants) or ninety-nine (Cubs) games.

What could the Giants have done better? Well, Merkle could have touched second base. That's one thing. Also, John McGraw could have played left fielder Spike Shannon less often than he did. Before the Giants sold Shannon in July, he played just about every day and batted .228 with some walks (in 1907, he'd ranked third in the league in walks) and virtually no power (he'd never had any power).

And here's my favorite fact regarding the 1908 pennant race in the National League: when the Giants sold Shannon, they sold him . . . to the Pirates, for whom he played even worse. In thirty-two games, Shannon batted .197. So for all the talk about Merkle, not to mention Matty and Honus and Three Finger, Spike Shannon might have played the biggest role of all, because all by himself he knocked two teams—his own teams—out of first place.

1908 Cleveland Naps (Tigers)

It was an incredible season, 1908. In the National League, three teams finished within a game of first place. In the American, three teams finished within a game-and-a-half of first place. Of course, all anybody remembers about 1908 is Merkle, but the pennant race in the other league was every bit as exciting (if absent the huge controversy).

The real blunder in 1908 was committed by the American League, which still didn't require contenders to play as many games as it took to determine a legitimate winner, even though the situation had come up in both 1905 and '07. So when the season ended, the Tigers were a half-game ahead of the Indians by virtue of having played one fewer game, but weren't required to make up the missing game. Of course, if the Indians had won just once more, then they would have benefited from the nonrule.

Should the Naps (as they were then called, in honor of player-manager Nap Lajoie) have won just once more? Before I get into the statistics, a brief history lesson. . . . In 1908, the average American League team scored 3.44 runs per game, which is the third-lowest figure in league history. The league on-base percentage was .288; slugging percentage, .304. If you hit .275 with fifty walks and thirty doubles, you were a hell of a hitter.

So that's the context. Still, it's hard to understand why Lajoie let Joe Birmingham play in center field nearly every day, considering that Birmingham had not been good as a rookie in 1907, and batted .213/.253/.257 in 1908. In fairness to Birmingham (and Lajoie), he *was* an outstanding fielder. But his glove wasn't *quite* good enough to carry his bat, at least not in 1908, and his regular presence in the lineup probably did cost Cleveland the pennant.

The White Sox deserve mention here, too. Though they finished a game-and-a-half behind the Tigers, they'd have finished a half-game *ahead* of the Tigers if they'd won their last game. The White Sox and Tigers closed the season with a three-game series; when it began, Chicago trailed by two-and-a-half games. But they won the first two games, 3–1 and 6–1. For the third game, White Sox manager Fielder Jones started Doc White, who'd pitched a complete game just two days earlier. White didn't have anything, but it probably wouldn't have mattered, as Detroit's Wild Bill Donovan tossed a 7–0 shutout.

So I won't fault Jones for pitching White on short rest (just a few days earlier, White Sox ace Ed Walsh had started, and won, both ends of a doubleheader). I will, however, fault Jones for playing Jiggs Donahue at first base more than he played Frank Isbell. Both batted left-handed, and here are their OPS+'s—that is, their OPS's adjusted for league and home ballpark, with 100 a baseline average—in 1906, 1907, and 1908:

	1906	1907	1908
Isbell	114	91	103
Donahue	102	92	69

Donahue was considered a fine first baseman in an era in which defense at first base was more important than it would become. But there's no way that Donahue's glove was good enough to carry his bat. Not with Isbell on the roster.

1922 St. Louis Browns (Yankees)

At first glance, the Browns' problem would seem to be the left side of their infield, in the persons of shortstop Wally Gerber (.267/.326/.334, 47 errors) and third baseman Frank Ellerbe (.246/.303/.319). But Gerber's forty-seven errors weren't an obscene number for his era, and overall he was probably better than half the everyday shortstops in the majors. Ellerbe, on the other hand, was truly awful: hopeless with the bat, deficient with the glove. But he'd batted .292 with the Senators in 1920 and .288 with the Browns in '21, and in '22 he was only twenty-six. He should have been better, and probably would have been if not for a knee injury suffered during his days as a football star at Wofford College.[1] Eventually the Browns gave up on Ellerbe, and plucked Eddie Foster—then batting .211 for the Red Sox—on waivers, and Foster did reasonably well as the everyday third baseman down the stretch.

On the pitching side, the Browns had six hurlers with at least one hundred innings, and the *worst* of these, Dixie Davis, went 11–6 with an ERA better than league average. Lefty reliever Bill Bayne racked up a 4.56 ERA in ninety-three innings. He didn't help. Neither did Dave Danforth, who pitched well—3.28 ERA in eighty innings—but got suspended for doctoring the baseball, then waived to the minor leagues (apparently because the Browns were tired of dealing with the controversy that followed Danforth wherever he went).

But what really hurt the Browns was terrible luck. Their run differential (+224) dwarfed that of the Yankees (+140). But the Yanks won a few more games than they should have and the Brownies lost a few more than they should have, and that was enough.

1940 Cleveland Indians (Tigers)

These were the famous "Cleveland Crybabies," so named because in the middle of the season about half the roster asked owner Alva Bradley to fire manager Ossie Vitt. Bradley might have done it, but the writers already had the story, and Bradley didn't want to fire the manager and have everyone know who really was running the asylum. The Indians played about the same after the rebellion as before, and were in the pennant race until the end.

The Tribe's only real weaknesses were outfielders Beau Bell and Jeff Heath. Bell played right field and Heath played left, but neither were full-timers (Ben Chapman played in right when Heath was in left, and in left when Bell was in right). I haven't done the research to determine whether or not they were (sort of) platooned for part of the season. They probably were, at times—Bell batted righty, Heath lefty—but considering that Bell played more than Heath, and that Heath finished the season with a .219 batting average, and that Heath was reportedly one of the ringleaders of the rebellion, it seems likely that Heath simply lost some of his playing time to Bell as the season progressed. Which might have been a mistake, but then again Heath *did* bat .219. So maybe he shouldn't have gotten the 356 at-bats that he did? Maybe. But Heath had batted .343 in 1938 and .292 (with power) in 1939, so patience was in order. And Bell, too, had been a good hitter in the past, though in his case it had been a few seasons since he'd actually made a positive contribution. Beau Bell wasn't the Indians' only weakness, but giving him 444 at-bats was probably their biggest mistake.

1944 Detroit Tigers (St. Louis Browns)

It's awfully tempting to give the Tigers a pass; after all, if Pete Gray could get into seventy-seven games in 1945, can you really blame the Tigers for letting shortstop Joe Hoover (.236/.301/.290) play 120 games in 1944?

Actually, Hoover would have played even more than he did, if not for a "stomach disorder."[2] His chief backup: Joe Orengo, who batted .201/.297/.266 in forty-six games (and those numbers were a fair representation of his abilities). In mid June the Tigers signed Leslie "Bubba" Floyd to spell Hoover. Floyd started at shortstop, went 4 for 9 while playing error-free in the field . . . and got sent to Buffalo,[3] where he spent the rest of the season and batted .257/.355/.294 in eighty-one games. Was Floyd better than Hoover? We don't know nearly enough about the defense of either, but we do know that the International League (home of the Buffalo franchise) was terribly weak due to the war, just as both major leagues were. If Floyd really was a better player than Hoover, it can't have been by much. (And by the way, neither Hoover nor Orengo nor Floyd played in the majors after the boys came home from the war.)

1945 Washington Senators (Tigers)

World War II didn't affect Major League Baseball much until 1943. Sure, a few players were drafted in '42 (and Bob Feller, along with a few others, actually enlisted). But the draft didn't begin to devastate the rosters until 1943, and then it got worse in '44 and '45.

Even the mighty Yankees were affected by the draft. In 1944 they won "only" eighty-three games, their fewest in nearly two decades. That same season, the St. Louis Browns—*the St. Louis Browns*—won their first (and as it turned out, only) American League pennant.

Meanwhile, the Washington Nationals (or "Senators," as they were more popularly known) finished in last place for the first time since 1909. And this just one year after a second-place finish (and *that* came one year after a seventh).

The standings during the latter stages of the war were volatile. A team might be up one year, down the next, and up again the next. Where you finished was a matter of management, yes, but it was largely a matter of who got drafted, who didn't, and (particularly in 1945) who got discharged from the service.

On September 23, 1945, the Senators split a doubleheader, leaving them just one game behind the first-place Tigers. There was a week left in the season.

Except the Nats were finished. Literally.

Washington played *forty-four* doubleheaders in 1945. A lot of teams played a lot of doubleheaders, to limit travel (as demanded by the War Department). But nobody else played forty-four doubleheaders, and nobody else played ten games in five days (as the Nats did in early August).

Why did the Senators' season end so early? According to Shirley Povich, owner "Clark Griffith, never suspecting that his club would be a pennant contender, had rented out his Stadium to the Washington Redskins for the last week in September and arranged the baseball schedule to crowd in the Senators' dates earlier. The double-headers had taken their toll of the Washington pitchers too."[4]

The real goat wasn't Griffith, though. That honor shall forever be reserved for outfielder George "Bingo" Binks. In Washington's penultimate game of the season—the first game of a doubleheader against the Athletics—the score was 3–3 in the bottom of the twelfth. With two outs and nobody on, the immortal Ernie Kish hit a can of corn to center field. Binks lost the ball in the sun, Kish landed on second base, and scored the winning run a moment later on George Kell's single. As Povich wrote a few years later, "The miscreant Binks was in trouble with his teammates. He had neglected to take his sunglasses into the outfield after the sun came out on what had been a gray day. An inning earlier, outfielder Sam Chapman of the A's had stopped the game to call for his sunglasses, but Binks never took the hint that the sun was now present. There were threats to deprive Binks of his World-Series or second-place money."[5]

A week later, on the season's final day, the Tigers won the first game of a doubleheader to take a one-and-a-half game lead over the second-place Senators, and the second game was washed out by rain, never to be made up. But if Binks had caught Kish's corn and the Nats had eventually won, Detroit's lead would have been just half a game after winning that first game of the doubleheader, and they'd have been forced to play the second. And who knows what would have happened next . . .

1948 Boston Red Sox (Indians)

All that's remembered about the '48 Red Sox is manager Joe McCarthy's decision to start Denny Galehouse in the one-game playoff for the American League pennant, but I cover that in some detail on page 65.

The lineup was solid—McCarthy's lineups were nearly always solid—and the only two weak spots on the pitching staff were Mickey Harris and Dave Ferriss, both of whom had pitched reasonably well in '47. But with the exception of backup catcher Matt Batts, the Red Sox bench was utterly nonproductive, which would hurt them down the road, too.

1949 Boston Red Sox (Yankees)

This pennant race has been immortalized by David Halberstam. For those of you who haven't read *Summer of '49*, the Red Sox owned a one-game lead over the Yankees with two games to play, but lost both games, 5–4 and 5–3, at Yankee Stadium to lose the pennant.

Jack Kramer went 6–8 with a 5.16 ERA, and might legitimately be blamed for the Red Sox's ultimate fortunes. But in 1948, Kramer went 18–5; he'd earned the 117 innings that he got in '49.

Another problem: Earl Johnson, who pitched only forty-nine innings but lost six games and posted a 7.48 ERA. But with Johnson, too, there was little hint of this before the season. In 1947 he'd been excellent, and in '48 he'd been decent. And even in '49, Johnson wasn't nearly as bad as his ERA; in forty-nine innings he gave up just one home run.

There was nothing wrong with the Red Sox lineup that season. The bench was another story, though. Aside from the regulars, three Red Sox batted more than fifty-two times, and none of them did much. Second-string catcher Batts did show some power, so he gets a pass. But what about first baseman Billy Hitchcock (.204/.291/.259) and outfielder Tommy O'Brien (.224/.336/.336)? The Red Sox's weak bench hurt them in 1948, and it hurt them again in '49. The real blunder was committed by general manager Joe Cronin, who didn't do enough to strengthen the bench in either season.

But just as the Red Sox's finish in '48 has always been blamed on something Joe McCarthy did in the last game of the season, so has their finish in '49.

With two games left in the season, the Red Sox led the Yankees by one game. There couldn't be a tie, because the two clubs would finish the schedule with two games at Yankee Stadium. All the Red Sox needed was one win. Just one lousy win.

On Saturday afternoon, the Sox jumped to a quick 4–0 lead, and they had Mel Parnell—the best pitcher in the majors that season—on the mound. And yet somehow they lost. With relief ace Joe Page pitching six scoreless innings and Johnny Lindell hitting a tie-breaking homer in the eighth, the Yankees pulled out a 5–4 victory and tied the Red Sox for first place.

In Sunday's winner-take-all, Ellis Kinder started for Boston, Vic Raschi for the Yankees. In the bottom of the first, the Yankees pushed across one run, but afterward Kinder was tough. Raschi was just as good, and when the Red Sox came up in the eighth they were still down 1–0.

Catcher Birdie Tebbetts led off, and grounded out. Ellis Kinder was due next, and of course he wanted to hit for himself (nearly all pitchers do). But McCarthy bumped him, instead sending rookie outfielder Tom Wright to the plate. Wright walked. Dom DiMaggio followed with a hard grounder, which Phil Rizzuto turned into a double play. And then in the bottom of the eighth, McCarthy's bullpen blew up. And for that, perhaps he does deserve some blame. First McCarthy turned to Parnell, who had pitched four innings just the day before. And then he tried Tex Hughson, who hadn't pitched in weeks. Neither was effective, and the Yankees scored four times (granted, the last three runs came on a bloop double to short right field). The Red Sox did rally for three runs in the top of the ninth, but fell short. For the second time in two seasons, they'd lost the pennant on the season's final day.

As the story goes, McCarthy shouldn't have removed Kinder. Batts later said, "There was no sense to taking him out. Why he took him out, God knows. That was the game. Nobody knows to this day why. Kinder was pitching a hell of a game."[6]

This strikes me as second-guessing at its very worst. And Batts wasn't the only one. Glenn Stout writes in *Red Sox Century*, "the righthanded Kinder could hit a little and was better than any lefthanded option on the Boston bench."

Really? At that moment, 1) Kinder's lifetime batting average was .115, and 2) Tom Wright, a left-handed hitter, had just batted .368 with 103 walks in the American Association. Vic Raschi, one of the toughest right-handers around, was pitching. You're telling me that there's not a *huge* difference between these two, in favor of Wright? And didn't Wright do what McCarthy wanted him to do? Wright was not a big power hitter. He was just supposed to set the table for the top of the Red Sox order, and that's exactly what he did.

The Red Sox hadn't scored a run in the last fifteen-plus innings. Was McCarthy really supposed to guess they would score three in the ninth? Managers had been losing games for decades because they were afraid to replace an effective pitcher with a pinch-hitter. McCarthy tried it the other way, which was the smart move.

I'll give the final word here to Mel Parnell, because I agree with him: "There was criticism of McCarthy, but it was unjust. You have to try to do something to get runs on the board. If Tom Wright could have started off an inning, it could have been explosive for us, and McCarthy would have been a genius. The way it worked, he wasn't."[7]

1949 St. Louis Cardinals (Brooklyn Dodgers)

Answer: Nippy Jones and Rocky Nelson.
Question: Who were the Cardinals' first basemen in 1949?
Bonus Question: Who cost the Cardinals the National League pennant, same season?

Of course, it's not really fair to blame Jones and Nelson for the Cardinals' fortunes. I'm sure they were doing the best they could. No, the blame lies with whoever thought Jones and Nelson would provide acceptable performance at first base.

Jones, twenty-four in 1949, had played a lot in '48 and batted .254/.307/.397. Nelson, also twenty-four in '49, spent all of '48 in the International League and batted .303 with seven homers. Taken together, Jones and Nelson might reasonably have been expected to give the Cardinals decent numbers. And Jones wasn't terrible. He wasn't *good*—he batted .300/.330/.426—but there were worse first basemen in the major leagues. Nelson, on the other hand, was truly awful. And though he would play in the majors as late as 1961, when he was thirty-six, Nelson's first good season in the majors was 1959. The Cardinals simply miscalculated. They thought Nelson could hit, and he didn't (though in fairness to Nelson, during the 1950s he put up some huge numbers in the high minors).

So anyway, the Cardinals didn't get enough production from their first basemen. At that time the Cardinals had two Class AAA teams, one in Columbus and another in Rochester. The first baseman in Columbus was Mike Natisin; he'd been one of the better hitters in the American Association for a few years, but in 1949 he was thirty-two. The first baseman in Rochester was Steve Bilko, who was just a baby, all of twenty years old. He tore up the International League—.310–34–125—but didn't get his first at-bat in the majors until September 22. Bilko played in six of the Cardinals' last eight games, reached base ten times, and knocked in a couple of runs.

Should the Cardinals have promoted Bilko earlier? Say, in July? Yeah, probably. But Bilko was just *so* young, and he wasn't much with the glove, and the Cardinals thought so little of Bilko that they didn't give him a real shot in the lineup until 1953.

(By the way, all of this would be moot if, eight years earlier, Branch Rickey—then running the Cardinals—hadn't traded Johnny Mize to the Giants for three nobodies and $50,000. When Rickey traded Mize, he was twenty-eight and clearly one of the best hitters in the majors. In 1949, Mize's best days were behind him, but he was still significantly better than the Jones/Nelson combo.)

1951 Brooklyn Dodgers (New York Giants)

You know the story, and you know the lineup. In 1951, even Billy Cox—today remembered solely for his defense at third base—did a pretty good job with the bat. They did give 118 at-bats to reserve outfielder Don Thompson, who batted .229 with only three extra-base hits (all doubles). But Thompson had batted .311 with the Dodgers' top farm club in 1950, and deserved a shot. It just didn't work out (and in 1952, Thompson returned to Montreal and batted .346).

1956 Milwaukee Braves (Dodgers)

This one's easy: in 1956, the Braves should have played Joe Adcock more and Frank Torre less.

Over the previous four seasons, Adcock had established himself as one of the better-hitting first basemen in the National League. But he wasn't much with the glove, and as Bill James once wrote, "In the spring of 1956 a fancy-fielding first baseman named Frank Torre showed up in the Braves camp, and manager Fred Haney took a liking to him."

Torre made the club and wound up playing in 111 games, mostly as a defensive replacement for Adcock. But he also picked up 159 at-bats, and batted .258 with *few* walks and *little* power. Specifically, Torre hit exactly six doubles and exactly zero home runs in those 159 at-bats.

1959 Milwaukee Braves (Los Angeles Dodgers)

See "Fred, Frank, and Felix," page 89.

1. Roger A. Godin, *The 1922 St. Louis Browns: Best of the American League's Worst* (Jefferson, N.C.: McFarland, 1991).

2. Sam Greene, "Detroit Banks on Success at Eastern Front," *Sporting News,* June 29, 1944, p. 7.

3. ".444 Hitter Released," *Sporting News,* July 6, 1944, p. 13.

4. Shirley Povich, *The Washington Senators* (New York: G.P. Putnam's Sons, 1954).

5. Ibid.

6. Peter Golenbock, *Fenway: An Unexpurgated History of the Boston Red Sox* (New York: Putnam, 1992).

7. Ibid.

BRAVES SIGN BABE

The season was begun with the acquisition of Babe Ruth and a grand flourish of trumpets, and it ended without Ruth and Boston deeper in the mire of defeat than it ever had been. Emil Fuchs, president of the club, severed his connection with it in early August. Throughout the season the club never functioned properly and was badly unsettled.

—*Spalding's Official Base Ball Guide* (1936)

Ask reasonably knowledgeable fans which 20th-century team had the worst record, and most will probably come up with the '62 Mets. For a long time that would have been my answer.

Until I discovered the 1935 Boston Braves, who won thirty-eight games and lost 115. That works out to a .248 winning percentage, just slightly worse than the Mets' sterling .250 (40–120). The Braves actually had some pretty decent players; they'd won seventy-eight games in 1934, and would win seventy-one in 1936. They had a damn good manager in Bill McKechnie, who'd won pennants in Pittsburgh and St. Louis and would later win two more in Cincinnati. He's in the Hall of Fame.

The '35 Braves also had a big fellow named George Herman Ruth, the subject of this particular essay.

Ruth had turned thirty-nine in 1934, and though he could still hit—in '34, Ruth was maybe the third-best hitter in the American League, behind only Gehrig and Foxx—he couldn't do much else. As Fred

Lieb later wrote, "The pipestems that served as legs would no longer carry, with any alacrity, the barrel that served as a torso." Yankees manager Joe McCarthy had seen enough of Ruth, because the Babe could neither field nor run and also because the Babe made no little secret of his ambition to manage the Yankees. Soon.

But the Yankees had a problem: the Babe was still immensely popular with the fans, and owner Jacob Ruppert was reluctant to unceremoniously dump Ruth (particularly if there was a real chance that some other American League club would snap up the slugger, who would then turn around and beat the Yankees with his prodigious circuit clouts). So instead, Ruppert dumped Ruth to the National League. Ceremoniously.

Ruppert actually explored a number of options, most of them involving Ruth taking over as manager of another club. Prior to the 1934 season, Ruppert offered

George Brace Collection

Well, at least he looked good in the uniform.

to make Ruth manager of the Yankees' Newark farm club. Ruth's wife and business manager both advised against going to the minor leagues, and he told the writers that going to Newark would be the same "as to ask Colonel Ruppert, one of the foremost brewers in the country, to run a soda fountain."[1]

There were talks about trading Ruth to the Reds, who would then trade him to the Dodgers. Connie Mack, who owned and managed the Philadelphia Athletics, considered replacing himself as manager with Ruth, but later told writer Joe Williams, "I couldn't have made Babe manager. His wife would have been running the club in a month."[2]

Ruppert called everybody he knew, but in early 1935 there simply weren't any openings for a major-league manager. And Ruth apparently would not settle for less.

Meanwhile, in Boston, Braves owner Emil "Judge" Fuchs was getting desperate. Once a solid draw, his club had slipped precipitously in 1934:

	Record	Attendance
1930	70–84 (6th)	465,000 (5th)
1931	64–90 (7th)	515,000 (5th)
1932	77–77 (5th)	508,000 (3rd)
1933	83–71 (4th)	518,000 (3rd)
1934	78–73 (4th)	303,000 (6th)

Attendance held steady in 1932 and '33, which was impressive because, with the Great Depression in full swing, attendance was down significantly around the league; leaving the Braves aside, National League attendance dropped eighteen percent in 1931, eighteen percent in '32, and twenty percent in '33. Expressed another way, while in 1930 the Braves accounted for roughly nine percent of National League home attendance, just three seasons later they accounted for sixteen percent.

But for reasons not apparent, attendance at Braves Field plummeted in 1934, even though the team was almost exactly as competitive as it had been in the two previous seasons. Meanwhile, Fuchs owed a lot of people a lot of money, and couldn't afford to pay the rent on Braves Field.

Faced with financial disaster—and prohibited by the National League from turning the ballpark into a venue for dog racing—Fuchs needed help. He got some from New England politicians, who threw their weight behind a season-ticket campaign that allowed Fuchs to pay off his existing debt. Still, the future looked bleak, as a $200,000 note would come due during the '35 season.

Colonel Ruppert knew an opportunity when he saw one. Fuchs needed a miracle, and who had done more miraculous things in baseball than the Babe? Nobody. Phone calls were made. Letters exchanged. Meetings held. And on February 26, in Ruppert's New York office, with Ruppert, Fuchs, Ruth, and a gaggle of reporters in attendance, the big announcement was made: Ruth would join the Braves as player, "assistant manager," and vice president. A reporter asked Ruth what a vice president does. He didn't know. Fuchs answered, "Advisory capacity; be consulted on club deals and so forth."[3] According to most of the writers, Ruth was being groomed to take over from manager McKechnie.

When Ruth signed his contract with the Braves, he believed that he really would be a sort of assistant manager, with the chance to either take over as manager—perhaps as early as 1936—or wind up with enough stock in the Braves to be an active co-owner. He believed those things because Fuchs, in a long letter delivered a few days before the press conference in New York, told him so.

However, Ruth's actual contract wasn't nearly so expansive. In fact, Ruth soon discovered that, rather than being given stock in the Braves, he was seen by Fuchs as a potential investor; the hope was that Ruth would sink $50,000 of *his* money into the club. Ruth also was expected to participate in various promotional events, and play in exhibition games (which were, in those days, frequent for most major-league clubs). But on May 12, with Ruth struggling at the plate, he told McKechnie and Fuchs that he wanted to retire. Fuchs convinced him to hang on for a few more weeks, as the Braves hadn't yet visited every National League ballpark where various Babe Ruth Days were scheduled.

There would be one last hurrah. On May 25 in Pittsburgh, Ruth hit a two-run homer in the first inning. In the third, he hit another. And in the seventh, he hit one more home run (this time with nobody on base). The latter two homers came against Guy Bush, who years later would say, "I never saw a ball hit so hard before or since. He was fat and old, but he still had that great swing. Even when he missed, you could hear the bat go swish. I can't remember anything about the first home run he hit off me that day. I guess it was just another homer. But I can't forget that last one. It's probably still going."[4]

Ruth had hit the ball over the Forbes Field roof, something nobody had ever done before. It was Ruth's last home run, and his last hit. And emblematic of the Braves' fortunes in 1935, despite Ruth's three home runs and six runs batted in—he'd also singled home a run—the Braves lost the game, 11–7.

Ruth could still swing the bat. But he couldn't run, and so he couldn't field or do more than trot around the bases, and McKechnie was facing a trio of mutinous pitchers who said they might refuse to take the mound if Ruth were in right field.

In the first game of a doubleheader on May 30, Ruth struck out in the first inning, then left the game after hurting his knee in the bottom of the inning. As Robert Creamer wrote, "His career ended not with a bang in Pittsburgh but with a whimper in Philadelphia."[5]

McKechnie didn't want Ruth on the team, and by this point neither did Fuchs. Now all everybody needed was an out. And Ruth gave it to them. The same day Ruth played in his final game, the *Normandie*—the world's newest, fastest, and largest ocean liner—left Europe, bound for New York. The Babe and his wife had been invited to a party celebrating its arrival in four days, and he desperately wanted to be there. He couldn't play ball anyway, not with his sore knee. Fuchs refused. After all, though the attendance at Braves Field might be paltry, the Braves had three exhibition games scheduled (one in Haverhill, Massachusetts, and then two in Boston against the Dodgers), and some significant number of those in attendance were expecting to see the Babe, even if only for a pregame bow.

Ruth thought about it. And on June 2, with the *Normandie* halfway across the Atlantic, he summoned reporters to the locker room after a game against the Giants (in which he did not play). "I'm quitting," he told them. Moments later, a message arrived from Fuchs: "I have given Ruth his unconditional re-

Jolly Cholly's Follies

In the annals of managerial inactivity, there's certainly a place reserved for Cubs manager Charlie Grimm. In Game 6 of the 1935 World Series, the Cubs and Tigers were tied at three runs apiece after eight innings.

But Stan Hack led off the ninth with a triple over the center fielder's head. The next hitter, shortstop Billy Jurges, struck out. Due next? Starting pitcher Larry French, who had given up ten hits and two walks in his eight innings of work, and batted .141 during the season.

Grimm let French bat for himself. French grounded weakly to the pitcher. The next batter, Augie Galan, flied out to left field. Threat over.

In the bottom of the ninth, Goose Goslin's two-out single off French ended the game and the World Series.

Years later, Cubs second baseman Billy Herman would say, "When I think back on the 1935 World Series, all I can see is Hack standing on third base, waiting for somebody to drive him in. Seems to me now he stood there for hours and hours."[7]

lease, and he is through with the Braves in every way."[6] Later there was a great deal of public sniping between the two men, with Ruth issuing pronouncements to the press and Fuchs responding with long written statements. In the end, neither got what they'd wanted. Ruth's opportunities with the Braves weren't worth the paper on which Fuchs's letter was written, and Fuchs's dream of packed ballparks was little but a fantasy, based on the ridiculous misconception that fans will pay good money to watch a player who can't actually play.

Ruth never did manage. Fuchs, unable to meet his financial obligations, lost control of the Braves within a few months of Ruth's retirement. And the Braves finished the season with the worst record in the National League since the Cleveland Spiders went 20–134 in 1899. In 1936, the franchise's new owners, eager to erase the stigma of what happened in '35, officially changed the club's name to "Bees" (and they remained the Bees until 1941).

1. Marshall Smelser, *The Life That Ruth Built: A Biography* (New York: Quadrangle, 1975).

2. Ibid.

3. Ibid.

4. Robert Creamer, *Babe: The Legend Comes to Life* (New York: Simon & Schuster, 1974).

5. Ibid.

6. Ibid.

7. Eric Enders, *100 Years of the World Series* (New York: Barnes & Noble, 2003).

THE SALE OF PEE WEE REESE

I was very disappointed. It was July, and I was going to an all-star game in Kansas City, the American Association all-stars against the Kansas City [Blues], who were leading the league at that point, and I was on the train, and one of the Louisville writers told me that I had been sold to Brooklyn. I said something like, "Gee Christmas, that's the last place in the world I'd want to go. All you ever read about is guys getting hit in the head by fly balls, three guys ending up on first base. I don't want to go there."

—Pee Wee Reese

The Red Sox's mishandling of Pee Wee Reese is one of the more interesting blunders in a long series that were committed during the franchise's eighty-six years in the wilderness. The Red Sox briefly owned Reese's contract in the minor leagues, but let him go because the owner gave in to the wishes of the club's field manager . . . who also happened to be the club's shortstop. How did this happen, and what did it mean?

In February 1933, Tom Yawkey turned thirty years old and, at the same time, came into an inheritance of several million dollars, and—here's what brings him into our little story—used a goodly chunk of that cash to purchase the Boston Red Sox. This being the Depression, Yawkey was perhaps the richest owner in the majors, and eager to spend his riches on this new toy. Straight off, Yawkey hired immortal second baseman Eddie Collins to be his general manager, and instructed Collins to buy all his favorite players from any fellow American League owners who needed a cash infusion (which of course was most of them). These early efforts were more successful than not—his strategy of simply purchasing stars and has-beens lifted the Sox from terrible to mediocre—but not so successful that the Red Sox actually challenged for a pennant.

In 1937, Yawkey changed direction by hiring longtime American League umpire Billy Evans to create a farm system. Yawkey bought minor-league teams, and Collins and Evans stocked them with young players. In 1938, Evans recommended the purchase of the American Association's Louisville Colonels almost solely because of their shortstop: Harold "Pee Wee" Reese, a top-shelf glove man who batted .277 that season, during which he turned twenty. Money changed hands—Yawkey purchased one-third of the franchise, with friends holding the rest—and Louisville became Boston's top minor-league club.[1]

Both Evans and Yawkey wanted a young shortstop because the incumbent, Joe Cronin, had noticeably slowed down in the field, a situation which was causing his pitchers to revolt. Lefty Grove regularly criticized Cronin to the writers, and Wes Ferrell had twice walked off the mound (and back to his hotel room!) after Cronin misplays. Yawkey sympathized with his pitchers—he always was a player's owner—and told Evans to go find a young replacement.

The tricky part was that shortstop Cronin was also *manager* Cronin.

The Red Sox of this era (and throughout much of their history, really) were beset with bizarre internal struggles for authority. The general manager (Collins), the farm director (Evans), and the manager (Cronin) all more or less reported directly to Yawkey, and so important moves were made (or not made) depending on who was in favor at the moment, or simply who'd spoken to Yawkey last. For that matter, many of the veteran players, especially Grove, went directly to Yawkey as well. The owner, a big fan of the spirits, drank with just about everybody employed by the club, with results all too predictable.

Cronin still saw himself as an everyday shortstop. He was less than thrilled with the purchase of Reese, and after watching him make a couple of misplays in a spring exhibition game between the Red Sox and Louisville, Cronin recommended to Yawkey that Reese be dealt. It took a while, be-

George Brace Collection

Pee Wee Reese

cause the other clubs figured if the Red Sox were willing to trade Reese, something must be wrong with him. But on July 18, 1939, Reese was traded to Brooklyn for $35,000 and four players to be named later (or perhaps more cash; we've not been able to find out if the Dodgers ever sent Louisville the promised players).[2] He remained with Louisville through the end of the season, batting .279 and wowing everybody with his fielding. In 1940, still only twenty-one, Reese took over at shortstop for the Dodgers . . . supplanting player-manager Leo Durocher, who wanted to win more than he wanted to guard his place in the lineup. Reese would eventually play in ten All-Star Games. Cronin held *his* place in the Red Sox lineup through 1941 and continued to post the big hitting numbers that were his hallmark.

This deal caused a lot of consternation in the local press at the time, and to this day it leads to teeth-gnashing among serious Red Sox fans. Most recent histories of the franchise suggest that the Reese fiasco cost the club several pennants. Did it?

In 1940, Reese batted .272 while playing part-time for the Dodgers. In Boston, Cronin drove in 111 runs. In '41, Reese hit .229 with little power and made forty-seven errors, while Cronin drove in ninety-five runs, started the All-Star Game, and finished eleventh in the MVP voting. As good a player as Reese became, at this point he wasn't nearly as good as Cronin, let alone good enough to push the Red Sox into a pennant race.

In 1942, Cronin handed his job to rookie Johnny Pesky, and sat himself on the bench. For all the criticism Cronin gets for dealing Reese, he was not at all reluctant to make way for a young shortstop in '42, just one season removed from his own fine performance (Cronin did hurt his arm late in '41, and played some games at third base). Pesky had hit .325 at Louisville in 1941—winning American Association MVP honors—and in his first season with the Red Sox, he batted .331 and paced the loop with 205 hits.

Both Reese and Pesky spent 1943, '44, and '45 in the service. In '46, Pesky returned to the lineup and batted .335, then .324 in '47; in both seasons, he led the American League in hits (he'd done that in '42, too). While Reese had become a fine player in his own right, it is fair to say that the Red Sox were not suffering at shortstop during these years.

In 1948, the Red Sox acquired All-Star shortstop Vern Stephens from the Browns. They now had two of the best shortstops in the majors, and moved Pesky to third base. In the next three seasons, Stephens drove in 137, 159, and 144 runs. In Reese's entire career, the Red Sox were serious contenders without winning in only three seasons . . . *these* three seasons, 1948 through 1950. It's not at all apparent that replacing Stephens with Reese would have made a difference.

YANKEES EAT CROW

Despite DiMaggio's second batting championship, the streak of pennants ended in 1940, partially because of a miscalculation by Barrow and Weiss who, deciding righthander Ernie Bonham needed another year in the minors, did not bring him up until August 12, after which he went 9–3 with a league-leading 1.90 ERA.

—Donald Dewey and Nicholas Acocella, *Total Ballclubs* (2005)

From 1921 through 1964, the Yankees won twenty-nine pennants and twenty World Series. They finished lower than third place only twice (seventh in 1925, fourth in '45). Their most dominant stretch was 1936 through '43; in those eight seasons they won seven pennants, and their *smallest* end-of-the-season lead was nine games.

The Yankees started their pennant skein in 1936 with 102 wins. They won 102 again in 1937, ninety-nine in '38, and 106 in '39. In '41 they won 101, in '42 103, and in '43 they won ninety-eight. The Yankees were a juggernaut, and in none of those seasons did anybody else in the league have a real shot at the pennant.

But in 1940 the Yankees won only eighty-eight games. The Tigers went 90–64 and won the pennant, one game ahead of the Indians and two ahead of the Yankees. Detroit's .584 winning percentage was the lowest ever for an American League pennant winner. Even a subpar season, by their standards,

would have put the Yankees in the World Series yet again.

So what were the problems? Nothing much. Just the pitching. And the hitting.

In 1940, Yankee pitchers Spud Chandler, Marv Breuer, Steve Sundra, and Lefty Gomez combined for fifty-nine starts, 463 innings . . . and a 4.90 ERA.

Gomez, only thirty-one, was basically done, and pitched only twenty-seven innings (racking up a 6.59 ERA). Sundra had somehow gone 11–1 with a 2.76 ERA for the Yankees in '39, but there was nothing in his past (or, as it turned out, in his future) to suggest that that performance was anything but a fluke, and in 1940 he started only eight games.

No, the big problems were Chandler, who started twenty-four games and posted a 4.60 ERA, and Breuer, a rookie who started twenty-two games and racked up a 4.55 ERA. The pair combined for sixteen wins and sixteen losses.

Chandler had pitched well in 1938 but missed most of the '39 season with a broken ankle,[1] and his numbers in 1940 suggest he was still recuperating. On the other hand, after struggling in his first four starts, Chandler pitched a shutout in late May, and from that game through the end of the season the Yankees were 14–6 when he started. So there was no obvious reason to yank him from the rotation (such as it was; McCarthy didn't employ anything resembling a rotation as we think of it today).

Meanwhile, Breuer actually pitched fairly well through the first part of the season. The Yankees won nine of his first thirteen starts, and it wasn't until late July that he started getting hammered regularly. And on August 5, Ernie Bonham debuted.

Yes, Bonham was better than Breuer. After going 10–4 with a 2.32 ERA with Kansas City, he joined the Yankees and went 9–3 with a 1.90 ERA down the stretch. And yes, the Yankees could have called him up sooner than they did. But there wasn't any compelling reason to do that.

The Yankees' other problem, the problem they could and should have solved, was their hitting.

In each season from 1936 through '39, the Yankees led the American League in both runs scored and runs prevented. In 1940, if they'd led the league in just one of those categories, they would have won another pennant. Instead, they finished third in both (and third in the standings).

Collection of Author

Joe McCarthy

Transcendental Graphics

Tiny Bonham

The '39 Yankees had scored 967 runs despite getting virtually nothing from two positions. At first base, Babe Dahlgren played all 144 games after Lou Gehrig removed himself from the lineup, and while Dahlgren did hit fifteen home runs, he also batted .235 with correspondingly poor on-base and slugging percentages. At shortstop, Frankie Crosetti led off in (literally) every game[2] and scored 109 runs, but batted .233 with little power, and his sixty-five walks should have been little consolation to the Yankees.

Crosetti was still a young man—he turned twenty-nine during the Yankees' World Series sweep of the Reds that fall—but his last good season with the bat was 1936, and management should have been at least *thinking* about the club's next shortstop.

Same goes for Dahlgren. He'd done some nice things in the minor leagues, but there was no reason for the Yankees to assume he would improve significantly in 1940.

As it happened, Dahlgren did improve a bit, but that was balanced by Crosetti's further decline. And with stars Bill Dickey and Red Rolfe unexpectedly suffering the worst seasons of their careers—nothing the Yankees could have done about that—the club scored only 817 runs, exactly 150 fewer than in 1939.

But did the Yankees have any alternatives at hand? Obviously, they could have traded for, or purchased, a shortstop or first baseman. Or simply called one (or both) up from the minors. At that time the Yankees controlled two top-level farm clubs, the Kansas City Blues and the Newark Bears. These were the top first basemen and shortstops with those clubs, the Blues listed first at both positions:

		Games	On Base	Slugging
1B	Johnny Sturm	144	.360	.397
	Ed Levy	137	.340	.463
SS	Phil Rizzuto	148	.400	.482
	George Scharein	134	.301	.290

One of those names and sets of numbers should stick out. Phil Rizzuto, for his efforts with Kansas City, would be named by *The Sporting News* as No. 1 Minor League Player of the Year. In the early 1980s, Gene Schoor wrote a book about Rizzuto, which includes the following paragraph (pay special attention at the end):

> Both [second baseman Jerry] Priddy and Phil were ready for the big leagues in 1940 and could very well have been called up by the Yankees. But, under the fabulous Joe McCarthy, the Yanks had won their fourth straight pennant and fourth straight World Series in 1939, and they had no shortage of talent. The Yankees had the best second baseman in the majors, Joe Gordon, and Frank Crosetti was an ace shortstop. McCarthy wasn't about to make a change in the starting lineup. Phil and Jerry had to bide their time in Kansas City for another year, and it did neither team nor ballplayers any harm.

That's Gene Schoor for you: never let the facts get in the way of a righteous lie. Leaving Rizzuto in Kansas City all season did no harm. Oh, except the Yankees finished third when they should have finished first.

I believe that Joe McCarthy ranks among the very greatest managers, right there with John McGraw and Bobby Cox. But according to McCarthy's biographer, during the 1940 season he and Yankees general manager George Weiss stopped off in Kansas City to see Rizzuto, Sturm, and Priddy. McCarthy concluded none of them were quite ready to help the Yankees.[3]

With the benefit of hindsight, we can guess that Rizzuto, who took over as the Yankees' starting shortstop in 1941 and batted .307, was more than ready. He should have taken over from Crosetti in the middle of the season. Or Ed Levy should have been summoned from Newark to play first base. Or

"Hey, is that catching?"

On August 8, the Yankees lost to the Red Sox at Fenway Park, dropping their record to 50–51. They were in fifth place, eleven-and-a-half games behind the first-place Tigers. This information wasn't anything that observers were able to get a real handle on. Sure, the Yankees had suffered all sorts of injuries, but still . . . *fifth place? Eleven and one-half games out?? In August??? The Yankees????*

So faced, as all sportswriters are, with the demand for an explanation, *New York Daily News* columnist Jimmy Powers came up with a real whopper: some of the Yankees were suffering from the same malady that was, at that moment, killing Lou Gehrig.

And they'd caught it from Gehrig. On August 18, Powers wrote, "Has the mysterious polio germ which felled Lou Gehrig also felled his former teammates, turning a once-great team into a noncontender? . . . Poliomyelitis, similar to infantile paralysis, is communicable. The Yankees were exposed to it at its most acute stage . . . It is hard to believe mere coincidence can explain away the wholesale failure of the individuals . . ."

But of course that's exactly what it was. And of course Gehrig was felled by ALS (not some form of polio), which of course isn't communicable. Gehrig served court papers to sue Powers for $1 million; Bill Dickey and other Yankees also threatened lawsuits. Legal actions were avoided when Powers wrote, and the *News* published, an extensive retraction on September 26.

And the Yankees saved their strongest rebuttal for the field: after Powers' initial article was published, the Yankees won thirty-two of their remaining forty-six games.

Levy's teammate Tommy Holmes should have been called up to play right field, with Tommy Henrich shifting to first base. Hell, the Yankees should have done *something*.

Joe McCarthy's loyalty and patience generally served him quite well, but in 1940 those qualities cost him another championship.

1. Rich Westcott, *Diamond Greats* (Westport, Conn.: Meckler Books, 1988).
2. Herm Krabbenhoft research, reported in e-mail to author, Sept. 29, 2005.
3. Gene Schoor, *Scooter: The Phil Rizzuto Story* (New York: Scribner, 1982).
4. Alan H. Levy, *Joe McCarthy: Architect of the Yankee Dynasty* (Jefferson, N.C.: McFarland, 2005).

DUROCHER: "I HAVE THE RIGHT TO REMAIN SILENT"

For many Dodger fans, it all began in October 1941 . . . I thought, "Why God, why? Why had God done it to us and given it to them? Why?"

—Dodgers fan Joel Oppenheimer

You're probably familiar with the play that changed the course of the 1941 World Series. How, in the ninth inning of Game 4, with two outs, nobody on base, and the Dodgers leading by a run, Hugh Casey struck out Tommy Henrich, only to have catcher Mickey Owen let the ball get away, allowing Henrich to reach first safely and precipitating a miraculous four-run rally.

To this day, controversy rages over whether or not Casey struck out Henrich with a spitter,* but what's most interesting is what happened after Henrich (and Casey, and Owen) so unexpectedly kept the inning alive. Or rather, what did *not* happen.

First, some backstory. Hugh Casey, a hard-drinking Georgian, was not the sort of fellow often described as easygoing or imperturbable. Late in the '41 season, furious over a dubious balk call, he had— it was generally believed—aimed beanballs at George Magerkurth. The plate umpire.

Just the day before, in the third game of the Series, Casey's failure to cover first base on a routine grounder had fueled the two-run inning that propelled the Yankees to a 2–1 victory. It might be an exaggeration to call him a head case, but he was undoubtedly a player who required some maintenance.†

How then to explain what *didn't* occur after Henrich reached?

Did Owen go to the mound for an apologetic chat? No.

Did Leo Durocher, never known for inaction, trot out to calm his volatile reliever? No.

The game simply continued as though nothing had happened.

---

* Casey maintained until the very end that he'd thrown a curveball, and that's what Henrich said, too.

† In 1951, Casey shot himself to death.

"You feel well enough to play?"

In 1941, the pennant-winning Dodgers won 100 games. In 1942, the Dodger won 104 games—to this day, the franchise's all-time record—but they didn't win the pennant, because the Cardinals won 106 games.

It's hard to fault Durocher for anything. After all, how are you supposed to win *more* than 104 games?

Except Durocher probably did cost the Dodgers at least two games with his stubborn refusal to put Pete Reiser on the bench, where he belonged.

Reiser was a phenom, arguably the game's greatest young talent until Mays and Mantle arrived in 1951. In 1941, at twenty-two, Reiser had paced the National League in both batting average (.343) and slugging percentage (.558). He got off to an amazing start in 1942, and was batting in the .360 range in mid July. But Reiser always had a problem with outfield walls, and on July 19 in St. Louis, he crashed into the concrete wall in deep center field. Reiser suffered a severe concussion and a fractured skull, and was advised to give up baseball for the rest of the year.[2]

Six days later, he was back in the lineup. And he stayed in the lineup, all while suffering headaches, dizziness, and occasionally double vision.

As Reiser later told Donald Honig, "Leo kept me in there, but I probably shouldn't have played. Fly balls I could stick in my hip pocket, I didn't see them until they were al-

Leo Durocher (and friends)

Transcendental Graphics

DiMaggio singled; runners on first and second. But the situation remained manageable; still, just one out was needed.

Any movement from Durocher? None.

Charlie Keller slammed a double, driving in the tying and lead runs. Even then the game was not irretrievably lost; down only one with the top of the order due in the bottom of the ninth. Yet Durocher remained as immobile as a tombstone. And one walk and another double later, the Dodgers were indeed ready for burial.

In retrospect, it's inexplicable. To Durocher's credit, in *Nice Guys Finish Last*, his wonderful 1975 autobiography (co-written with Ed Linn), he acknowledged his failure.

> It wasn't the pitch to Henrich that did it, anyway. There was still only a man on first with two out. It was what happened afterwards. And right there is where I do think it is possible for a manager to second-guess himself. Considering Casey's actions within a very short period of time—pitching too quickly in Cincinnati, throwing those bean-balls at Magerkurth in Pittsburgh, and freezing twice within a matter of minutes the previous day—I should have called time and gone to the mound to remind him that he still only needed one out to end the ball game. To slow him down, in other words, until I was absolutely sure that he was in full control of himself.[1]

Durocher's regrets included a faulty memory. Quoting Leo: "The next batter was Charley Keller, a left-handed hitter. I had Larry French, a veteran left-hander . . . warming up in the bullpen. Given everything that had been happening, the situation screamed for me to replace Casey with French."

But he didn't have French.

French had relieved Kirby Higbe in the fourth inning, faced one batter, and been pinch-hit for in the bottom half. So Larry French was not an option.

Okay, anyone is entitled to forget who was not in their bullpen thirty years after the fact, but there's more to it than that. Many, perhaps most, of the best managers are obsessive men who can never, ever let go. When Earl Weaver's autobiography appeared in the '80s, he was still furious about the famous shoe-polish play in the '69 Series. Whitey Herzog, who wrote his memoirs in the late '90s, remained absolutely nutty about Don Denkinger's infamous call in the '85 Series.

It was the same with Durocher . . . except he had no umpire to blame. Over the course of thirty years, he must have replayed that fateful half-inning over and over in his mind, to the point where he was second-guessing himself over alternatives that never actually existed. The man they called "The Lip" was not exactly the most sympathetic character in baseball history, but in this single instance one can almost feel sorry for him.

Almost.

—*Mike Kopf*

most past me. I went from .380 down to .310. But the big thing wasn't the batting average; it was the fly balls that I couldn't run down. That's what hurt us. So we blow the pennant. I say blow—we won 104 ball games! But there's no question in my mind that by being stubborn, I cost the Dodgers the pennant in 1942."[3]

Reiser didn't blame Durocher. He blamed himself. But among the managers' many duties is to tell a player that he's just not healthy enough to play.—*R.N.*

1. Leo Durocher with Ed Linn, *Nice Guys Finish Last* (New York: Simon & Schuster, 1975).
2. Sidney Jacobson, *Pete Reiser: The Rough-and-Tumble Career of the Perfect Ballplayer* (Jefferson, N.C.: McFarland, 2004).
3. Donald Honig, *Baseball When the Grass Was Real* (New York: Coward, McCann, & Geoghegan, 1975).

BROWNS PLAY PETE GRAY

The worst thing that happened to our ballclub in 1945, which we should have won the pennant, was Pete Gray. And honestly I think if we hadn't had Pete . . . we could have won the pennant in 1945.

—Babe Martin

Over the years, a number of old St. Louis Browns argued that Pete Gray cost them the American League pennant in 1945. But did he?

What was Gray, a thirty-year-old man who'd lost his arm as a six-year-old boy, doing on the club in the first place? Had wartime demands for soldiering, sailoring, and manufacturing really depleted the manpower pool so badly that there was room in the majors for the partially limbless? The cynics of the day—and there were more than a few—saw the presence of Pete Gray as little more than grandstanding (or, more precisely, an attempt at grandstand-filling).

Had one of the two Philadelphia teams or the Boston Braves—the only three clubs consistently at or near the bottom of the standings throughout the war—given Gray a job, the intent would have been apparent. But when the Browns purchased the contract of Pete Gray from the Southern Association's Memphis Chicks on September 29, 1944, the Browns were tied for first place.

This, at least, was their defense when Gray made the big club the following spring. It's silly to suggest the Browns weren't thinking about public relations, considering the franchise had trouble drawing a million people over the entire length of the Great Depression. But Pete Gray was not plucked from a sandlot. He'd done impressive things with Memphis, like hitting well over .300, stealing sixty-eight bases, and being named the league's Most Valuable Player.

On the other hand, lots of players were piling up high batting averages in 1944. In the American Association—a tougher loop than the Southern—men like Red Marion, Cosmo Cotelle, and Wayne Blackburn posted big averages, yet never did play in the majors. In fact, Gray's .333 mark in '44 was just eleventh-best in his league.

So yes, Gray probably got a shot in the majors because he had an angle. What of it? He wasn't the first or the last. He is, though, the one who has caught the most heat for it over the years.

"He screwed up the whole team," said Ellis Clary (he of the 566 OPS in forty-one plate appearances). "If he's playing, one of them two-armed guys is sitting in the dugout pissed off."[1]

Had Gray been more of a hail-fellow-well-met sort, it is possible that comments like this would not exist for the record. Instead, Gray was all business and it rubbed a lot of his teammates the wrong way. We've seen it happen countless times in baseball history where a well-liked player with no tangible skills is hailed by his mates as a big contributor. Gray could not get by on personality alone.

He did have his moments, as any semiregular player is bound to. By and large, though, his was a lost season on the field. What worked in Memphis was not working in St. Louis. Bunting for hits was much tougher against the big leaguers, and stealing was something he tried rarely. Gray's greatest ability as a hitter was laying the bat on the ball, and he struck out just once every twenty-four plate appearances (but even that seems more impressive today than it did then).

Was Gray the worst hitter in baseball in 1945? These are the ten lowest OPS's among all 1945 players with at least 150 plate appearances.

OPS	Player	Team	Pos	PA	Post-'45 PA
447	Red Hayworth	Browns	C	168	0
479	Tony Daniels	Phillies	2B	250	0
482	Greek George	A's	C	159	0
492	Skeeter Webb	Tigers	SS	449	325
506	Al Cihocki	Indians	Inf	307	0
520	Pete Gray	Browns	OF	253	0
522	Mike Guerra	Senators	C	154	1367
526	Babe Martin	Browns	LF	203	21
527	Frank Drews	Braves	2B	169	0
529	Buddy Rosar	A's	C	325	1618

Gray wasn't even the worst hitter on the Browns. That honor goes to reserve catcher Red Hayworth, who did precious little in his fifty-six games. And given the quote at the top of this essay, the appearance of Babe Martin on this list rates very highly in the delicious irony department, as Gray's and Martin's contributions with the bats were practically identical.

George Brace Collection

Pete Gray

Another knock on Gray was his fielding. While the speedy Gray was famously adept at snaring fly balls, it is said that he wasn't so smooth on balls hit his way on the ground. Said third baseman Mark Christman:

> Pete Gray cost us the pennant in 1945. There were an awful lot of ground balls hit to him when he played center field. When the kids who hit those balls were pretty good runners, they could keep on going and wind up at second base. I know that lost us eight or ten ball games because it took away the double play or somebody would single and the runner on third would score, whereas if he had been on first it would take two hits to get him to score.[2]

Certainly, Gray was at a disadvantage when it came to making the transfer from glove to hand and then throwing. Upon fielding the ball in his glove (left) hand, he quickly tucked the glove under his upper right arm, and let the ball roll into his left hand. It all happened in a split-second—half a century later, Jim Abbott would use essentially the same technique—but it was enough for baserunners to occasionally take an extra base. But what was the practical impact of this?

Gray played in seventy-seven games. In twenty-four of those games he either pinch-ran, pinch-hit, or played a little bit in the field, batting fewer than three times. In these part-time games, the Browns were abysmal: three wins, twenty-one losses. Gray played the field in eight of those games, seven of which were losses. Of those seven losses, only two were by one or two runs. Two were 11–0 blowouts, and the rest were lost by at least three runs.

There were fifty-three contests in which Gray batted at least three times. Here's a breakdown of all Gray's games:

	W	L	Pct.	R/G for	R/G against
Gray w/3 or more PA	32	21	.604	4.11	3.38
Other Browns games	49	49	.500	3.87	3.77

The Browns were significantly *better* when Gray played all or most of the game than when he didn't. This is not to suggest he made them better. Given his offense, that would take a leap of logic greater than the premise that he cost them the pennant.

But the Browns finished six games out of first place. To win the pennant outright, the Browns would have to have gone 39–14, instead of 32–21, in Gray's games. Can seven of those twenty-one losses really be laid directly at his feet?

In his fifty-three games, the Browns went 10–8 in one-run games. Without Gray, they were 19–18 in one-run games. Once again, their record in these circumstances is better with him than without him. In order for Christman's recollections to be on the money, we would have to believe that Gray was solely responsible for most or all of these eight one-run losses or the two in which he played the field part-time.

If that happened, it's not showing up in the numbers. Gray's defensive stats—which, it should be said, do not account for baserunners taking liberties—are roughly neutral. He seems to have been slightly above average at tracking down drives to the outfield.

One would be hard-pressed to prove that *any* position player who saw the limited action Gray did cost his team six games in the standings, unless he was keeping Babe Ruth on the bench. And the Browns' other outfielders that season bore little resemblance to the Babe.

Of course, a number of Browns have argued that Gray's very presence disrupted the team. Denny Galehouse—who pitched for the Browns in '44, spent '45 in the service, then returned to the club in '46—cited complacency and Gray in the team's failure to repeat: "There was a very disturbing influence in that Pete Gray was there, that one-armed guy, and he tended to hurt

Missing Sigmund?

According to Ellis Clary, Browns pitcher Sig Jakucki derived a great deal of pleasure from tormenting Pete Gray, who didn't take the abuse in good humor. Clary: "We would have won the pennant again if it hadn't been for Pete Gray. He broke up the damn team over there. We would have won it again. Finally Luke [manager Luke Sewell] had to kick Sig off just before the season ended . . . The coming of Gray ultimately was the end of Jakucki for all the shit he pulled."[5]

Jakucki was suspended on August 31. Sewell said, "Jakucki has been suspended indefinitely for being out of condition, for insubordination, and because I believe it is for the general good of the team. I actually believe the ball club will be stronger without him."[6]

At the time, Jakucki was 12–10 with a 3.51 ERA. That looks pretty good until you discover that in this pitcher's year, the Browns finished the season with a 3.14 *team* ERA. So Sewell must have known it wouldn't be that hard to replace Jakucki's contributions.

Too, when a player was suspended for being "out of condition," it usually meant he was drinking so much that it showed up on the field. And then there's the story about Jakucki getting on a train with the rest of the team, and threatening to kill his manager. Supposedly, Sewell was holding money out of Jakucki's paychecks so the pitcher would have enough money to get home to Texas after the season. And Jakucki didn't like that, because it left him with less cash for booze.

So the facts don't support Clary's contention that Pete Gray cost the Browns Jakucki, which in turn cost the Browns the pennant. Jakucki was, by all accounts, a serious drunk, and would have been in trouble with Sewell whether Gray was around or not. And in terms of performance, it's not at all clear that losing Jakucki hurt the Browns. The same day they suspended Jakucki, they brought up pitchers John "Ox" Miller, Al LaMacchia, and Cliff Fannin from their Toledo farm club. Miller (2–1, 1.59), LaMacchia (2–0, 2.00), and Fannin (0–0, 2.61) all pitched well, with Miller doing better in his three starts than Jakucki would have.—R.N.

things, I think . . . the Pete Gray thing kind of interrupted the normal routine of things."[3]

But if Gray's impact on chemistry was so great, why did the Browns play so much better *with* him in the lineup? Are we to believe the disgruntled Brownies brooded when he was on the bench? Did they play harder when he was in the lineup because they were trying to compensate for his presence? If the latter were the case, doesn't that mean he actually helped the team when he played?

Was it, then, a blunder for St. Louis to have carried Gray all season?

He *was* a gate attraction. While total attendance was down, the Browns' attendance-per-home-date actually increased by nearly 7 percent (there were more doubleheaders in '45, which knocked down the overall numbers). And Gray was also a draw in road games, at least early in the season; on May 27, a dark and rainy day, nearly 40,000 fans showed up at Yankee Stadium to see a Browns-Yanks twin bill.[4]

And Gray's performance on the field, though perhaps less than useful, was by no means debilitating, considering his relatively spare playing time and the Browns' relatively distant finish. In the end, Pete Gray did not cost his team the pennant any more than Babe Martin did.

—*Jim Baker*

1. David A. Heller, *As Good as It Got: The 1944 St. Louis Browns* (Charleston, S.C.: Arcadia, 2005).

2. William C. Kashatus, *One-Armed Wonder: Pete Gray, Wartime Baseball, and the American Dream* (Jefferson, N.C.: McFarland, 1995).

3. Ibid.

4. James P. Dawson, "Yanks Top Browns, 10–9 in 14th and 3–1," *New York Times*, May 28, 1945, p. 14.

5. Peter Golenbock, *The Spirit of St. Louis: A History of the St. Louis Cardinals and Browns* (New York: Avon, 2000).

6. Fred Lieb, "Jakucki Put Off Browns' Train—And Off the Club," *Sporting News*, Sept. 6, 1945, p. 4.

MCCARTHY STARTS GALEHOUSE

I thought of Denny Galehouse as nothing but a relief pitcher. When Mc-Carthy picked him to start that game, the whole ballclub was upset about it. The whole twenty-five ballplayers. I don't think there was one of them that wasn't upset about it. There was mumbling and grumbling going on. You could hear the players, "Why in the hell is he pitching him?"

—Matt Batts in *Fenway: An Unexpurgated History of the Boston Red Sox*
(Peter Golenbock, 1992)

In 1948, for the first time in American League history, two teams finished the schedule tied for first place. On October 4, the Red Sox would host the Indians in a one-game playoff for the pennant and the opportunity to meet the Boston Braves in the World Series. Red Sox manager Joe McCarthy's problem? Who to start against Cleveland.

Six pitchers started at least ten games for the Red Sox in 1948. One of them, Mickey Harris, went 7–10 with a 5.30 ERA. Another, Joe Dobson, had started a day earlier. And another, Jack Kramer, had started two days earlier. That left three real possibilities:

	Age	W-L	ERA	Rest
Mel Parnell (L)	26	15–8	3.14	3
Ellis Kinder (R)	34	10–7	3.64	4
Denny Galehouse (R)	36	8–7	3.86	7

There were good arguments to be made for and against all three. Parnell was the best pitcher, but with the least rest and the least experience. Gale-house was probably the worst of the three, but had the most rest and the most experience. Kinder was right in the middle.

McCarthy chose Galehouse, who didn't escape the fourth inning. Kinder gave up four runs while pitching six innings in relief, and the Indians won 8–3 on their way to the World Series. Parnell didn't pitch. And McCarthy's choice of Galehouse became, according to author David Kaiser, "the most controversial choice of a starting pitcher in the history of baseball."[1]

Birdie Tebbetts was the Red Sox catcher that afternoon, and for decades he hinted at a secret reason for McCarthy's decision to start Galehouse instead of Parnell (or Kinder, who doesn't seem to have been seriously considered). In his book, published posthumously, Tebbetts wrote,

The story of why he picked Denny Gale-house is so logical and clear that I just don't understand why it hasn't been explained by some of these so-called expert journalists who are so completely dependent upon statistics. Stats are a great thing, but they only take you so far, and then your own logic and experience has to guide you to a decision. I will say this: I have written the reasoning of Joe McCarthy in my diaries and they are there to be read and pondered after I'm gone. If anybody cares. But his decision was so completely rational I don't understand why nobody has figured it out.[2]

Tebbetts has been gone for seven years now. And there are a lot of people who care. Me among them. But my efforts to read Tebbetts's diaries have, to this point at least, gone unrewarded.* So for the moment we're left to divine McCarthy's reason with the information at hand.

In those days, most managers figured if a starting pitcher had three days of rest, he was good to go. McCarthy wasn't most managers, though. As David Kaiser has noted, in 1948, "McCarthy had started pitchers on three days' rest on only nine occasions, and he had never started a pitcher on three days' rest twice in succession." Parnell had started on September 26 and he'd started on September 30; October 4 would make two straight starts on three days rest. And Parnell hadn't been particularly effective in those two previous starts.

What's more, by all accounts the wind was blowing out to left field when McCarthy woke up on the morning of the playoff game. Much of the Indians' power—Joe Gordon, Ken Keltner, Lou Boudreau—was right-handed. Parnell threw left-handed. On the other hand, Parnell was *exceptionally* stingy with the long ball; in 212 innings that season, he gave up only seven home runs.

According to Parnell, when he arrived at Fenway Park that morning, he found a baseball under his cap, signifying that he would start the game. But then, "while I was getting dressed, McCarthy came up from behind. He tapped me on the shoulder and said, 'Kid, I've changed my mind. I'm going with the right-hander. The elements are against the left-hander. The wind is blowing out strong to left field."[3]

Shortly after the game, McCarthy talked to reporter Joe Cashman from the *Boston Record*. He expressed concern about Parnell's relative inexperience and his left-handedness, and also said, "Mel wasn't too well rested and hadn't looked too good in his last start."[4]

---

* Tebbetts's diaries, if they really exist, currently reside with his heirs, somewhere in Florida.

Joe McCarthy (and friends)

Collection of Author

Second-Guessing the Winner

Lou Boudreau's selection of knuckleballer Gene Bearden to start for the Indians in the playoff was as questionable as any move Joe McCarthy made.

In the last two weeks of the season, Boudreau used a three-man rotation: Bearden, Bob Feller, and Bob Lemon. Feller and Lemon wound up in the Hall of Fame. Bearden did not. Lemon, though, wasn't pitching all that well down the stretch. Bearden was. On September 28 he shut out the White Sox, and four days later he whitewashed the Tigers.

The day before Bearden beat the Tigers, Lemon lost to them; the day after, Feller lost to them. This necessitated the one-game playoff for the pennant. Afterward, Boudreau actually discussed the decision about the next day's starting pitcher with his entire team. According to Boudreau, the only player who raised an objection to Bearden was second baseman Johnny Berardino, who said, "You can't pitch a left-hander in Fenway Park."[11]

Boudreau did have a great many options. Aside from Lemon, he had Sam Zoldak and Steve Gromek, both of whom had pitched exceptionally well that season in somewhat limited action (and both had pitched well in their last starts, a few weeks earlier). A lot of people thought Feller was the man for the job, as he'd pitched only two and two-thirds innings before getting knocked out of the previous day's game. Meanwhile, Bearden had pitched nine innings just two days earlier.

Fair enough. That narrowed the choices to Kinder and Galehouse, both of them right-handed. They were roughly the same age, and had been, roughly speaking, equally effective during the season. Other than the Red Sox, the two best teams in the league were the Indians and the Yankees. Galehouse had, during the season, beaten the Yankees twice and the Indians once. Among Kinder's ten victories were one over the Yankees and none against the Indians.

Also, Galehouse had a great deal of experience and success in big games. He was, at the time, one of only four active American League pitchers who'd won at least one hundred games. In 1944, while with the Browns, he started two games in the World Series and completed both of them, allowing only three runs. And on July 30, 1948, he'd relieved Parnell in the first inning of a game against the Indians, gone the rest of the way, and allowed only two hits. But, writes Glenn Stout, "McCarthy ignored the fact that Cleveland had later belted him for nine runs in five innings, and that after winning two games in early September he had pitched only twice since September 12 and been shellacked each time."[5]

This "fact" wasn't a fact, though. Not all of it. Galehouse pitched against the Indians three times in 1948. In addition to the fine relief outing on July 30, he started against Cleveland twice. On June 17, he gave up five runs in three-plus innings. And on August 25—the "later" Stout refers to—he gave

Yes, Bearden was a knuckle-baller. But Bearden wasn't a knuckleballer the way we think of them now. In those days, a "knuck-leballer" relied on the pitch but not exclusively. According to Ted Williams, in the playoff game, "Every ball he threw was a little knuckleball or a little breaking curve. Knuckle or curve. Knuckle or curve. We got four hits." [12] Bearden did throw mostly knuckleballs (roughly eighty percent, according to Boudreau) but was known to throw the occasional fastball and slider, too. And for another thing, *knuckleballers get tired, too* (if they didn't, Wilbur Wood and Phil Niekro would have started eighty games per season rather than forty).

Boudreau also made a couple of questionable lineup choices. In the interest of packing his lineup with right-handed hitters who might take advantage of the wind and the Wall, Boudreau started outfielder Allie Clark at first base, though Clark hadn't played the po-sition since 1942, when he was in the Piedmont League; and Bob Ken-nedy in right field, though Kennedy had started only a few games for the Indians since coming to the club in an early-June trade.

Neither Kennedy nor Clark did anything (Clark was pulled for de-fense in the fourth inning), and Bearden didn't actually pitch all that well: five hits, five walks, and three runs in nine innings. But he was plenty good enough.

up seven hits and four runs in one and two-thirds innings. (It's possible that Stout conflated these two starts; if you combine them, you get nine runs and *nearly* five innings.)

On the other hand, it's true that Galehouse got shellacked in his two out-ings after September 12: six and two-thirds innings, thirteen hits, and six runs.

On yet another hand, what's so special about September the 12th? On the 11th, Galehouse started against the Athletics and pitched a complete game, limiting the A's to just one run.

McCarthy told Joe Cashman that Galehouse was "more experienced . . . an old hand at pressure pitching [with] a better record than Kinder against the Indians." [6] And McCarthy had an incredible memory, which allowed him, throughout his career, to choose his starting pitchers based on factors that we can, even today, only guess about.

There's one more thing, though . . . Galehouse might not have been any better rested than Parnell. Yes, on paper he was plenty rested: seven days worth. But forty years later he recalled, "I had been in the bullpen Sunday"—during a must-win game against the Yankees—"from about the fourth in-ning on. Mr. McCarthy told me to go down to the bullpen and get loose and stay up when we were at bat and when the Yankees were at bat. So I threw six innings the day before. I don't think people in Boston knew I'd threw for those six innings. That's something that hasn't been brought out at all." [7]

McCarthy had to have known, though. McCarthy was famous for know-ing everything. We are left, then, to assume that either McCarthy knew Galehouse had pitched six "innings" in the bullpen and didn't care, or that Galehouse was, forty years and plenty of blame later, exaggerating the ex-tent of his fatigue. After all, if he'd really been so tired, he could have simply told McCarthy.

Like many controversial decisions, this one wasn't quite so controversial when it happened. In the *Sporting News*, Ed McAuley wrote,

> Most of the baseball writers had guessed that McCarthy would start ei-
> ther Ellis Kinder or Mel Parnell in this large contest, but this observer
> has read no criticism of Marse Joe's choice of Galehouse. Doylestown
> (O.) Denny is known as a money pitcher. He was well rested and once
> earlier in the summer he had held the Indians to two hits in eight and
> two-thirds innings. [8]

In the *New York Times*, columnist Arthur Daley allowed that McCarthy had "gambled on the ancient" Galehouse. [9] But he didn't make a fetish of it. In ret-rospect, it's clear that Parnell probably would have been a better choice than

Galehouse or Kinder. As McCarthy supposedly told Parnell afterward, "I made a mistake. I'll just have to live with it." [10]

But if we had been Joe McCarthy in 1948 and we knew everything that he knew, we might well have made the same decision he made.

1. David Kaiser, *Epic Season: The 1948 American League Pennant Race* (Amherst: University of Massachusetts Press, 1998).

2. Birdie Tebbetts with James Morrison, *Birdie: Confessions of a Baseball Nomad* (Chicago: Triumph, 2002).

3. Peter Golenbock, *Fenway: An Unexpurgated History of the Boston Red Sox* (New York: Putnam, 1992).

4. Glenn Stout and Richard A. Johnson, *Red Sox Century: One Hundred Years of Red Sox Baseball* (Boston: Houghton Mifflin, 2000).

5. Ibid.

6. Ibid.

7. Ibid.

8. Ed McAuley, *Sporting News*, Oct. 13, 1948.

9. Arthur Daley, "Sports of the Times," *New York Times*, Oct. 5, 1948, p. 33.

10. Alan H. Levy, *Joe McCarthy: Architect of the Yankee Dynasty* (Jefferson, N.C.: McFarland, 2005).

11. Lou Boudreau with Russell Schneider, *Covering All the Bases* (Champaign, Ill.: Sagamore Publishing, 1993).

12. Ted Williams as told to John Underwood, *My Turn at Bat: The Story of My Life* (New York: Simon & Schuster, 1969).

"HEADS, YOU WIN. TAILS, I LOSE."

I had a boyhood buddy named Noel Moran. Noel's grandfather was watching the 1951 playoff game against the Giants, and he was in his eighties. When Branca threw the pitch, and Thomson knocked it out, he bent over, called Branca a "dago bastard," spit at the screen, and keeled over dead.

—Dodgers fan Joe Flaherty

The Brooklyn Dodgers, of course, lost the 1951 pennant on the last pitch of the last game of their best-of-three playoff series with the New York Giants. With the benefit of hindsight, we can guess the Dodgers wouldn't have blown that huge August lead over the Giants if they'd done one of two things: 1) called up, sooner than they did, right-hander Clem Labine, who spent much of the summer fooling American Association hitters, or 2) pitched Labine more often, once he was up, than they did.

After joining the club in August, Labine initially pitched in relief, but on the 28th he started for the first time, and earned his first of four straight complete-game wins. On September 21, though, Labine gave up a first-inning grand slam to Phillies third baseman Willie "Puddin' Head" Jones. As Labine would later tell the story, he wanted to pitch from the stretch, manager Charlie Dressen wanted him to take the full windup . . . and when Labine pitched

from the stretch *and* gave up the homer, Labine went straight into Dressen's doghouse, and wouldn't pitch in any of the Dodgers' next eight games. Two of those games were one-run losses, and it's certainly possible that Labine would have made a difference.

It's not all that likely, though. And perhaps due to all the extra rest, Labine pitched a shutout in the second game of the playoff series (see sidebar).

There's another decision, far more obscure, that just might have cost the Dodgers the pennant.

With the Dodgers and Giants tied at the conclusion of the 154-game schedule, they would play a best-of-three series to determine the National League championship. A few days earlier, there was a coin flip in New York, at National League headquarters, to determine the game sites. The Dodgers won.[1]

Which meant they lost. As Ralph Branca later recalled,

For some reason, when the Dodgers won the toss for the playoffs in 1946, they elected to go to St. Louis to play the first game and then come back and play the next two in Brooklyn. I do not know who made the decision, but because of it we had to travel by train to St. Louis, which was a twenty-six-hour trip, and we were exhausted, and of course, we lost.

And the reason I bring that up, now it's 1951, and we're in Philadelphia, and the Giants are in Boston, and we have a playoff with the Giants, and they toss a coin, and the Dodgers win the toss again. Only this time, no one is around because they're all in Philadelphia, and they call a guy named Jack Collins, who was ticket manager. Collins remembers that the '46 decision was wrong, that we went all the way to St. Louis and then all the way back, and so he makes the decision that we'll play the first game at Ebbets Field and the next two at the Polo Grounds.[2]

Was Jack Collins really powerful enough to be given this decision? Doesn't seem likely. I ran Branca's story by Buzzie Bavasi, who in 1951 was, among other things, Dodgers owner Walter O'Malley's right-hand man. Bavasi's take?

"Ridiculous. No one but Charlie Dressen made the decision . . . Charlie told me what to do and that was it."[3]

So how did Collins get the goat horns? Well, he, unlike Dressen and Bavasi, was in New York and might well have announced the Dodgers' decision after the coin flip went their way. Dressen, who never made a mistake he couldn't blame on somebody else, probably told anybody who'd listen that the pointy-headed ticket manager was the one who screwed up. And shortly after the season, Collins—who, according to Bavasi, wasn't one of O'Malley's favorite people anyway—was fired, and thus wasn't around to defend himself.

So it was Dressen. But was there *any* good reason for potentially playing two of three on the road?

Both clubs were outstanding that season in both home and road games. The Giants were 49–27 at the Polo Grounds, 47–31 away from home. The Dodgers were 49–28 at Ebbets Field and 47–30 on the road. And of course the twin advantages of not traveling beforehand and sleeping in one's own bed weren't operative here, as the entire proceedings would take place within the confines of two New York boroughs.

Historically, though, the Giants struggled at Ebbets Field. From 1947 through '51, the Giants fared well against the Dodgers at home: 28–26. In

The Blame Game

Coach Clyde Sukeforth lost his job because he recommended Branca rather than Carl Erskine, when Charlie Dressen called the bullpen.

Sukeforth didn't do anything wrong, nor did Dressen. Preacher Roe was the Dodgers' second-best pitcher (behind Newcombe), but Roe was left-handed and wasn't going to face the right-handed-hitting Thomson. Carl Erskine was getting loose alongside Branca, but Erskine wasn't throwing particularly well, and anyway that season he wasn't particularly effective, posting a 4.46 ERA.

Meanwhile, Branca had pitched effectively in the first game of the playoff series, and his 3.26 ERA that season would rank tenth-best in the league. Much has been made of Thomson's home run off Branca two days earlier, and another earlier in the season. Overall, though, Branca had done decently enough against Thomson in their careers: in fifty-three plate appearances, Thomson had batted .265 (with four walks and three home runs).

Maybe Dressen made a big mistake in the second playoff game, though. The Dodgers blew out the Giants, 10–0, with rookie Clem Labine tossing a six-hitter. A complete game. If Labine hadn't pitched all nine innings—the Dodgers went ahead 6–0 in the top of the seventh, then 8–0 in the eighth—maybe he, a ground-ball pitcher, would have been available the next afternoon, just to face Thomson (actually, Labine did finally get loose in the bullpen, but not until Branca entered the game). Exactly fifty years later, Bob Brenly would make exactly the same mistake with Randy Johnson in Game 6 of the World Series. But nobody remembers Brenly's gaffe, because in the end it didn't cost him anything.

Brooklyn, though, the Giants were awful, going just 18–38 (including 2–9 in 1951).

You probably know what happened next. Branca started the first game, in Flatbush, and gave up three runs, two of them coming on a Bobby Thomson home run that would, according to Branca, have been a routine fly ball in the Polo Grounds. The Dodgers lost, 3–1. Branca relieved in the third game, in Harlem, and gave up Thomson's pennant-winning home run that would, according to Branca, have been an out in Ebbets Field.

Of course, considering the vast difference in the two stadiums' geometries, it's highly unlikely that all the other events would have occurred similarly. But then, that's sort of the point. We *know* it makes more sense to play two of three games at home, and we *know* the Dodgers lost the series, two games to one.

Would the Dodgers have won the pennant if Dressen had made a different choice? I believe they would have. The Dodgers won the second game, 10–0, and they just barely lost the other games. I think they would have won one of those other games, if they'd been played in the other ballpark.

1. John Drebinger, *New York Times*, Sept. 28, 1951, p. 43.

2. Peter Golenbock, *Bums: An Oral History of the Brooklyn Dodgers* (New York: Putnam, 1984).

3. Buzzie Bavasi, e-mail to author, Sept. 16, 2005.

BAD TRADES (PART 1)

or

"HEY, IT SEEMED LIKE A GOOD IDEA AT THE TIME . . ."

Men go shopping just as men go out fishing or hunting, to see how large a fish may be caught with the smallest hook.

—Henry Ward Beecher, *Proverbs from Plymouth Pulpit*

Disclaimer 1: This article is not meant to be a comprehensive list of the worst trades in major-league history, but rather just a list of lousy trades that I feel like writing about, but at no great length.

Disclaimer 2: We have an incredibly incomplete understanding of which trades really were the worst. Sure, we can talk about the *results* of a trade with some precision. But let's say there are two young minor leaguers: Joe Hitter and Jim Pitcher. Given the omnipotence of The Almighty, we know that Joe Hitter's chances of becoming an outstanding player is ninety percent; Jim's chance of becoming a fantastic pitcher is five percent.

But the Mammoths don't share our omnipotence, and they foolishly trade Joe to the Mundys for Jim, straight up. Terrible trade for the Mammoths.

Except Joe flops, and Jim wins two-hundred games. Now who made the terrible trade?

I don't know that anything precisely like this has happened in the real world, but I'm sure that things like it have happened. Trades that looked one way on paper—perfect paper, I mean, if such a thing existed—wound up working out the other way. What's more interesting—at least in the context of this book—are those trades that shouldn't have made sense to one side or the other, *at the time.* We'll certainly find some of those. But they're not as common as you might think.

Short Explanation of Statistics: With each trade, after each listed player there is one number: the sum of all Win Shares earned by that player after the trade in question.

December 12, 1903: Cardinals trade Mordecai Brown (284 Win Shares) and Jack O'Neill (9) to Cubs for Jack Taylor (71) and Larry McLean (73).

This looked like an awfully strange deal at the time. Brown was twenty-seven, had pitched in only one major-league season and gone 9–13—albeit with an excellent 2.60 ERA—in that one season. Meanwhile, Taylor was only two years older than Brown, and over the previous two seasons, he'd won forty-four games and posted ERAs even lower than Brown's. In 1902, Taylor had actually been the best pitcher in the National League, and in '03 he'd been the second-best starter for a team that finished 82–56.

So why was Cubs president James Hart willing to trade Taylor? According to one source,

> . . . Taylor had gotten into trouble with ownership as a result of his performance in the postseason exhibition series against the White Sox. Taylor was uncharacteristically roughed up in his four starts and finished with a 1–3 record. After the series—which ended in a 7–7 tie—Hart became suspicious that Taylor had "thrown" the games for profit. Although Hart did not push for charges against Taylor, the Chicago magnate obviously was no longer interested in his services.[1]

So Hart showed up at the December owners' meetings with the intention of trading Taylor. Which he did, sending Taylor and rookie catcher Larry McLean to the Cardinals in a swap for Brown and veteran backstop Jack O'Neill.

O'Neill couldn't hit, and was nearly finished. McLean could hit a little, but spent most of 1904 on the bench and all of '05 and '06 in the minors before resurfacing with the Reds in 1907. So essentially this came down to Brown for Taylor.

And what a mismatch that was.

In his first season with the Cardinals, Taylor did win twenty games. He slumped in '05, but came back so strong in '06 that the Cubs—by then under new management—made a trade to bring Taylor *back* to Chicago, and he went 12–3 in the second half as the Cubs finished 116–36 (still the best record in major-league history). Taylor's career ended in 1907, though.

Meanwhile, Brown had become a huge star immediately upon joining the Cubs. From 1904 through 1910, there was nobody better—not even Christy Mathewson—as Brown went 160–66 with a 1.56 ERA, and also served as the National League's top reliever (not that anybody really noticed in those days).

July 25, 1910: Philadelphia Athletics trade Joe Jackson (294) to Cleveland Naps for Bris Lord (46).

It's fun to wonder how history might have been different if Connie Mack

Joe Jackson

hadn't traded Jackson. Would the A's have won more pennants than they did? Well, the A's *did* win in 1910 and 1911, with Lord playing quite well in both seasons (and '11 was the first of Jackson's many brilliant seasons). In 1912, Lord dropped off badly while Jackson was going gangbusters with Cleveland, but the A's finished fifteen games out of first place so Joe wouldn't have made a real difference. In 1913, the A's returned to first place and beat the Giants in the World Series. And in 1914 they won another pennant, but got swept by the Miracle Braves in the Series.

After that, Mack broke up the club, selling or trading nearly all his best players. If Jackson were still with the A's, Mack probably would have dumped him, too. Would Jackson have eventually wound up with the White Sox, and helped throw the Serious in 1919? It's impossible to know, but there were only a few American League teams—in those days, good players didn't switch leagues—with the wherewithal to acquire a superstar like Jackson.

Why did Mack trade Jackson?

It just didn't work out in Philadelphia. Jackson, a former millhand from South Carolina, was barely nineteen when he debuted with the Athletics in 1908. He spent most of 1909 in the minors—and batted .358 to lead the Sally League—before being summoned back to Philadelphia in September. The A's were in a pennant race with the Tigers, but Jackson didn't seem all that interested. He didn't like Philadelphia, he didn't like his teammates, and he had a habit of skipping morning practice sessions. One day, while riding a streetcar to the ballpark, Jackson hopped off and spent the afternoon at a burlesque house.

Mack had seen enough. In 1910, he loaned Jackson to New Orleans, and later that summer traded him to the Cleveland club, owned by Mack's friend Charlie Somers.

Many years later, Jackson said of his time with the A's, "It wasn't anything I had against Mr. Mack or the ball club. I just didn't like Philadelphia."

May 22, 1913: Giants trade Heinie Groh (270), Red Ames (77), Josh Devore (9), and $20,000 to Reds for Eddie Grant (10) and Art Fromme (14).

and

July 20, 1916: Giants trade Edd Roush (286), Bill McKechnie (20), and Christy Mathewson (1) to Reds for Buck Herzog (55) and Red Killefer (0).

John McGraw was, one of the all-time great judges of talent. But without these twin misjudgments, there probably would have been one hell of a pennant race in 1919. That season ranked among the finest for both Groh and Roush. Here's what Groh and Roush did in 1919, along with what the Giants who played the same positions (third base for Groh, center field for Roush) did:

		Shares
Reds	Roush	33
	Groh	30
Giants	Kauff	24
	Z'man	14

Replace Benny Kauff and Heinie Zimmerman with Edd Roush and Heinie Groh, and you pick up twenty-five Win Shares: something like eight wins. The Giants finished nine games behind the Reds that season.

Eight-and-a-half seasons after McGraw traded Groh, the Giants made another Groh-related blunder when they sent two players and $150,000—a gigantic amount of money in those days—to the Reds in exchange for Groh, who had just turned thity-two and was, as the Giants discovered, well past his prime. The Giants did win three straight pennants immediately after Groh rejoined the club, and he did play a role in those championships (not to mention hitting .474 in the '22 World Series). But that $150,000 certainly could have been spent more wisely, and after 1925 the Giants didn't win another flag until 1933.

May 6, 1930: Red Sox trade Red Ruffing (265) to Yankees for $50,000 and Cedric Durst (3).

Durst was just an old fourth outfielder with a sub-.300 on-base percentage who went back to the minors after the season. But in fairness to the Red Sox, it should be noted that $50,000 was an awful lot of money in 1930. In those days, most of the minor-league clubs were still independent, and you could buy a pretty good player for $50,000.

Ruffing's record with the Red Sox was really quite amazing. He debuted with them in 1924, shortly after his nineteenth birthday, but didn't earn a decision in twenty-three innings and spent most of that season in the minors. He made it back for good in 1925; these were his W-L from '25 through '29: 9–18, 6–15, 5–13, 10–25, 9–22. The Red Sox were terrible, though, and Ruffing didn't pitch all that poorly. His ERA+ in those same seasons: 90, 92, 90, 106 (he went 10–25), 88.

In 1930, Ruffing was still only twenty-five. But he started the season 0–3 with a 6.38 ERA, and the Red Sox were ready to deal. The Yankees weren't great in 1930—they finished third—but they were plenty good for Ruffing, who didn't pitch a whole lot better but won fifteen games (and lost only five) in his five months with the Yanks. In 1931, Ruffing again didn't pitch any better than he had with the Red Sox, but won sixteen games. His first great season was 1932—18–7, 3.09 ERA, and 190 strikeouts—and then in 1935 he began a five-year run as one of the American League's best starting pitchers.

And as improbable as it would once have seemed, the pitcher who began his career with thirty-nine wins and ninety-six losses eventually was elected to the Hall of Fame.

December 3, 1936: Dodgers trade Frenchy Bordagaray (45), Dutch Leonard (210), and Jimmy Jordan (0) to Cardinals for Tom Winsett (10).

Not exactly a major deal, but I need an excuse to repeat this wonderful little story about then-Cardinals general manager Branch Rickey,* from Dewey and Acocella's *Total Ballclubs*:

> Branch Rickey was second to nobody in building up untalented prospects as a prelude to trading them for more than they were worth. One of his most successful deceptions was a promotion of outfielder Tom Winsett, whom he constantly described as "a coming Babe Ruth" and whom he managed to palm off on Brooklyn . . . After Winsett had

---

* Later, Rickey would run the Dodgers during most of the 1940s, and the Pirates during much of the '50s.

hung up his spikes with a grand total of eight homers over parts of seven seasons, Rickey offered a more honest evaluation of the outfielder: "Woe unto the pitcher who throws the ball where Winsett is functioning. But throwing it almost anywhere else in the general area of home plate is safe."[2]

Yes, it's a wonderful little story. I doubt if the Dodgers were fooled by Rickey's talk about Babe Ruth, though. Winsett had just turned twenty-seven, and his major-league stats included a .218 batting average and exactly one home run in 101 at-bats.

But in 1936, while playing for the Cardinals' farm club in the fast American Association, Winsett had batted .354 with fifty home runs and 154 RBI. The year before, it was .348–20–90. I don't know about you, but I'll take my chances with a guy who can put up those numbers, hole in his swing or not.

And the players Rickey swindled from the Dodgers? Jordan didn't play in the majors after the deal. Bordagaray hung around for a while as a utility man, his career extended a few years by the war. And Leonard, by far the best player in the deal? A knuckleballer, Leonard was sent to New Orleans in 1937, then lost to the Senators in the Rule 5 draft before throwing a single pitch for Rickey's Cardinals.

December 11, 1941: Cardinals trade Johnny Mize (114) to Giants for Ken O'Dea (42), Bill Lohrman (17), Johnny McCarthy (10), and $50,000.

The figures for the ex-Giants are inflated by the soft competition of the war years. O'Dea, for example, posted sub-.300 on-base percentages in 1941 and '42, then jumped to .345, .343, and .359; when the boys came back in 1946, his OBP plummeted and he was out of a job. McCarthy spent 1942 in the minors, returned to the majors (with the Braves), and batted .304 before he got the letter from Uncle Sam.

Essentially, absent World War II the only notable commodities exchanged in this trade would have been Mize and the cash.

Why did Cardinals general manager Branch Rickey let Mize get away? It's not because he had some great prospect waiting in the wings. In both '42 and '43, first base for the Cardinals was manned by Ray Sanders and Johnny Hopp, both of them good hitters, neither of them in Mize's class (and both batted left-handed, so there wasn't a natural platoon there). I think Rickey was just looking ahead. This deal was made four days after the Japanese attacked Pearl Harbor. Could Rickey have been figuring that Mize would eventually be drafted, and if the Cardinals were going to get anything for him, it would have to be now? At that time, there were people who thought the war might last another four or five years, maybe longer. Mize was about to turn twenty-nine, so if the war lasted five years he wouldn't be back until he was thirty-four . . . well past his prime. One of Rickey's most famous aphorisms was, "Trade a player a year too early rather than a year too late."[4]

As things turned out, 1) Mize was drafted after the '42 season, 2) the war lasted three more years, 3) Mize returned to the majors in 1946, when he was thirty-three, and though Mize certainly could still hit, he played more than 115 games in only two seasons after the war. So maybe Rickey knew what he was doing

Oh, and there's this: when Rickey sold a player to another club, he received a bonus of ten percent of the sale price. In 1941, five thousand dollars bought a lot of cigars.

December 14, 1948: Washington Nationals trade Mickey Vernon (181) and Early Wynn (243) to Indians for Ed Klieman (4), Joe Haynes (6), and Eddie Robinson (107).

Let's look at what these guys did in the three previous seasons.

Hitters	Age	Games	Avg	OBP	Slug
Vernon	30	452	.287	.345	.410
Robinson	27	237	.256	.314	.422

Pitchers	Age	Innings	W-L	ERA
Wynn	28	552	33–39	4.32
Klieman	30	187	8–6	3.13
Haynes	31	509	30–25	3.34

An interesting mix of players. Vernon certainly had a more extensive—and thus more reliable—track record than Robinson, but he was three years older than Robinson, and Vernon's three-year stats are heavily inflated by his fantastic '46 season; in the next two seasons he was first decent and then awful. Considering their ages and recent performances, one could certainly have made a reasonable argument for Robinson being the better player. In fact, neither of them looked like particularly good players, considering the standards for first basemen.

And looking at the pitchers, it's Haynes, and not Wynn, who looks like the class of the group. What the chart doesn't tell you (*stupid chart*) is that three weeks before the trade, Haynes "underwent an operation for calcium deposits in his right shoulder at Johns Hopkins hospital." So why would Washington want him included in the deal? He was the owner's son-in-law. Over the next four seasons, all of them with the Senators, Haynes went 10–21 with a 5.42 ERA. Even allowing for Haynes's injury, it should be noted that Klieman was more than just a throw-in. Pitching for Cleveland in 1947, he'd led the American League in games pitched—fifty-eight, all in relief—and in '48 his 2.60 ERA made him one of the better relievers in the league. He barely pitched after the Senators got him, but it's hard to fault them for that.

Of course, Wynn wound up pitching his way into the Hall of Fame. Vernon didn't do quite that well, but he certainly ranked as one of the better first basemen in the majors over the next eight seasons. To the Senators' credit, though, they did get him back from the Indians in 1950, and they got him really, really cheap, as Vernon batted .189 in his first twenty-eight games, leading the Indians to give him up for nothing (the Indians did have Luke Easter, a fine hitter, and Easter could play only at first base).

Like most deals, this one looked pretty even at the time. But occasionally trades that look perfectly balanced wind up being incredibly lopsided, and this is a prime example.

November 10, 1948: Tigers trade Billy Pierce (246) *and* $10,000 to White Sox for Aaron Robinson (32).

One could, I suppose, come up with some sort of system to place a dollar value on a Win Share at any particular point in history. This occurs to me as I wonder if $10,000 alone might have been fair compensation for catcher Aaron Robinson's thirty-two Win Shares after the deal.

And then of course there's Billy Pierce, who won 208 games after the trade, 186 of them with the White Sox.

October 19, 1949: A's trade Nellie Fox (298) to White Sox for Joe Tipton (29).

Within a year, two brilliant trades for the ChiSox.

At the time of this one, Tipton was twenty-six. In 1947, he'd batted .375 in the Eastern League and skipped straight to the majors in '48, batting .289 in limited action with the Indians, who traded him to the White Sox for a pretty decent pitcher (the above-mentioned Joe Haynes). Tipton slumped to .204/.306/.309 with the White Sox in '49, and then Connie Mack gave up Nellie Fox to get him.

Why? It's hard to say. The A's did need a catcher, but any evidence that Tipton was significantly better than Mike Guerra and Joe Astroth—Mack's catchers in 1949—seems to have disappeared. Yes, Guerra was getting up there in years, but he had one more good year left in him, and Astroth was younger than Tipton.

Fox, a twenty-one-year-old rookie in '49, had batted .255 with thirty-two walks and only nine strikeouts in eighty-eight games, and showed the flashy defense for which he would eventually become famous. Mack's other second baseman? Pete Suder, a veteran who could play every infield position, and who had just set career highs with ten homers and seventy-five runs batted in only 118 games. Suder was thirty-three, and would never play nearly as well again.

When Connie Mack made this deal—a terrible misjudgment of talent, as Fox proved within a few years—he was nearly eighty-seven years old, and it's possible that he simply didn't know what he was doing. Or that he didn't do anything at all; by that point, his son Earle was doing much of the work, and perhaps he deserves the blame for trading a future Hall of Famer for a backup catcher.

August 30, 1951: Yankees trade Lou Burdette (178) and $50,000 to Braves for Johnny Sain (40).

There's nothing new, or even all that notable, about trading a young minor-league pitcher (Burdette) for a grizzled veteran (Sain) with something left, and Sain was an important piece of the Yankees' pennant- and World Series–winning puzzles from 1951 through '53 (and in '54, when they won 103 games but finished behind the Indians, Sain led the American League with twenty-two saves).

This one deserves special mention, though, because in 1957—by which point Sain was an ex-pitcher—the Braves met the Yankees in the World Series, and Lou Burdette* essentially beat the Yankees all by himself, going 3–0 with three complete games, including shutouts in Games 5 and 7. And in a bizarre turnaround, one year later the Yankees beat Burdette in Games 5 and 7 for a very particular sort of revenge.

December 5, 1957: Redlegs trade Curt Flood (221) and Joe Taylor (3) to Cardinals for Marty Kutyna (16), Willard Schmidt (9), and Ted Wieand (0).

Flood was a fantastic prospect. In 1956, he made his pro debut with High Point–Thomasville in the Carolina League. Only eighteen, he must have been one of the youngest players in the league, but still managed to lead the

---

* Burdette's full name was Selva Lewis Burdette Jr. and all the sources spell his nickname as "Lew." But Burdette *signed* his name as "Lou," so that's what I call him.

The Mahatma Misfires

Most of the stories about Branch Rickey's trades involve him fleecing some poor National League club or another. In 1938, Rickey sent a sore-armed Dizzy Dean to the Cubs, and all he wanted in return was Curt Davis, a couple of other useful players . . . and $185,000. In 1947, Rickey sent Dixie Walker—who, as his nickname might suggest, didn't particularly enjoy having Jackie Robinson as a team-mate—along with Hal Gregg and Vic Lombardi, to the Pirates for Preacher Roe and Billy Cox. There are many other examples, most of which involve Rickey getting paid large sums for players you've never heard of.

For the record, though, here's one example of Rickey getting the raw end of a deal. In the early 1930s, Rickey was running the Cardinals and Bill Veeck's father was running the Cubs. According to Veeck, one of Rickey's favorite games was to offer a potential trading partner two players, trusting that his partner would choose the wrong player. According to Veeck, though, "You take risks when you play that game, of course. I know that Branch got caught early in the game when he offered my daddy the choice between Big Bill Lee, a right-hander, and Clarence Heise, a lefty. The Cubs were solid in right-handers . . . and they had only one lefty." (Ah, Rickey must have figured: they'll take the lefty.) "They also had a scout named Jack Doyle who was an incomparable judge of minor-league talent. My daddy quickly took Lee, who went on to

loop in batting average (.340) and walks (102) while also hitting twenty-nine home runs. Willie McCovey was in the same league that year. He and Flood were born eight days apart in 1938. McCovey was excellent in '56, but Flood—an outstanding defensive center fielder—was better.

In 1957, Flood moved up a level, to the South Atlantic League. His power and batting average dropped off, but .299–14–82 were still plenty good considering his age and his defense.

Oh, except that summer the Reds turned Flood into a third baseman. Then, that winter in Venezuela they turned him into a second baseman. And the next spring, they traded him to St. Louis. In his autobiography, Flood wrote,

> The Reds wished me luck. Hail and farewell. I learned later that Cincinnati had been impressed by Vada Pinson's work during his first minor-league season, 1957. Because he was the bigger of us, and the faster, and because they neither needed me for third base nor cared particularly for an all-black outfield of Robinson, Pinson and Flood, they unloaded me to the Cards.[5]

I'm not sure how fair that is. Pinson, as things turned out, really was the better player. And with first Jerry Lynch and later Wally Post, the Reds were set in left field before Tommy Harper took over in 1963 (giving the Reds an all-black outfield). That said, this was just a horrible, horrible trade for the Reds. If they didn't have room in their outfield for Flood, they should have held on to him for another season, then traded him when his value was higher.

June 15, 1964: Cubs trade Lou Brock (320), Jack Spring (1), and Paul Toth (10) to Cardinals for Ernie Broglio (6), Doug Clemens (14), and Bobby Shantz (3).

Commentary from another book with my name on the cover:

> The Cubs haven't made a lot of great deals over the years, but they haven't made a lot of bad ones, either. Even Lou Brock for Ernie Broglio . . . what a lot of people forget is 1) Brock's only position was left field, and the Cubs already had a pretty good one there, and 2) Brock wasn't a great player, anyway. He did enjoy some great seasons with the Car-dinals, of course, some borderline MVP-level seasons. But most years he was merely very good, with his great speed and good batting aver-

age balanced somewhat by a moderate number of walks and poor defense.[6]

I'm going to stand by what I wrote in that other book (he wrote, as courageously as ever). The club had all kinds of problems in center field, but Brock could barely play left; he'd have been a disaster in center. Another thing people forget: Broglio was a damn good pitcher. In 1962 and '63, he was 30–17 with a 2.99 ERA. He wasn't pitching as well when the Cubs traded for him—3–5, 3.50 ERA after eleven starts—but then Brock wasn't exactly tearing things up, either: .251/.300/.340 with two homers and ten steals in fifty-two games.

Of course, 1) Brock started hitting immediately upon joining the Cardinals and didn't stop until a dozen or so years later, and 2) Broglio pitched worse, not better, after going to the Cubs, and after 1964 would win only three more games in the majors. I'm not sure how anybody could have known those things would happen, though.

win 169 games. Heise won one game for the Cardinals."[3]

Veeck's not known for the accuracy of his memory, and in fact Heise did not win one game for the Cardinals. He pitched in one game, but did not win (or lose). Still, like most of Veeck's stories, this is a good one (and Big Bill Lee did win 169).

1. Fred Eisenhammer and Jim Binkley, *Baseball's Most Memorable Trades* (Jefferson, N.C.: McFarland, 1997).
2. Donald Dewey and Nicholas Acocella, *Total Ballclubs: The Ultimate Book of Baseball Teams* (Toronto: SPORT Media Publishing, 2005).
3. Bill Veeck with Ed Linn, *The Hustler's Handbook* (New York: G.P. Putnam's Sons, 1965).
4. Paul Dickson, *Baseball's Greatest Quotations* (New York: Harper Collins, 1991).
5. Curt Flood with Richard Carter, *The Way It Is* (New York: Trident Press, 1971).
6. Rob Neyer, *Rob Neyer's Big Book of Baseball Lineups* (New York: Scribner, 2003).

A'S TRADE ROGER MARIS

During the next few years, we traded some of our best players to the Yankees, including Clete Boyer, Enos Slaughter, Art Ditmar, Bobby Shantz, Ryne Duren, and Harry Simpson. There was a real shuttle operating between Kansas City and New York—and too many of our good young players went, and we wound up with players the Yankees no longer wanted.

Lou Boudreau[1]

It's true. The Athletics did trade some of their best players to the Yankees. The A's moved to Kansas City in 1955, and when they traded Roger Maris to the Yankees in 1959, it was just the latest of many transactions between the two clubs. "We have tried unsuccessfully to trade with other clubs in both leagues," said Yankee general manager George Weiss. "The Yanks and Kansas City have faith in each other."[2]

It's true. They did have faith in each other. There's no way of knowing how hard the Yankees tried to trade with other clubs, but they certainly didn't have much success. The Yankees made their first deal with Kansas City—a sale of three players, actually—on March 30, 1955, shortly after Arnold Johnson took over as Athletics owner. Johnson died in March 1960 (he was only fifty-three). In those five seasons, the Yankees completed fifteen transactions with the A's, and eleven transactions with all the other fourteen major-league clubs. And that difference is even more pronounced when you consider the numbers of players involved. Most of the Yankees' deals with other teams were either sales or purchases of negligible players (with all due respect to Tom Lasorda and Bobby Del Greco). Many of the Yankees' deals with the Athletics involved multiple players, some of them with big names.

Why the cozy relationship? Without going into all the details, suffice to say that Arnold Johnson was exceptionally chummy with Yankees co-owners Dan Topping and Del Webb. To name just one of the trio's ventures, Johnson—as part of a (legal) tax dodge—purchased Yankee Stadium and Kansas City's Blues Stadium, then leased the stadium back to the Yankees. And everybody made out like bandits. As John E. Peterson writes in *The Kansas City Athletics*, Johnson "did not have a great deal of money himself but had a remarkable ability to work out mutually profitable deals involving millions of dollars without any individual investing much of his own money. The purchase of the Athletics was similar to all the other transactions he arranged in which all the parties benefited."[3]

And as Peterson points out, Johnson and the Athletics did pretty well in all their dealings with the Yankees. In fact—and here's the surprising thing—really it's not that close. Purely in terms of the future performance that was exchanged by the two teams, the A's came out way, way ahead. If we look at the first seasons after each deal, the A's come out ahead, 175 Win Shares to 104 Win Shares. And if we look at the entire careers of all the players involved, again the A's make out better: 1,041 Win Shares for players after they were traded to Kansas City, 727 Win Shares for players after they were traded to New York.

Yes, the Yankees got Bobby Shantz, Clete Boyer, Ralph Terry, Hector Lopez, and (of course) Roger Maris.

But the A's got Bob Cerv, Ralph Terry, Woodie Held, Russ Snyder, Jerry Lumpe, and Norm Siebern.

The A's side of the equation gets forgotten, I suppose, because

- they traded Terry *back* to the Yankees, for whom he pitched well,
- they traded Held and Snyder too early to other clubs, after which both became solid major-leaguers, and
- people forget that Lumpe and Siebern were pretty damn good for a few years.

These numbers include only the deals before Charlie Finley bought the team in 1960. Upon taking over, Finley declared that the A's would no longer be doing business with the Yankees. To emphasize this point, Finley bought an old bus, painted "Shuttle Bus to Yankee Stadium" on the side . . . and burned it![4]

Roughly six months later, Finley traded Bud Daley, arguably the club's best pitcher, to . . . the Yankees! That was one hell of a contradiction. It was also one hell of a trade, in favor of the A's. Daley won twenty games in three-and-a-half seasons with the Yankees, posting league-average ERAs. The A's got Deron Johnson, who played in the majors for another fifteen years.*

Nobody today would talk about the Athletics-Yankees "shuttle" if not for one deal in particular: on December 11, 1959, the A's traded Roger Maris to the Yankees for Norm Siebern. And within two short years, Maris had won two MVP Awards and broken Ruth's Record. What's worse, ever since then

---

* True, the A's didn't get any value out of Johnson. But getting him from the Yankees wasn't the problem. The problem was trading him (and for not much) before he showed his stuff in the majors.

Finley's Follies

Trading Roger Maris to the Yankees wasn't the blunder that forced the A's from Kansas City. The real blunder was born of Charlie Finley's arrogance.

When Arnold Johnson bought the Athletics and moved them to Kansas City in 1955, the franchise was practically destitute in terms of player development. There were only three full-time scouts, and about as many legitimate prospects in the minor leagues. Johnson tried to improve things, but this was before the amateur draft, and he was reluctant to pay the bonuses required to sign top talent. Still, within a few years the farm system was producing talent, and meanwhile the A's were doing respectably enough, attendance-wise, despite fielding noncompetitive teams.

Johnson died during spring training in 1960 and the club struggled all season, both on the field and at the gate. After nearly nine months of intense machinations, insurance magnate Charles O. Finley purchased controlling interest in the franchise roughly a year after the A's traded Maris.

Finley was good for the A's (who would, just more than a decade later, become the American League's powerhouse) and he was good for Kansas City (which, thanks to Finley, would eventually have a powerhouse of their own) . . . but he was decidedly bad for the A's of Kansas City.

Finley, as it turned out, had absolutely no idea how to sell tickets, or broadcast rights, for baseball games. He thought he could

National Baseball Hall of Fame, Cooperstown, New York

Roger Maris: who knew?

it's been suggested that the Yankees essentially "parked" Maris with the Athletics until they thought he was ready for the big time.

I'm not buying it.

In 1959, Maris got off to a great start, then suffered an appendicitis attack and spent most of June on the disabled list. He came back strong, and on the morning of July 30, Maris was batting .342 and the A's were in fourth place, with a shiny .500 record; a few days later Maris started in right field in that season's second All-Star Game. Things had never been better, for Maris or the Athletics.

All was not well, though. From July 30 through the end of the season, Maris batted .162 with two home runs and sixteen RBI in fifty-three games. He was at his very worst in August—only seven hits and two RBI in twenty-eight games—then seemed to come out of his funk somewhat in September. But as Maris went, so went the A's, who went 16–38 in August and September and undoubtedly left a sour taste in management's collective mouth.

A couple of years later, Yankees general manager George Weiss said, "If Maris hadn't slumped in '59, I doubt whether Johnson would have traded him."

Johnson probably *couldn't* have traded him. The local fans and sportswriters would have strung him up. We know the A's *should* have kept Maris, and if we'd been running the A's then, we probably *would* have kept him. But the A's traded him because they thought it was the right thing to do, not because they considered themselves a Yankee farm club.

Of course, after leaving the A's, Maris was fantastic for a few years. But Norm Siebern could play a little, too. Here are their Win Shares in the five seasons following the trade:

	1960	1961	1962	1963	1964
Maris	31	36	25	17	25
Siebern	21	23	27	18	20

No, Siebern wasn't the player Maris was. But the difference between them certainly wasn't huge, particularly considering that Maris probably enjoyed at least some advantage from batting just ahead of Mickey Mantle in the Yankee lineup (not to mention playing in an organization that didn't have its collective head up its collective rear end).

The Yankees, as you probably know, won pennants in each of these five seasons.

Did trading for Maris make the difference for any of those pennant-winning teams? From '60 through '63, the Yankees finished eight, eight, five, and ten-and-a-half games ahead of the runners-up. They'd have won those titles with Siebern in right field rather than Maris. Not in 1964, though, when they beat out the second-place White Sox by just one game. It's likely that if they didn't have Maris that season, the Yankees wouldn't have won.

Did trading Maris hurt the A's? They didn't finish within twenty games of first place in any of those five seasons (and wouldn't until 1969, by which point they were in Oakland and both Maris and Siebern were finished).

And here's something that's often forgotten: before the A's traded Maris, *he wasn't all that good.* As a twenty-two-year-old rookie with the Indians in 1957, Maris batted .235 in 116 games. He hit for power and drew sixty walks, both positive markers. But then in 1958, split between Cleveland and Kansas City, he batted .240, again with power but with fewer walks. In '59, Maris's first (and only) full season with the Athletics, he upped his numbers a couple of notches, to the point where you could see a future star poking out.

But certainly not where you could guess that Maris would be the MVP in each of the next two seasons. Certainly not where you could guess that he would break *Ruth's Record.*

Would the A's have benefited from Maris's talents? Undoubtedly. Would he have hit sixty-one home runs if he'd been playing in Kansas City? No. If Maris had remained with the Athletics, they would have won a few more games than they did . . . but probably not enough that anybody would have

sell tickets like he sold insurance, so shortly after taking over he spent $100,000 on brochures mailed to 600,000 people in the Kansas City area. The result? Twenty thousand dollars in ticket sales. As Joe McGuff later wrote, "Finley has done nothing to promote season ticket sales. He has never had one salesman on the street." The A's sold roughly half as many season tickets under Finley as they had under Johnson.

On the other hand, Finley did know how to build a farm system. In 1967, the A's last season in Kansas City, they finished in last place, but their roster included Sal Bando, Bert Campaneris, Catfish Hunter, and Reggie Jackson. A few years after moving to Oakland, the A's thrived in the standings . . . but still they struggled at the gate, because Finley never did learn to sell tickets. And Kansas City got another team, which in 1976 supplanted Finley's A's in first place.

noticed. They would still have been the most pathetic team in the American League, and they would still have moved to Oakland in 1968.

1. Lou Boudreau with Russell Schneider, *Covering All the Bases* (Champaign, Ill.: Sagamore Publishing, 1993).

2. Fred Eisenhammer and Jim Binkley, *Baseball's Most Memorable Trades* (Jefferson, N.C.: McFarland, 1997).

3. John E. Peterson, *The Kansas City Athletics: A Baseball History, 1954–1967* (Jefferson, N.C.: McFarland, 2003).

4. Joe King, "Love Feast Ends," *Sporting News*, May 17, 1961, p. 14.

FRED, FRANK, & FELIX

For most of his career, Fred Haney was no doubt a fine manager. In 1959,
Fred Haney had the worst season of any major league manager in history.

—*The Bill James Guide to Baseball Managers*

Fred Haney managed the Milwaukee Braves. He'd managed them in 1956 when they'd blown a good-sized lead down the stretch, and he'd managed them in 1957 and '58 when they won National League pennants. In '59 the Braves never could get much traction, and spent most of the season trading places with the Dodgers and the Giants at the top of the standings. The Braves did win their last two games, thus forging a first-place tie with Los Angeles. And in those days, that meant a best-of-three playoff series for the pennant (these days, it would be just a one-game playoff). The Braves lost the first playoff game. About the second, Bill James wrote,

> Facing Don Drysdale in the one hundred fifty-sixth and deciding game of a 154-game season, Haney chose as his cleanup hitter not Henry Aaron (.355 with 39 homers), or Eddie Mathews (.306 with 46 homers), or Joe

Adcock (.292 with 25 homers in 404 at bats) or Wes Covington or Del Crandall, both of whom were pretty good hitters. He chose Frank Torre, who had hit .228 with 1 homer in 115 games.[1]

It was an odd choice. But regarding this particular instance, I think James was a little too rough on Haney. Because in that 156th game, Torre was pretty good. In the first inning, Torre's two-run single gave the Braves a 2–0 lead against Drysdale. He also drew three walks, and it was hardly Frank Torre's fault that he didn't score any runs that afternoon. Oh, and Drysdale was exceptionally tough on right-handed hitters. He didn't throw sidearm but that's how it looked to the right-handed hitters, and Drysdale's best pitch was a fastball that bore down and in against the righties. According to Retrosheet, from 1960 through 1962 right-handed hitters managed to bat just .212 against Drysdale. One could reasonably argue that playing Torre instead of Adcock was the most effective (if not necessarily the smartest) discretionary decision that Haney made that day.

The Braves blew a 5–2 lead in the ninth, and lost in the twelfth when second baseman Felix Mantilla—then playing shortstop because starter Johnny Logan retired in the seventh with an injury—uncorked a wild throw that skipped past Torre.

So while one might reasonably argue that Torre should not have started (let alone batted cleanup) in that last game, the fact is that Torre did play well and certainly did not cost the Braves the game.

A more substantive charge might be that Haney gave Torre too much playing time during the first 154 games. Before the playoff with the Dodgers, Torre played in 115 games and batted roughly three hundred times (including walks). He started sixty-four games, all of them at first base. In retrospect, we can see that he played more than his performance warranted . . . but did he play more than you or I would have played him? I'm not at all sure that he did. But let's figure it out.

Frank Torre signed with the Boston Braves in 1951. He batted .313 in the minors that season, but—oddly, for a first baseman—didn't hit a single home run in eighty-seven games. Torre then spent a couple of seasons in the service (as many players did at that time). He returned to baseball in 1954 and batted .294 in the Southern Association, and this time around he hit nine homers. In '55 he moved up to the American Association and batted .327 with a touch of power.

So in 1956, Frank Torre was twenty-four and he was, by all indications, ready. But he struggled in limited duty with the Braves that season, and was just decent in '57.

In 1958, though, Torre was a pretty damn good player. That actually presented a small problem, because it gave the Braves two first basemen who (apparently) deserved to play, the other being Joe Adcock (who was a truly fantastic hitter). So both played in a sort of semiplatoon, which meant more time for Torre since he was the lefty-hitting half of the duo (Adcock also played occasionally in the outfield). And here's the thing: Torre actually played just as well as Adcock. Sure, their histories suggested that Adcock was fundamentally the better hitter. But there was not then, and probably is not now, a manager in the world who wouldn't have thought that Torre deserved plenty of at-bats in 1959, based on what he'd done in '58.

So when the '59 season opened, Torre was in the lineup when the Braves faced a right-handed starting pitcher. On the other hand, in April and May the Braves faced a left-handed starting pitcher ten times; Torre started just one of those games.

But when he did play, he didn't hit. Through May 24, he'd played in thirty-four games and batted just .242 with *one* home run. And that essentially cost Torre his job. For the rest of the season he was in and out of the lineup, but mostly out. Torre did play regularly for a week in June, a week in July, and—most damning, if one is making a case against Haney—for two weeks beginning in late August. After September 5, though, Torre started only once before the second playoff game against the Dodgers.

When Haney did write Torre's name on the lineup card, it was certainly unorthodox considering prior events. But it worked. Torre got on base four times.

Bill James doesn't restrict his criticism to Haney's employment of Frank Torre. He also writes of Haney, "Lacking an established second baseman after Red Schoendienst went down with tuberculosis, he refused to decide who he wanted to play second base. He ran second basemen in and out all year, getting worse performance from all of them than he could possibly have gotten from any of them."

In rough order, here's who played second base for the Braves in 1959, along with their stats for the season:

	Games	OBP	Slug
Felix Mantilla	60	.266	.271
Chuck Cottier	10	.222	.167
Joe Morgan*	7	.280	.261
Johnny O'Brien	37	.271	.259
Casey Wise	20	.267	.237
Mel Roach	8	.152	.097
Bobby Avila	51	.330	.331
Red Schoendienst	4	.000	.000

* No, not *that* Joe Morgan; the one who managed the Red Sox after John McNamara.

Pretty ugly, huh? Mantilla was the Opening Day starter but quickly lost his job, and was in and out of the lineup the rest of the season. On July 21, general manager Birdie Tebbetts stabilized the position, finally, by getting Bobby Avila from the Red Sox in a waiver deal. Avila, who'd won a batting title in 1954, didn't have much left (this would be his final season in the majors), but he obviously was an improvement over all who'd come before him

The Wisdom of Hindsight

Perhaps the point of this little essay belongs in the introduction, but it's going here because this is where I decided to put it . . .

One of the tricky things about analyzing personnel decisions after the fact is that we're not *there*. In the case of the 1959 National League pennant race, for example, we would be questioning Dodgers manager Walter Alston instead of Roy Haney if only the Braves had been able to win just one more of their first 154 games. And if Alston were the subject of our inquisition, we could easily point to Don Zimmer, who was unbelievably awful that season. In ninety-seven games and 249 at-bats, Zimmer managed to hit just .165. He did draw some walks. But there simply isn't any way to sugarcoat .165.

So Alston was foolish to give Zimmer that much playing time, right? That very nearly cost the Dodgers the pennant.

Zimmer did start the season as the Dodgers' regular shortstop. But he deserved to. In 1958 he'd batted .262/.305/.415 (with seventeen homers in 127 games). Not great, but perfectly acceptable for a shortstop. But he got off to a horrible start in '59 and wound up losing his job to Bob Lillis. Lillis didn't last long, either, and on June 6 the Dodgers put Maury Wills into the lineup.

I know what you're wondering: "What took them so long to give Wills a shot?"

Well, Maury Wills was not a real prospect until that summer. He was twenty-six, and in '58 he'd batted .253 in the Pacific Coast League.

The Tigers had him in the spring of '59 on a conditional basis, but sent him back to the Dodgers. Back in the PCL, though, Wills was batting .313 on June 1, and the Dodgers sent for him.

He got off to a lousy start, and didn't nail down the everyday job at shortstop until the middle of August.[2] Wills was the best shortstop the Dodgers had; we know that now. But *at the time*, there was no compelling reason for Alston to think that Wills was better than Zimmer (and in fact, Zimmer would play decently for the Cubs in 1960 and '61).

In retrospect, my only real gripe with Alston in '59 is that he gave far too many at-bats to Ron Fairly, who batted .238 with scant power in 244 at-bats. Fairly would later become a fine hitter, but in 1959 he turned twenty-one and wasn't quite ready for the National League.

(at least as a hitter). Schoendienst, just beginning to recover from the tuberculosis, played in a few September games (including the last one).

Should Haney have picked one of those pre-Avila second basemen and stuck with him until help arrived?

Perhaps. Mantilla, particularly, would later have some good seasons. On the other hand, Cottier was a .220 lifetime hitter in the majors; Morgan, .193; O'Brien, .250 but most of that was in 1954; Wise, .174; Roach, .238.

Roach was probably the best of the bunch. In 1958 he'd batted .309 in forty-four games, and in 1960 he would bat .300 in forty-eight games. But Roach wasn't really available, as he spent most of the '59 season recovering from a knee injury that had abbreviated his '58 campaign.

Yes, Haney probably should have just given the job to Mantilla or O'Brien until Avila arrived. If he hadn't screwed around with Cottier and Morgan and Wise and Roach, the Braves probably would have won just one more of their first 154 games, and they wouldn't have been forced to play 155 and 156. But as I suspect Bill James has discovered since going to work for the Red Sox, it's not easy to keep your wits about you in the midst of a pennant race.

Also, shouldn't we save at least a bit of the blame for Birdie Tebbetts? It was Tebbetts who left Haney with such lousy options at second base. And presumably it was Tebbetts who stocked Haney's bench with decrepit veterans like Enos Slaughter (43) and Mickey Vernon (41), neither of whom had anything left at all. And it was Tebbetts who left Haney with two first basemen and only one first base.

And finally, it's probably worth mentioning that the Braves were extraordinarily unlucky that season. The Braves scored nineteen more runs than the Dodgers, and allowed forty-seven fewer. Based on their run differentials, we would have expected the Braves to win ninety games, the Dodgers eighty-two. Was this Haney's fault? Maybe. But from Haney's hiring in 1956 through the end of the '58 season, the Braves' runs scored and allowed were typical of a team with 254 wins; they actually won 253.

Five days after losing the playoff to the Dodgers, Fred Haney resigned. During his three seasons and four months at the helm, Haney's Braves had won more games than any other team in the major leagues. He never managed again.

---

1. Bill James, *The Bill James Guide to Baseball Managers from 1870 to Today* (New York: Scribner, 1997).

2. Maury Wills as told to Steve Gardner, *It Pays to Steal* (Englewood Cliffs, N.J.: Prentice-Hall, 1963).

GIANTS MOVE INTO CANDLESTICK

Almost petrified with cold in his outdoor radio booth during a game early during the 1960 season, Joe Garagiola, the St. Louis broadcaster, was asked if he wanted some hot coffee. "Never mind the coffee," Garagiola advised. "Get a priest."

—Charles Einstein, *A Flag for San Francisco* (1962)

Given enough time, almost anything, no matter how unsightly or terrible, can become a source for amusing memories—just ask Roberto Benigni—and that's essentially what happened to Candlestick Park.

During the first 1961 All-Star Game, Giants pitcher Stu Miller was blown off the pitching rubber by a gust of wind.

Funny.

In 1963, Mets manager Casey Stengel shepherded his squad to the field for batting practice . . . but before all those future superstars could take their cuts, a gust of wind picked up the batting cage and deposited it on the pitcher's mound.

Hilarious.

For many years, any fan who managed to make it through an entire extra-innings night game was rewarded, upon exiting the ballpark, with a *"Croix de Candlestick"* pin.

Oh, that's just so . . . colorful.

At the time, though, it really wasn't so funny.

How did this happen? Why did they build a ballpark in perhaps the single worst place for a ballpark in the entire Bay Area? In 1962, Giants chronicler Charles Einstein wrote,

Giants president Stoneham has maintained that the final location of Candlestick Park . . . was the only practical solution. It afforded, for one thing, a large parking area, most of which, however, was under water and had to be filled by earth that some critics believe was taken off a hill which in turn was what kept the wind from blowing when the area was first surveyed.

Others believe that the site survey did not take place during afternoon hours, which are

Park Effects

It's been written many times that if not for Candlestick, Willie Mays might well have broken Babe Ruth's record, might even have hit 800 home runs. Certainly, Mays himself believes that.

The facts, however, do not lend themselves to that theory.

Mays spent the first six seasons of his career in Harlem's Polo Grounds, the next two in San Francisco's Seals Stadium, and the next twelve (plus a month) in Candlestick.

Before the Giants moved into Candlestick, Mays averaged one home run for every 16.3 at-bats. After the Giants moved into Candlestick, he averaged one home run for every 16.2 at-bats.

Why the misconception? In 1960, Candlestick's first season, the ballpark was awfully tough on power hitters. The Giants hit only forty-six home runs in their seventy-seven home games (they hit eighty-four homers away from Candlestick); Mays hit twelve homers at home, seventeen on the road.

The Giants weren't stupid. They weren't paying Mays all that money to hit long fly balls in front of the home fans. So after just one season, the Giants pulled in the fences, ten feet all the way around. And from 1961 through his last game with the Giants in 1972, Mays hit 190 home runs in his home games and 177 in his road games. Candlestick didn't *help* Mays; most players enjoy a real home-field advantage, just by virtue of being home, and of course there's that '60 season. But there's little evidence that Candlestick particularly hurt him, either.

when the wind blows. Charles Feeney, vice-president of the Giants, recalls driving out to the Candlestick site while construction was going on and seeing whole carloads of cardboard boxes and other objects sail past him through the air.

"Does the wind always blow like this?" Feeney asked a workman.

"Only between the hours of one and five," the laborer responded.[1]

The significance of one and five? Those typically were the hours during which day games were played. And the Giants played a lot of day games—in 1961, fifty-four of seventy-seven—because it was so often bitterly cold at night. (I experienced this firsthand when I visited Candlestick in 1998. My first game was an evening affair, and I was moderately comfortable only because I was wearing a quilted jacket and fur-lined gloves. I went back the next afternoon, and enjoyed a wonderful summer afternoon punctuated by occasional gusts of gale-force wind. This was in July.)

What did Candlestick cost the Giants? Here's where they ranked in National League attendance, from 1960—the first year of Candlestick—through 1968, graphed against their place in the National League standings:

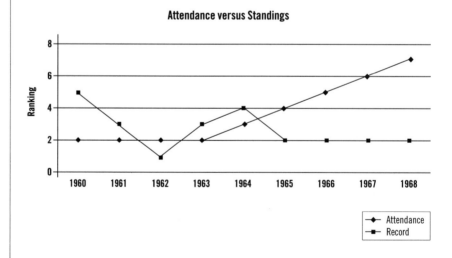

Attendance versus Standings

There was obviously a honeymoon in Candlestick's first four seasons, with the Giants finishing behind only the Dodgers (who were breaking all sorts of attendance records). Actually, attendance held fairly steady through 1965, in terms of fannies in the seats (as opposed to league rank, which is pictured here). But in 1967 the bottom fell out, as the Giants finished second in the standings but drew only 1.24 million fans.

In 1968 the bottom *really* fell out, as the Giants again finished second but barely drew 830,000 paying customers. Sure, maybe the fans were just tired of all those second-place finishes . . . but if that were the case, why didn't the fans come out in 1971, when the Giants won the National League West but ranked just tenth in the league in attendance?

So when the Giants were good, nobody showed up. And when the Giants were bad? Train wreck. And the A's weren't helping. In 1968, with the A's having just moved from Kansas City to Oakland, the Giants' attendance dropped by roughly a third, and in 1972—just one season removed from their first division title—the Giants drew only 647,744 customers, slightly fewer than in their last season (1957) in New York.* In 1974 and '75, with the Giants tanking in the standings, they drew barely half a million fans per season, ranking last in the majors both seasons.

Considering that the A's were winning the World Series every year but not drawing well, either, there was a fairly persuasive argument being made that the Bay Area simply couldn't support two franchises. In 1975, Horace Stoneham very nearly sold the Giants to a Canadian brewery, which intended to move the club to Toronto, where the transaction was considered a done deal (San Francisco Mayor George Moscone was able to delay proceedings long enough for local developer Bob Lurie to step in and buy the franchise). And when the A's were supposedly bound for Denver in 1978 or '79, there was some sentiment toward changing "San Francisco Giants" to "Bay Area Giants," with the club playing half its home schedule in Oakland.

Of course, everybody stayed put. And in 1989, when the Giants and Athletics both reached the World Series, the A's sold nearly three million tickets and the Giants—for the first time ever—sold more than two million.

The Giants played on Candlestick Point for forty years. In all that time, they drew two million fans three times (1990, and also 1993 and 1999); by contrast, the small-market Royals drew two million fans in eleven seasons between 1978 and 1991. It's virtually impossible to know how many fans the Giants might have attracted to a *temperate* ballpark. We do know, however, that since moving into PacBell Park in 2000, the Giants have sold more than three million tickets and ranked in the top three in National League attendance every year.

---

1. Charles Einstein, *A Flag for San Francisco* (New York: Simon & Schuster, 1962).

---

* In case you're wondering, after moving to San Francisco in 1958, the Giants played in old Seals Stadium for two seasons.

CASEY SAVES WHITEY

Howard Cosell mentioned every year for ten straight years that Casey made a mistake in not starting Whitey Ford in the opening game. But it was my best year. I was 15–9 to Whitey's 12–9. Yes, as it worked out, Whitey might have won three games, but anyone can second-guess. Casey and his coaching staff made the decision based upon the respective seasons we had.

—Art Ditmar[1]

Just the bare bones, because we've got a lot of stuff to get to . . .

In 1959, the Yankees finished fifteen games out of first place, leading some to wonder if maybe ol' Casey Stengel was finally too ol' to manage the modern ballplayer. And on the morning of September 5, 1960, the Yankees trailed the first-place (and decidedly upstart) Baltimore Orioles by two games . . . from which point the Yankees mounted one of the great stretch runs in major-league history, winning twenty-two of their last twenty-six games, including their last fifteen straight, to finish eight games in front. Next up: the Pittsburgh Pirates, playing in their first World Series since they were swept by the Yankees in 1927.

Enough bones. Here's where it gets interesting . . .

According to Peter Golenbock in *Dynasty*, Stengel

was unsure who to pitch in the opening game . . . All the coaches—Ed Lopat, Ralph Houk,

and Frank Crosetti—agreed to withhold Ford until the teams returned to New York for the third game because of Ford's unbeatable record in the Stadium, but the disagreement then arose as to who should start the first one. Lopat, the pitching coach, pushed hard for Stengel to start the rookie Stafford. "This kid is the closest thing I've seen to Whitey Ford," Lopat said over and over. "He doesn't care who he's pitching against and he knows what he's doing all the time." Stengel agreed, but Houk and Crosetti were violently opposed to starting a rookie in the first game of a World Series. They felt Ditmar should start.[2]

Ditmar did start instead of Stafford, who had turned twenty-one just a few weeks earlier and spent most of that season in the Eastern League. We might quibble with that choice, but the Conventional Wisdom was then—and is now, right?—that given a choice between a veteran and a rookie in a big game, you go with the veteran. And while Stafford certainly had pitched well since joining the Yankees in August—in eight starts, he'd posted a 1.62 ERA—Ditmar led the Yankees with 200 innings, and his 3.06 ERA ranked fourth in the American League.

But why not Whitey Ford? That's what Whitey wants to know . . .

> I had missed the first six weeks of the season because of a bad shoulder, and I didn't pitch well during the first half of the season. But I finished strong and wound up 12–9. I was very strong in my last four starts, so I figured I would get the opening-game assignment against the Pirates in the World Series. Casey held me back until Game 3. He said something about my pitching in the comfort of Death Valley. But I didn't agree with him. It's the only time I was ever annoyed with Casey. Holding me back till the third game prevented me from pitching three times. I pitched two shutouts. I was pitching the best ball of my life at that time. If he had given me three more starts, I would have given him three wins, and we would have been the world champs again.[3]

The source for that quote is Dom Forker's *Sweet Seasons*, an entertaining book most notable for its consistently—one might even say habitually—inaccurate memories. Ford did *not* miss the first six weeks of the season. In his first start he pitched seven shutout innings, and after a good start on May 20, his ERA never reached even 3.30 the rest of the season. Did Ford finish strong, as he says? In his last four starts, he gave up ten runs in twenty innings (and by the way, three of those four starts were against bottom-feeders Kansas City and Washington). He wasn't pitching *poorly*, but he certainly wasn't pitching the "best ball" of his life. Not close.

Nevertheless, when you read interviews with the players on that team, the one thing about which all of them (except Ditmar) agree is that Ford should have started Game 1. To a man, they believed that Ford was their best pitcher and that your best pitcher should pitch the Series opener. So why didn't he?

First let's check with Ralph Houk, then a Yankees coach (and manager-to-be):

> I sat in on the meetings with Casey and the coaches when we discussed the rotation for the World Series. I think there was concern about Whitey starting in Pittsburgh with that hard infield our scouts had talked about. Whitey got a lot of ground balls and the Pirates had all those right-handed hitters . . . [4]

Next, Yankees pitcher Ralph Terry:

> Going by what Houk says, that's a strange pick they made, isn't it? If Pittsburgh had such a hard infield, why start a sinkerballer like Art Ditmar. And right-handed, left-handed, who cares? This is Whitey Ford we're talking about, he got everybody out. I know Casey wanted Whitey to start that first game in Yankee Stadium. You couldn't beat Whitey at home. But, here's the thing. Whitey could only start one game of the three in Yankee Stadium. So what difference would it have made if he started Game Four there instead of Game Three?
>
> . . . I still can't figure this one out. One thing no one mentions is that the dimensions of Forbes were very much like Yankee Stadium, so that was a great park for Whitey. He proved that in Game Six when he shut the Pirates out . . . [5]

Was Ford better at home? From 1958 through the end of the 1960 season, Ford was 22–15 with a 2.87 ERA at home, and 20–12 with a 2.57 on the road (all these stats include the '58 World Series against the Braves). That's not to suggest that on some sort of fundamental level, Ford wasn't a more effective pitcher at home; most pitchers are. But considering the similarity between Yankee Stadium and Forbes Field, this seems practically irrelevant.

Had Ford been effective in World Series games? In a dozen Series starts, he'd won five games, lost four, and posted a 2.81 ERA.

But of course Ford did not start Game 1. Ditmar did, and lost. He also started Game 5, and lost that one, too.* Casey went with Whitey in Games 3 and 6 (and he pitched shutouts in both). That decision's been made, and can't be unmade. So who pitches Game 7, if not Ford? Stengel's options were Ditmar (15–9, 3.06 during the regular season), Bob Turley (9–3, 3.28), Ralph Terry (10–8, 3.40), Jim Coates (13–3, 4.29), Eli Grba (6–4, 3.67), and rookie Bill Stafford (3–1, 2.25).

At this point, Stengel had no confidence in Ditmar. Coates obviously was not one of the Yankees' top starters, and Grba apparently wasn't a serious candidate, either (he'd spent much of the World Series either pitching batting practice or warming up in the bullpen).

That left Turley, Terry, and Stafford as reasonable options.

Turley, 1958's Cy Young Award winner, had been one of the premier power pitchers in the game just a few years earlier. But by 1960 he'd become a finesse pitcher. Turley had started Game 2 of the Series, and beat the Pi-

---

* In fairness to Ditmar, he didn't pitch all that poorly in either of his starts, but was yanked very early in both.

Transcendental Graphics

Bobby Shantz and Casey Stengel

rates 16–3 despite giving up thirteen hits and three walks (while failing to strike out even one Buc).

Terry had started Game 4 and got hung with a 3–2 loss, but pitched well in his six-plus innings.

Stafford, coming out of the bullpen in Game 5, tossed five shutout innings while giving up only three hits (and all of them were ground balls that skipped past or bounced over infielders).

According to Stafford, "Casey came to me the night before Game 7 and said, 'Get a good night's rest. You're going to start tomorrow.' Well, he changed his mind. You know that he liked to go with veterans in big games. But some of the coaches were opposed to the switch, as they told me later."[6]

Turley started. After six batters—three of whom reached base—Stafford replaced him, but was bumped for a pinch-hitter after pitching just one inning. Next out of the bullpen: Bobby Shantz. In 1952, he'd been named American League MVP after going 24–7 for the Athletics, but the 5'6" left-hander threw 280 innings that season and was never the same afterward. Still, he'd done a fine job since coming to the Yankees in 1957, first as a spot starter and lately as a reliever. In '60, his 2.79 ERA was tops in the Yankee bullpen.

Shantz was fantastic in Game 7. When he came in, the Yankees trailed 4–0. He pitched five scoreless innings—allowing just one single and one walk—while the Yankees mounted a steady comeback. After six innings,

Out to Pasture . . .

Whitey Ford later recalled, "I was so mad at him that I wouldn't talk to him on the plane ride home to New York after the seventh game. But two days later I felt sorry about that. The Yankees fired Casey. So in the end Casey's move hurt him more than it did me. Overall, I enjoyed playing for him. It was the only disagreement we ever had. He let you go out and play, and if you did your job, he left you alone."[8]

Did Stengel's questionable tactics—and Mazeroski's home run—get Casey fired after the season? There were many who believed, at the time, that if the Yankees had won the World Series, the club would have been compelled to keep Stengel around for at least one more season. Stengel didn't believe that, though. In his 1962 autobiography, he said, "The last month and a half of the 1960 season I could tell I was through as manager of the Yankees. The attitude of people in the office that I knew and liked was different. They knew that things were going to change.

". . . A few things went wrong in the 1960 World Series against Pittsburgh, and we lost to them in seven games. But if we'd been a little luckier and won, it wouldn't have made any difference about whether I was going to stay on."[9]

It's hard to say for sure what would have happened if the Yankees had won (and considering that they outscored the Pirates 55–27, they easily could have won). There certainly would have been an immense amount of pressure from the writers—most of whom adored

New York owned a 5–4 lead, and in the top of the eighth they made it 7–4. And they weren't necessarily finished yet. With two outs and runners on second and third, Shantz was due up.

On the bench, Stengel still had Bob Cerv and Dale Long as prospective pinch-hitters.

Stengel let Shantz bat. He lifted a fly ball to right field, ending the half-inning.

And in the bottom of the eighth, everything fell apart for the Yankees. The first three Pirates singled—the second hit was a bad-hop grounder that struck shortstop Tony Kubek in the throat, knocking him out of the game—and Stengel summoned Jim Coates from the bullpen to replace Shantz. With one run already in, the next batter sacrificed the runners to second and third. Roberto Clemente hit a ground ball to the right side, and was safe when Coates was slow to cover first base. Catcher (and ex-Yankee) Hal Smith hit a three-run homer, and suddenly the Pirates were ahead, 9–7.

The Yankees came back in the ninth with two runs to tie, but Bill Mazeroski mooted that rally with his leadoff homer in the bottom of the ninth. Neither Ryne Duren nor Luis Arroyo, two of the Yankees' better relievers, ever got into the game.

And what was Bob Turley's opinion?

> . . . Casey was losing it. He would call out for pinch hitters or relievers who had been long since traded from the club and he made moves that were questionable, not quirky . . .
>
> . . . that seventh game, for instance, which I started and got knocked out in. Casey brought in Bobby Shantz to relieve me and Bobby did a great job, even though his arm was killing him. Casey knew it, too, but he told Bobby to keep going as long as he could. Meanwhile we have Ryne Duren, all rested and ready to pitch . . . Luis Arroyo sat there, too . . . Instead of calling for either of them, he's got Bobby pitching all those innings in pain, Ralph Terry warming up so many times he's draining himself, and then he brings in Jim Coates instead of Arroyo or Duren to give up that three-run homer to Hal Smith, and that just killed us . . .
>
> No, those weren't hunches backfiring. Stengel had been a great manager, and I don't mean to speak ill of him, but that was a man who should have retired the season before. He just didn't have it any more.[7]

I cannot say with any confidence that Stengel's wits weren't about him during the 1960 World Series. He'd always done things his own way, and his own way worked more often than not. But Casey should have started Whitey Ford three times, and he screwed up Game 7 six ways to Sunday.

Stengel—to keep him around at least until the Yankees failed to win a pennant (which didn't happen until 1965). But management was worried about losing Ralph Houk, who had been anointed Stengel's successor and supposedly was receiving feelers from Kansas City about taking over as manager of the Athletics.

1. Dom Forker, *Sweet Seasons: Recollections of the 1955-64 New York Yankees* (Taylor, 1990).

2. Peter Golenbock, *Dynasty: The New York Yankees 1949—1964* (Englewood Cliffs, N.J.: Prentice-Hall, 1975).

3. Forker, *Sweet Seasons*.

4. Richard Lally, *Bombers: An Oral History of the New York Yankees* (New York: Crown, 2002).

5. Ibid.

6. Forker, *Sweet Seasons*.

7. Lally, *Bombers*.

8. Forker, *Sweet Seasons*.

9. Charles D. Stengel and Harry T. Paxton, *Casey at the Bat* (New York: Random House, 1962).

BILL VEECK TRADES THE FARM

So the Sox suddenly had Minoso, who hit .311 with 20 homers and 105 RBI in '60; Sievers, who hit .295 with 28 homers and 93 RBI; and Freese, who hit .273 with 17 homers and 79 RBI. But future standouts like Callison, Cash, Battey, and Romano were gone. And the Sox wound up third in '60 and a distant fourth in '61—the year Veeck left baseball for health reasons. Many South Side fans have yet to forgive Veeck for mortgaging their future. Veeck, however, will defend his deals to the death.

—Bob Vanderberg, *Sox: From Lane and Fain to Zisk and Fisk* (1982)

In 1959, the Chicago White Sox won their first pennant in forty years, then lost to the Dodgers in the World Series. Shortly thereafter, owner-operator Bill Veeck, acting as his own general manager, set about remaking the lineup. Veeck made three big trades (and one little one) prior to Opening Day, 1960 . . .

- **December 6:** White Sox trade catcher John Romano, third baseman Bubba Phillips, and minor-league first baseman Norm Cash to Cleveland for outfielder Minnie Minoso, catcher Dick Brown, pitcher Don Ferrarese, and minor-league pitcher Jake Striker.
- **December 9:** White Sox trade outfielder Johnny Callison to Philadelphia for third baseman Gene Freese.
- **April 4:** White Sox trade catcher Earl Battey, minor-league first baseman Don Mincher, and

$150,000 to Washington for first baseman Roy Sievers.
- **April 18:** White Sox trade pitcher Barry Latman to Cleveland for pitcher Herb Score.

All four trades were absolute disasters. Nobody remembers that last one (the little one), but Latman for Score deserves brief mention. Latman, a fastball/slider pitcher, had gone 8–5 with a 3.75 ERA for the White Sox in '59. He would never be a good pitcher, really, for even one full season, but he did win forty-seven games after the trade. Score won six.

The first three deals, though, are what cost the White Sox at least two American League pennants.

Let's look just at the first eight seasons following those trades. (Why only eight? Because the White Sox were pretty good from 1960 through '67, but fell deep into the second division in '68 and weren't again competitive until '71 or '72.) Below are the

Win Shares earned by every player in the three trades in each of the eight seasons; "Coming" includes every player Veeck got, and "Going" every player he traded away . . .

	1960	1961	1962	1963	1964	1965	1966	1967	Totals
Coming	76	77	23	34	12	3	2	0	227
Going	66	125	120	109	87	113	96	70	786

If I hadn't cut off the comparison in 1967, of course, the difference in value exchanged would be even more dramatic. Callison and Mincher both were useful players as late as 1970, and Cash was still helping the Tigers in 1973.

Aside from a great many wins, what did this massive transferal of talent cost the White Sox? Here's how many games they finished out of first place in each of those eight seasons:

	1960	1961	1962	1963	1964	1965	1966	1967
Behind	10	23	11	10½	1	7	15	3

So what on earth was Veeck thinking that winter? Well, for one thing, he'd been after Roy Sievers for a while. Here's Veeck on the '59 White Sox in *Veeck—As in Wreck:*

> I should have listened to Al Lopez. Al told me from the beginning that we were going to win it. "This," he kept telling me, "is my kind of team." I have always respected Al's ability and judgment. I had, after all, been the first operator to look upon him as a major-league manager. But as far as I was concerned, it was his kind of team and he could have it. Al got his chance to prove his point mostly because I wasn't able to make a deal for any of the power hitters I was after. Particularly Roy Sievers. I offered Cal Griffith as much as $250,000 for him, plus players. As much as Cal wanted the money he was afraid of the reaction of his Washington fans.[1]

Sievers didn't play particularly well for the Senators in 1959, which probably knocked his price down a bit; all Veeck had to give up after that season was $150,000, plus Earl Battey and Don Mincher. (That's all.) And in 1960 it didn't look like a bad deal, as Sievers played well while Battey and Mincher

Don Zminda, who knows as much about the White Sox as anybody you'll meet, weighs in with the following response to this essay . . .

In fairness to Veeck:

- Norm Cash came pretty much out of nowhere after the trade (and in fact Frank Lane dealt him to the Tigers—for Steve Demeter!—before he'd played a game for the Indians). In December of '59, Cash was twenty-five and hadn't played much above the low minors. I can't think of anyone who imagined he'd have the kind of career he wound up having. (Just wondering . . . what part did corked bats play in his success?)

- Battey's minor-league record had indicated more hitting potential than he'd displayed in his spotty appearances with the Sox through 1959 (.209 in 358 AB, albeit with thirteen home runs), but his development into an All-Star, like Cash's, was a pretty big surprise.

- Don Mincher's eventual success was more predictable based on his minor-league record, but it did take him a while, and he was a platoon player for most of his career.

- Callison was considered the big star of that group, but his career had a big downturn after 1965 and never quite matched the buildup he was given.

were still establishing themselves as major leaguers. Minoso also played well, leading the American League in both games and hits. The Sox finished third, ten games behind the Yankees, but that was as good as things got for Veeck. After the season, suffering from various physical ailments, he sold his share of the White Sox.

And that's really why he traded all those young players for veterans. Veeck never stayed anywhere for long. He bought the Indians in 1946 and sold them in 1949. He bought the St. Louis Browns in 1951 and sold them in 1953. He bought the White Sox in 1959 and sold them in 1960. Veeck, who was always buying teams with other people's money and thus never had any real security, was essentially incapable of thinking more than a year or two ahead. Maybe he didn't know how good Norm Cash and Johnny Callison and Earl Battey would become, or maybe he just didn't care because he figured he wouldn't be around to enjoy them anyway.

In 1962 the White Sox finished in fifth place, eleven games behind the Yankees. But what if they had Johnny Romano and/or Earl Battey behind the plate, instead of Cam Carreon and Sherm Lollar? And Norm Cash at first base, instead of Joe Cunningham? And Johnny Callison in right field, rather than Mike Hershberger? I'm not at all sure the Sox would have beat out the Yanks—the Sox catchers and Cunningham weren't really so bad in '62—but they would have come a lot closer than they did.

In '63, the White Sox again finished well behind the Yankees: ten-and-a-half games. Their three catchers—J. C. Martin, Carreon, and Lollar—combined for a .307 on-base percentage, .322 slugging. Meanwhile, Earl Battey was batting .285 and hitting twenty-six home runs for the Twins. The Sox had four outfielders who saw most of the action in the garden: Floyd Robinson (.361 OBP, .419 slugging percentage), Mike Hershberger (.338/.361), Dave Nicholson (.319/.419), and Jim Landis (.316/.369). Meanwhile, Callison was in the middle of a four-season stretch as one of the best outfielders in the National League; in '63 he batted .284 and hit twenty-six homers. At first base, Cunningham split time with Tommy McCraw. Neither was good. Meanwhile, Norm Cash was thriving with the Tigers. Again, it's not apparent the White Sox would have finished ahead of the Yankees . . . but they certainly would have put a scare into them.

In 1964, the White Sox finished one game out of first place. There's no question about it: if Veeck hadn't made those three big trades—hell, if he'd made only two of them, *any* two of them—the Sox are in the World Series.

In 1965, the Yankees were finally dethroned as American League champions. Not by the White Sox, though. The Twins finished in first place, seven games ahead of the second-place ChiSox. Catchers J. C. Martin and Johnny

Romano (back with the White Sox after five seasons in Cleveland) played well . . . but not as well as Battey played for the Twins. First baseman Bill Skowron played well . . . but not nearly as well as Norm Cash played for the Tigers. Left fielder Danny Cater played well . . . but not nearly as well as Johnny Callison played for the Phillies. Battey, Cash, and Callison totaled seventy-four Win Shares; Martin/Romano, Skowron, and Cater totaled sixty-two Win Shares. That's a four-game theoretical difference in the standings—everything else being equal, of course—and suddenly the White Sox are right on the Twins' heels.

In 1967, Chicago finished fourth, but only three games out of first place in a fantastic four-team race. McCraw played first base for the White Sox and batted .236/.288/.362. Granted, that was a pitcher's year and the Sox played in a pitcher's ballpark; as a *team*, the White Sox batted .225/.288/.320. But Norm Cash batted .242/.352/.430, and that's not all park effects. Cash earned twenty-one Win Shares, against twelve for McCraw. Considering that three Win Shares theoretically equals one victory, we've just put the White Sox in a tie for first place. But we can do even better than that, if instead of keeping Cash throughout the 1960s we keep Don Mincher. As it happens, 1967 was Mincher's finest season—twenty-eight Win Shares— and there's an *excellent* chance that if the White Sox had Mincher at first base in '67 they'd have won the pennant.

Bill Veeck is generally regarded as one of the game's canniest executives. Fair enough. But the biggest thing he ever did . . . bigger than signing Larry Doby, bigger than bringing Satchel Paige to the major leagues, bigger than sending Eddie Gaedel to the plate . . . the biggest thing he ever did was remake the lineup of the 1959 American League champions. And with those three trades, he certainly cost the White Sox two pennants, and perhaps as many as five.

In 2005 the franchise finally won its first World Series since World War I. But if not for Bill Veeck, the wait might well have been forty years shorter.

So some of this is wisdom developed in hindsight, but Veeck definitely deserves most of the criticism he was given. To me his biggest sins were:

- trading *both* of the team's young catchers;
- trading three young players— Callison, Romano, Mincher— who could reasonably have been expected to develop into real power threats; and
- not just trading the young players, but trading them for players who clearly had at most a couple of good years left (Sievers and Minoso).

My eighty-six-year-old father and I are still upset about it.—*D.Z.*

---

1. Bill Veeck with Ed Linn, *Veeck—As in Wreck: The Autobiography of Bill Veeck* (New York: G. P. Putnam's Sons, 1962).

CUBS CONVENE COLLEGE OF COACHES

There were at least 100 good reasons to try this experiment; as it turned out, there were at least 101 reasons to call it a monumental bust. Even today, when mention is made of the College of Coaches, it brings out the laughter and disrespect that was immediately associated with the Cubs teams I played on in the early 1960s.

—Ron Santo[1]

The inevitable end of multiple chiefs is that they fade and disappear for lack of unity.

—Napoleon I

The following appeared in the 1961 edition of the Chicago Cubs' media guide:

The custom of having a manager has been followed for 90 years in baseball—that is, ever since the professional game started in 1871.

The manager set-up has meant constant turnover both in personnel and style of play. In the last 14 years in the two major leagues, 103 changes of managers have been made. And each new manager generally meant a new style of play and a new set of coaches who, for the most part, were special friends of the manager.

The core of the new Cubs program is a standard system of play, administered by a stable, good-sized group of coaches. The coaches are selected on the basis of merit, knowledge of the game, and ability to teach, rather than personal favoritism.[2]

The "new Cubs program" was called the "College of Coaches." Chicago sportscaster Chet Coppock called it "the dumbest single coaching situation in the history of modern sports."[3] It was a completely radical experiment, and it failed utterly. But like asbestos and the Concorde, it began as a decent enough idea.

In 1959, the Chicago Cubs finished in seventh place. It was the Cubs' fourteenth straight second-division finish—fifth place or worse in the eight-team National League—and there were a lot more sevenths and eighths than fifths and sixths.

Owner Phil Wrigley decided to make a change. During the World Series, manager Lou Boudreau asked for a new contract, to run two or three years.[4] Mr. Wrigley declined Boudreau's generous offer, and instead announced, on December 20, the birth of his new brainchild: the College of Coaches (though it's not clear whether or not the brainchild actually had

The professors in Mesa, Arizona. Left to right, front row: Elvin Tappe, Goldie Holt, Bobby Adams, Harry Craft. Left to right, back: Verlon Walker, Rip Collins, Vedie Himsl, Charlie Grimm.

that name, initially). The idea was that eight top coaches would rotate through the entire organization, from Class D all the way up to the big club, ensuring that players at every level were taught the same ways to botch rundowns, miss cutoff men, ground into double plays, and so forth.

Who would manage the Cubbies?

They wouldn't figure that out until the eight-man coaching staff was completely assembled. As Wrigley put it, "We're getting together our army before picking the general."[5]

And according to the original plan, there *would* be a general. According to El Tappe, who'd served as a player-coach since 1958, the whole thing was his idea. Wrigley liked Tappe, and after the '61 season he asked for Tappe's advice, which was essentially to hire whomever he wanted as manager, but keep the same coaches so the franchise would maintain some consistency of instruction, whatever the inevitable managerial changes (the Cubs had three managers in '59 and '60).

As Tappe remembered, "My idea was to hire eight guys. Four of them would be coaches in the major leagues. Four of them would be in the minor leagues. We had a hitting coach, pitching coach, catching coach, infield-outfield coach. We had them all different ages . . . I went out and hired all of them. And all of them were organizational people. They were not buddy-buddy to the manager."

Sounds pretty good so far, right?

But then Wrigley asked Tappe, "Well, could one of the rotating coaches be a manager?"

Tappe answered, "Well, yeah."[6]

So the Cubs would have no "manager"; rather, each (or as it happened, some) of the eight would take his turn as "head coach" before rotating back to the minor leagues. How would this work, in practice? Nobody knew, which was apparent as the season progressed and there was absolutely no discernible pattern regarding who was designated as head coach at any particular time. Here are the four head coaches for 1962, in order and with their wins and losses during each stint:

	W	L
Vedie Himsl	5	6
Harry Craft	4	8
Himsl	5	12
El Tappe	2	0
Craft	3	4
Himsl	0	3
Tappe	35	43
Lou Klein	5	6
Tappe	5	11
	64	90

As you might imagine, the players didn't have any idea what the hell was going on. As Cubs pitcher Don Elston says in Peter Golenbock's *Wrigleyville:*

> I don't think you will talk to one ballplayer who played under that system that's going to say anything different than it *was* very hurtful, and it was a very bad situation. In 1961, it all went to hell, no question about it . . .
>
> Our concern as players was that not one of them helped one of the others. My impression was that whoever was the manager—or the head coach—was pretty much on his own. All they did was wait until it was their turn.[7]

The following January, Wrigley defended the system, but allowed that eventually the Cubs might employ one "leader" for an entire season, though he would still be called a head coach.[8] Clearly, Tappe was Wrigley's favorite.

And when the 1962 season opened, Tappe was again the head coach. According to the *Chicago Tribune* that spring, "It was generally accepted by newsmen that Tappe's tenure will last as long as the Cubs are playing something akin to winning baseball."[9]

Further, Vedie Himsl seemed to have coached himself out of the head coach picture, as Lou Klein and new Collegian Charlie Metro were supposedly the "only two candidates waiting in the wings for the No. 1 position" (Harry Craft, meanwhile, had been hired to manage the expansion Houston Colt .45s).

Anyway, early on the Cubs played something greatly akin to losing baseball. On April 30, with the Cubs' record just 4–15, the *Tribune* quoted an anonymous player saying, "We need somebody to kick us in the rear. I've never seen morale so low on any club I've ever been on—majors or minors."[10]

That evening in Los Angeles the Cubs lost their seventh straight, and Lou Klein took over from Tappe. He lasted for thirty games—twelve wins, eighteen losses—after which Metro took over, and held the job the rest of the season.

Shortly after the World Series the Cubs fired Metro, perhaps because he wasn't the easiest guy in the world to get along with. As the *Tribune* observed, Metro was "an outspoken critic of many Cub policies and a man who was at odds with some of his fellow coaches thru much of the dismal campaign . . ."[11] One of Metro's particular crimes was forbidding his players from shaving in the clubhouse after a game (the reason for this rule is apparently lost to history).

In 1963, the Cubs added Bob Kennedy, who'd managed Salt Lake City in '62, to the College. However, Kennedy was designated as "head coach" for all of '63 and '64, giving the Cubs a de facto manager.

"We have had several head coaches for the Cubs," Wrigley said, "and we learned that, despite our grand plan, each of the head coaches had his own individual style. The aim of standardization of play was not achieved because of the various personalities. We learned that the players didn't know where to turn. Each coach had a different idea. I guess it was something like the Irish policeman who said, 'It's not that I bait you because I hate you, but just to show my authority.'"[12]

(I have no idea what that means.)

Kennedy was kicked upstairs in June of '65, and replaced as head coach by Lou Klein, an original faculty member. The Cubs finished eighth, and Wrigley hired Leo Durocher, who got the three-year deal that Boudreau didn't and said, "If no announcement has been made of what my title is,

"Leo? Meet our programmer . . ."

It's sort of a shame that Wrigley's early-1960s Cubs are remembered for the College of Coaches, and little else. I mean, it's fair that they are, because the experiment failed so spectacularly. But Wrigley had some other ideas, and nearly all of them were good ones.

In 1962, the Cubs invited North Carolina track coach Dale Ranson to spring training, to tutor the youngsters in the fine art of sprinting.

On May 29, 1962, the Cubs signed Buck O'Neil as a coach for the major-league club. O'Neil, who'd served with the organization as a scout since 1956, was the first black coach in major-league history.[14]

On January 10, 1963, Wrigley hired Robert Whitlow, a retired Air Force colonel, as the franchise's first "athletic director." Whitlow is best remembered for leading the Cubs in their morning calisthenics during spring training. Military-style. That went over about as well as you'd expect, but at least Wrigley wasn't sitting on his hands.

And here's Wrigley's most interesting innovation: in the same *Chicago Tribune* story that broke the news about the College of Coaches, this item appeared: "The Cubs have installed an IBM system which gives instantaneous information on all players on National League rosters. Wrigley said he eventually hopes to expand into the minor league field."

I've found little mention of Wrigley's shiny computer system after this. Considering that teams *today* are still figuring out how to compile and disseminate data to those who are willing to use it, we shouldn't be surprised that Bob Kennedy and Leo Durocher weren't poring over computer printouts before every game. Phil Wrigley wasn't a great baseball man. But he did have some good ideas.

I'm making it here and now. I'm the manager. I'm not a head coach. I'm the manager." [13]

1. Ron Santo with Randy Minkoff, *Ron Santo: For Love of Ivy* (Chicago: Bonus Books, 1993).

2. Quoted in George Castle, *The Million-to-One Team: Why the Chicago Cubs Haven't Won a Pennant Since 1945* (South Bend, Ind.: Diamond Communications, 2000).

3. Ibid.

4. Jerry Holtzman, *The Sporting News*, Oct. 12, 1960, p. 7.

5. Edward Prell, "They'll Cost $120,000 and Help Pick Pilot," *Chicago Tribune*, Dec. 21, 1960, p. B1.

6. Rick Phalen, *Our Chicago Cubs: Inside the History and the Mystery of Baseball's Favorite Franchise* (South Bend, Ind.: Diamond Communications, 1992).

7. Peter Golenbock, *Wrigleyville: A Magical History Tour of the Chicago Cubs* (New York: St. Martin's Press, 1996).

8. Edward Prell, "Owner of Cubs Sees the Light!" *Chicago Tribune*, Jan. 12, 1962, p. C1.

9. Richard Dozer, "Pick Tappe as Season's First Chief," *Chicago Tribune*, March 25, 1962, p. B1.

10. "A Cub Says: 'We Need Kick In Pants,'" *Chicago Tribune*, April 30, 1962, p. C1.

11. Richard Dozer, "Cubs Fire Metro; Coach Plan Stays," *Chicago Tribune*, Nov. 9, 1962, p. C1.

12. Castle, *Million-to-One Team*.

13. Edgar Munzel, "Bruins Give 3-Year Pact to Durocher," *The Sporting News*, Nov. 6, 1965, p. 3.

14. Richard Dozer, "Cubs Sign Negro Coach," *Chicago Daily Tribune*, May 30, 1962, p. C1.

ALSTON GOES 0 FOR 6

The Dodgers and Giants each won 101 games, forcing a three-game play-off series. I relieved in the first two games, and then, in the third game, Walt brought me in for Podres in the sixth inning with two on and no one out. And I was still pitching in the ninth inning. There was no such thing then as being a setup man. We got beat in the ninth. That was terrible. That was pressure. You don't get paid for playing those playoffs, and if you lose, you don't get into the World Series. Jesus, I was tired. I just wanted to get it over with. It seemed like the season was endless.

—Ed Roebuck [1]

The National League was born in 1876. Among its first seventy seasons, not even one season ended with two teams tied for first place. And then there were four in a hurry: 1946, 1951, 1959, and 1962, with the Dodgers being involved every time.

The similarities between 1951 and 1962 were striking. In both seasons, the Dodgers held a substantial lead in the middle of the season, only to wind up tied with the Giants at the conclusion of the schedule. In both seasons, the Dodgers and Giants split the first two games of their best-of-three play-off series. And in both seasons, the series ended with the Dodgers blowing a ninth-inning lead in the third game.

In 1962's first playoff game, Koufax started for the Dodgers but didn't have anything—still recovering from a serious finger injury, he hadn't turned in a good start since July 12—and Billy Pierce pitched a three-hit shutout for the Giants. In the second game, the Dodgers were behind 5–0 in the seventh but exploded for seven runs, then mooted a Giants comeback with a run in the bottom of the ninth.

And that set up the third game, winner-take-all.

Juan Marichal started for the Giants, Johnny Podres for the Dodgers. In the top of the sixth, with the Giants leading 2–1, they loaded the bases against Podres, who was relieved by sinkerballer Ed Roebuck. Roebuck wriggled out of the jam with no damage.

The Dodgers went ahead with two runs in the bottom of the sixth, and added one more in the seventh for a 4–2 edge. Roebuck gave up a single in the eighth, but that runner was erased by a double play and he got the next guy on a pop to second.

What happened over the next inning-and-a-half has been described many times in the decades since, and I'd like to let the participants speak for themselves when possible, beginning with Dodgers coach Leo Durocher:

Durocher: Roebuck had come into the game in the sixth inning and pitched out of a jam. Got by the seventh and struggled to get through the eighth. Pitching has always been one of my strong points, and I could see that his arm was hanging dead. "How do you feel, buddy?" I asked him, as he was coming off.

He said, "My arm feels like lead. Man, am I tired."

I didn't go to Alston. I went to the pitching coach, Joe Becker, who was standing practically alongside him in the corner of the dugout near the bat rack. That's the right way to do it. You don't go over the pitching coach's head. "Get somebody ready," I said to Becker. "Don't let this fellow go out in the ninth inning. He can't lift his arm."

Becker didn't say a word. Alston didn't say a word. It was like I wasn't there.

I said, "Walt, he told me he was tired. He's through." And Alston said, more to Becker than to me, "I'm going to win or lose with Roebuck. He stays right there."[2]

In the bottom of the eighth, with the Dodgers still leading 4–2, Tommy Davis stood on third base with two outs. Oddly, manager Alvin Dark ordered intentional walks to each of the next two batters, John Roseboro and Willie Davis. Presumably, Dark ordered those walks because Davis was followed in the batting order by Eddie Roebuck.

Should Alston have pinch-hit for Roebuck? His bench was exceptionally long in numbers—technically this was still the regular season, so all the September call-ups were available—but exceptionally short on talent. Right-handed Don Larsen was on the mound for the Giants, and Alston had already loaded his lineup with left-handed batters because the right-handed Marichal had started for the Giants. Alston had at least seven non-pitchers on his bench, but only one batted left-handed and none could hit worth a damn.

If Alston were inclined to use a pinch-hitter, the obvious choice would have been Tim Harkness, who 1) was the lone lefty available, and 2) would, as things developed, go into the game as a defensive replacement just moments later. But Alston had decided to stick with Roebuck on the mound, so Roebuck had to bat for himself. He grounded to third base, ending the inning.

Roebuck: The tireder I got, the more the ball sunk, which is probably one of the reasons why Walt didn't take me out of the game. But I was really beat. It was the most uncomfortable I've ever felt in a game. The smog was just hanging in the park, it was hot, and I was thinking how happy I was going to be when this thing was over.[3]

Durocher: When I came back in and took my seat at the other end of the bench, Drysdale, Koufax, and Johnny Podres—who had started the game—were standing right there. "Don't let them send Roebuck back out," they pleaded. "Tell him he's got to make a change. Don't let him do it, Leo."

Don't let him? "What the hell do you want me to do, I'm not managing the club. There's not a goddam thing more I can say than I've said."[4]

Outfielder Duke Snider: Our pitchers were worn out by this point— Koufax, Podres, Ron Perranoski, Stan Williams, Ed Roebuck—all of them—except one, Don Drysdale. Roebuck was pitching. Big D was sitting next to me when the ninth inning started and I said to him, "Don, go down there and tell Alston you want to warm up. We could still lose this thing if we're not careful. It's only 4–2. In '51 it was 4–1 and we lost."

Don says, "I already told him."

"What did he say?"

"He said he's saving me for tomorrow." That would be the first game of the World Series, against the Yankees.

"Do you realize there might not be a tomorrow? Our staff is tired. Go down there and tell him again."

He came back a minute later and I asked him the same question: "What did he say?"

"He said I'm pitching tomorrow against the Yankees."[5]

Shortstop Maury Wills: You want to know why he didn't put Drysdale in? Durocher got real vocal in our dugout. He kept saying that Drysdale should go in. Well, Alston didn't like that it was Durocher's idea and not his. So he kind of cut off his nose to spite his face.[6]

Just the day before, Drysdale had thrown 102 pitches.[7] Alston could have known this, and probably did. Durocher was a jerk who, according to a number of Dodgers, did his best that season to undermine Alston. But there's no real evidence that Alston let it bother him, and if he'd thought using Drysdale was the right move, he'd have made it.

Pinch-hitter Matty Alou led off the ninth against Roebuck with a base hit to right field.

First baseman Ron Fairly: Now Harvey Kuenn comes to the plate and he hits a perfect double-play ball, a one-hop to Wills. But unfortunately somebody had moved Larry Burright, our second baseman. They moved him over toward first base. If he's playing a normal second base, we turn the double play and Kuenn is out by ten feet.[8]

Roebuck: The ball is hit to Maury, but he has to wait for Burright to get to the bag. The throw finally got there and Larry made a hell of a pivot, but too much time had elapsed and Kuenn beat the relay at first.[9]

Pitcher Larry Sherry: Everybody was screaming, "Who moved Burright?" Because we knew it was either Alston or Durocher. But nobody ever took the blame for it.

The situation at this point was still less than dire. The Giants had a runner on first base, but the Dodgers were only two outs from the pennant and they had an accomplished sinkerballer on the mound. Unfortunately, the sinkerballer proceeded to walk both Willie McCovey and Felipe Alou, loading the bases. With Willie Mays up next.

Roebuck: Alston came out to the mound and asked me if I felt okay, and I just said that I wanted to finish this thing one way or the other.

That particular year, I'd had pretty good luck against Willie. [*Au.— That's true; before October 3, Mays was just one for seven against Roebuck in '62.*] So now I'm thinking I just want to get a groundball and hope he hits it at somebody. Somehow, he hits my inside pitch back up the middle, which is a very tough thing to do. This white blur was coming right at me. I had one of these huge gloves on, a model I think they called "The Claw." The ball hit in the web and if it had been a smaller glove, it probably would have stuck there and I could've gotten as many outs as I wanted. But it rolled out on the grass and was sitting there spinning while a run scored. I knew we were in big trouble then. So Walter took me out and brought in . . . [10]

Alston didn't have a great many options. In that entire season, only twelve pitchers saw action with the Dodgers. Only ten pitched more than ten innings. One of those ten, Phil Ortega, went 0–2 with a 6.88 ERA. Another was twenty-two-year-old rookie Pete Richert, who'd pitched sparingly in September and struggled in each of his last four outings. Another was nineteen-year-old rookie Joe Moeller, who hadn't pitched for the

Dodgers since July. Another was Podres, who'd started the game. Another was Roebuck.

That left only five possibilities: three starters, two relievers.

The starters were Drysdale, Koufax, and Stan Williams. Williams was the only one of the four who had spent much time in the bullpen that season, and just the day before he'd earned a victory with 1⅔ scoreless innings against the Giants. Koufax had gotten hammered two days earlier, and clearly wasn't healthy. Drysdale had started twenty-six hours earlier, had not pitched particularly well, and was slated to start Game 1 of the World Series (Alston never sent Drysdale to the bullpen).

The relievers were left-hander Ron Perranoski and right-hander Larry Sherry. Both pitched well during the season, but Perranoski was clearly the better pitcher. In 107 innings he posted a 2.85 ERA, saved twenty games, and—most impressively—somehow allowed just one home run all season. That latter number was fluky, but Perranoski was an outstanding reliever (he'd been good as a rookie in 1961, would be brilliant in '63, and ranked as one of the game's top firemen through 1970).

Orlando Cepeda, a strong right-handed hitter, was scheduled to bat next. Understandably, Alston wanted a right-handed pitcher to face Cepeda. Both Williams and Sherry were warming up, but Sherry was having trouble getting his arm loose. It had to be Williams. Left-handed-hitting Ed Bailey would bat after Cepeda. As Williams was leaving the bullpen, the lefty Perranoski said to him, "You get Cepeda, and I'll get Bailey."[11]

> **Catcher John Roseboro:** We all worried about Williams. He was wild and inconsistent. On Alston's orders, Durocher came out to the mound to make the change, and while we waited for Williams, Durocher said to me, "He'll walk the ballpark." I said, "He'll be okay." I wanted him to be.[12]

Williams did get Cepeda. Sort of. Cepeda hit a fly ball to right field, deep enough to drive in the tying run from third base.

> **Stan Williams:** So now there's two outs, it's 4–4 and the only right-handed hitter they've got left is John Orsino, a kid who they weren't going to use in that situation. So that means Bailey, a left-hander, is next. I figure that's it for me—Ronnie will be pitching to him—so I started walking to the dugout, then looked up and saw Alston wasn't coming.[13]

> **Roseboro:** Trying to throw one by Ed Bailey, Williams threw into the dirt. I made one of the better blocks of my career and kept the runner

on third, but the runner on first went to second. That was critical because it opened up first base, and Alston decided to give Bailey an intentional walk to load the bases and set up the force play at any base. This was quite a burden to load on the wild Williams, and he got too careful pitching to Jimmy Davenport and walked him, forcing in the lead run. That was it.[14]

Williams: It never bothered me that much because I gave it all I had and it didn't work out. Had I let up and thrown a half-assed fastball and the guy had gotten a base hit, I never would have forgiven myself. But I walked him at 100 m.p.h., giving my best shot.[15]

Williams was a pretty good pitcher. But in 186 innings that season, he walked ninety-eight batters while striking out only 108. As a reliever—when he presumably focused on throwing 100 m.p.h. more than anything else—Williams struck out twenty-one batters in twenty-five innings . . . but he also walked twenty-one.

Finally, Alston summoned Perranoski from the bullpen. Another run scored, though, when Burright kicked a grounder. Perranoski then struck out pinch-hitter Bob Nieman, and the nightmarish inning was finally over. In the bottom of the ninth the Dodgers went down in order, and the 1951 Replay was complete.

Reviewing the questionable moves . . .

- Not pinch-hitting Tim Harkness for Ed Roebuck in the bottom of the eighth, with two outs and the bases loaded;
- Not replacing Roebuck with another pitcher to start the top of the ninth;
- Shifting Larry Burright too far from second base to turn a double play;
- Not replacing Roebuck with another pitcher after (or just before) he walked Willie McCovey and Felipe Alou to load the bases;
- Not replacing Stan Williams with Ron Perranoski;
- Again not replacing Williams with Perranoski.

If you or I were managing the Dodgers in some super-sophisticated baseball simulation, we might make some of the same moves that Alston made. Probably not all of them, though. And if Alston had decided differently in just half of them, the Dodgers would probably have won the game and the pennant.

What keeps nagging at me, though, is the knowledge that 1) Alston won a whole lot of games over the years, and 2) all of these moves were at least somewhat defensible. Drysdale *had* thrown 102 pitches just twenty-four hours earlier. Perranoski *had* struggled down the stretch (in his previous eight outings, he'd give up twenty-two hits and thirteen runs in eleven innings). Harkness was *not* much of a hitter.

This certainly wasn't the best game Alston ever managed (and by the way, he had very little to say on the subject in either of his two autobiographies). But you know who I think deserves some mention here? General manager Buzzie Bavasi. In the first playoff game, with the Dodgers trailing 7–0 in the eighth inning, Alston felt compelled to bring in Perranoski to face a few batters. Why? Because he didn't trust anybody else.

In 1962 the Dodgers had two Class AAA farm teams, in Omaha and Spokane. In Omaha, a kid named Nick Willhite went 18–14 with a 3.33 ERA. In Spokane, Howie Reed—only twenty-five, but a triple-A veteran— went 12–8 with a 3.01 ERA. Another Spokanite, Ken Rowe, went 9–9 with a 3.44 ERA in seventy relief outings.

None of these guys would become even decent major-leaguers, but that's not the point. The point is that the Dodgers had, in their organization, at least a few pitchers who could have performed mop-up duties in August and September without completely embarrassing themselves or the ball club. And that would have lessened the strain on a trio of relievers that combined for more than three hundred relief innings. I believe that if Perranoski, Roebuck, and Sherry had been better rested at the end, the Dodgers would have won the pennant.

1. Danny Peary, ed., *We Played the Game: 65 Players Remember Baseball's Greatest Era, 1947–1964* (New York: Hyperion, 1994).

2. Leo Durocher with Ed Linn, *Nice Guys Finish Last* (New York: Simon & Schuster, 1975).

3. David Plaut, *Chasing October: The Dodgers-Giants Pennant Race of 1962* (South Bend, Ind.: Diamond Communication, 1994).

4. Durocher, *Nice Guys*.

5. Duke Snider and Bill Gilbert, *The Duke of Flatbush* (New York: Zebra, 1988).

6. Steve Delsohn, *True Blue: The Dramatic History of the Los Angeles Dodgers, Told by the Men Who Lived It* (New York: William Morrow, 2001).

7. Retrosheet.org.

8. Plaut, *Chasing October*.

9. Ibid.

10. Ibid.

11. Ibid.

12. John Roseboro with Bill Libby, *Glory Days with the Dodgers: And Other Days with Others* (New York: Atheneum, 1978).

Second Place Money

According to the more colorful accounts of the third game's aftermath, various Dodgers cried, got crazy drunk, and hurled epithets toward Alston's closed office door. Tommy Davis screamed over and over, "You stole my money! You stole my money!" Somebody else supposedly called Alston a "gutless son of a bitch."[16]

At the time, the general feeling among the Dodgers was that finishing second to the Giants cost them something like $10,000 per man, perhaps even $12,000.

That estimate was well off, though. If they'd lost the World Series—the likely outcome, considering Koufax's injury and Drysdale's probable fatigue, not to mention the state of the bullpen—their individual shares would have been roughly $7,000 per man. But every Dodger actually did receive $1,860 for finishing second (in those days, the players on the second-, third-, and fourth-place teams all received postseason bonuses). So losing to the Giants actually cost them slightly more than $5,000 apiece. Not an inconsiderable amount of money—Ed Roebuck's salary was something like $14,000 that season—but considerably less than $12,000.

13. Peary, ed., *We Played the Game*.

14. Roseboro, *Glory Days*.

15. Peary, ed., *We Played the Game*.

16. Glenn Stout and Richard A. Johnson, *The Dodgers: 120 Years of Dodgers Baseball* (Boston: Houghton Mifflin, 2004).

MANAGERS WHO PROBABLY SHOULDN'T HAVE BEEN

or

"WAIT A MINUTE . . . YOU WANT ME TO TAKE ORDERS FROM *THIS* GUY?"

> The leader must know, must know that he knows, and must be able to make it abundantly clear to those about him that he knows.
>
> *Making Good in Management*, Clarence B. Randall (1964)

> A chief is a man who assumes responsibility. He says, "I was beaten." He does not say, "My men were beaten." Thus speaks a real man.
>
> *Flight to Arras*, Saint-Exupery (1942)

I could devote half this book to managers who were not only failures, but were such *spectacular* failures that everybody realized, almost immediately, that a horrible mistake had been made. Did I say half the book? One could write an entire book about bad managers, and have plenty left over for a revised edition with forty percent new material. Instead, consider what's below as a completely idiosyncratic and utterly unfair list of *some* of the managers who, as events transpired, were less than perfect for the job.

Holly Hollingshead (1875, 1884)

A Washington boy, Holly Hollingshead played in the outfield for D.C.'s entry in the National Association in 1873 and '75; in the latter season, he was still only twenty-two but captained the Nationals in twenty games, in which the club went 4–16 (the Nats played eight other games under the guidance of pitcher Bill Parks, and lost seven of them). Nine years later, by now an ex-player, Holly Hollingshead managed Washington's American Association team—again called the Nationals—to a 12–50 mark. These Nationals, in their first season in the American Association, expired in early August; the franchise was "surrendered" to Richmond. Holly Hollingshead did not survive the transition.

(Of course I have absolutely no real evidence that Holly Hollingshead was anything but a brilliant tactician and an able handler of his fellow men. I just like to write "Holly Hollingshead" as many times as I can, and I don't know when I'll get another chance like this.)

Frank Bowerman (1909)

During the 1908 season, Braves catcher Bowerman "lost no opportunity to discredit [Joe] Kelley's ability as manager."[1] After the season, owner George Dovey fired Kelley, then visited Bowerman, who said if he weren't hired as manager, he would quit the club.

The weight of this threat is unclear, considering that 1) in 1908, Bowerman had batted only .228, and 2) in 1909 he would be forty years old, which was an awfully advanced age for a catcher (or any other sort of player) in those days. Nevertheless, despite his only apparent qualification as manager being that he once played for John McGraw, Bowerman was hired.

The Doves (as they were then generally called, in honor of Dovey) actually got off to a good start, winning eleven of their first twenty-one games; at the close of play on May 13, the Doves were in third place, only two-and-one-half games behind the Pirates.

And then the roof caved in. The Doves lost thirteen straight, won a game (1–0 over the Dodgers), lost six straight, won a game (4–2 in Chicago), then lost eleven straight. Thirty-two games, thirty losses.

In August the Doves lost fifteen straight, but by then Bowerman was gone. Earlier, he'd left the team for a stretch, returning to his home in Michigan. But according to the *Boston Daily Globe*, upon his return, "[t]he team continued to drop game after game, and did not appear to work consistently, so that the rest he got at that time did him very little good, and he was soon as badly off as he was before he went away."[2]

On July 16, Bowerman resigned after another loss dropped his club to 22–54.

George Sisler (1924–1926)

Sisler, a great first baseman who'd missed the 1923 season with a vision problem, returned to the Browns in 1924 as player-manager.

Writing in the *Post-Dispatch* on June 7, J. Roy Stockton opined of the Browns, "They have loafed and retrograded. Men have lost their speed and their punch because they have not worked . . . Sisler has suffered already for his kindness. There have been howls for his scalp . . ."[3]

As Sisler's biographer wrote, "Stockton's words were biting. His reference to Sis's kindness, a backhanded compliment at best, was probably the truest assessment of the failure of George Sisler as a manager."[4]

Fred Lieb later wrote, "Sisler was never meant to be a playing manager; he wasn't tough, lacked the aggressiveness of a Cobb or Speaker, the drive of a Hornsby, or the boyish enthusiasm of a Harris."[5]

Lou Boudreau (1942–1950)

If there's one rule by which every baseball executive should live, it's this: *Don't pay any attention to the wild-eyed advice offered by your local sports columnist.*

After the 1940 season, with the Indians looking for a new manager, *Cleveland Press* scribe Franklin Lewis wrote, "If Clark Griffith owned the Indians, he would put Boudreau in charge of the team even if he were only twenty-three years old."[6]

Boudreau, the Indians' impressive young shortstop, *was* twenty-three. And Clark Griffith, who actually owned the Washington Senators, had previously appointed young middle infielders Bucky Harris (1924) and Joe Cronin (1933) as manager. And both Harris and Cronin had won pennants in their very first seasons at the helm.

Spurning Lewis's advice (of sorts), Indians owner Alva Bradley hired Roger Peckinpaugh (himself a former shortstop/manager, way back in 1914 with the Yankees). A year later, though, after general manager Cy Slapnicka quit his job, Peckinbaugh was kicked upstairs, and again the Indians needed a new manager.

Boudreau, who'd aged a year—and they say the twenty-fourth is the most important—called Bradley and asked for the job. As Boudreau later wrote, "I cited my experience as captain of the basketball and baseball teams at Illinois and emphasized my personal conviction that I could do a good job for him."

A few days later, he got the job.

If Boudreau hadn't been blessed with one of the best players in the American League—himself—he wouldn't have lasted more than three or four seasons. The Indians were respectable enough, but didn't make a move toward first place even during the 1943–1945 period when everything turned upside down. On the other hand, Boudreau was one of the very best players in the American League, which is what you'd expect considering the low level of play in those years (Boudreau's draft status was 4-F, due to his bad ankles).

When Bill Veeck took over in 1946, he knew very well what had to be done.

> Problems we had aplenty. My first problem was that the best shortstop
> in baseball was, in my opinion, not the best manager, an opinion that

was not greatly altered by a close, intimate and—as it turned out—unbreakable association in Cleveland.

... At twenty-eight, he was still a faintly bewildered Boy Manager. The team I inherited was in sixth place; I thought Lou should have had them higher.

My main objection to Lou was that he managed by hunch and desperation. You ask Casey Stengel why he made a certain move and he will tell you about a roommate he had in 1919 who had demonstrated some principle Casey was now putting into effect. You ask Lou and he will say, "The way we're going, we had to do *something*." If there is a better formula for making a bad situation worse, I have never heard of it.[7]

Veeck didn't do anything then, because he didn't want his first move to rile every baseball fan in north Ohio. But after the 1947 season, he tried to make a deal that would have sent Boudreau and two outfielders to the Browns—who probably would have immediately flipped Boudreau to another club—in exchange for Vern Stephens and a couple of good pitchers. But the deal fell through when the Browns wanted more cash than Veeck was willing to spend, and eventually Boudreau—who said he wouldn't play for the Indians unless he was also the manager—got a new two-year contract.

Granted, if Stephens had played shortstop in 1948 rather than Boudreau, the Indians would have won neither the American League pennant—they had to beat the Red Sox in a one-game playoff just to accomplish that—nor the World Series. As things played out, not trading Boudreau was one of Veeck's best moves. It's true that in 1949, '50, and '51, Stephens was better than Boudreau. But the Indians finished eight, six, and five games out of first place in those seasons, and it's not likely that Stephens would have made up those games by himself.

Then again, Veeck's first choice as Boudreau's replacement was Casey Stengel. Now, we certainly don't *know* if Stengel would have been a genius in Cleveland, and anyway Al Lopez—who took over as manager in 1951— knew a thing or three, too.

But the problem wasn't Veeck's decision to keep Boudreau; in the short term, that worked out, and anyway Veeck rarely bothered thinking too far ahead. No, the problem was the hiring of Boudreau in the first place. If the Indians hadn't hired Boudreau to manage, when he was only twenty-four, they'd still have enjoyed his brilliant presence in the lineup and also had the flexibility to hire the best manager for the job.

Tommy Holmes (1951–1952)

A hero in Boston since 1945, when he was the best player in the National League, Holmes quit playing after 1950—even though he was only thirty-four, and still a fine hitter—and took over as manager of the Braves' farm club in Hartford. In June of '51, Billy Southworth quit as Braves manager, and Holmes was promoted to the big club.

His quick apprenticeship in Hartford probably wasn't enough. He treated his players like teammates—which of course they'd been, just the season before (and still were to some extent, as Holmes remained on the active roster and occasionally pinch-hit)—and he insisted on coaching third base, the result being a great many runners nailed at the plate.[8]

Holmes returned in 1952, and chose Jack Cusick over Johnny Logan as his shortstop. Cusick batted .167 for the season, but Holmes missed most of it; with the Braves in seventh place after thirty-five games, he got canned.

Joe Adcock (1967)

Bill James: "Adcock began his managerial career"—with the Indians in '67—"with no experience, no real preparation, and it was a disaster . . . Like Hornsby, Adcock tended to expect his players to work as hard at the game as he himself had worked."[9]

Rocky Colavito: "Without question Adcock was the worst manager I ever played for. He had a sour disposition. He was vindictive."[10]

Adcock had never managed or coached at any level before, and he managed like it. Here's one nugget: according to second baseman Vern Fuller, Adcock "fell in love" with second baseman Gus Gil, who got ninety-six at-bats and batted, wait for it, .115 (Gil actually wasn't that bad; two years later he hooked on with the Seattle Pilots and jacked his average all the way up to .222).

Larry Shepard (1968–1969)

From 1965 through 1975, the running story about the Pittsburgh Pirates was whether or not Danny Murtaugh felt good enough to manage the club. Murtaugh took over as manager in 1957, led the Pirates to the World Series in 1960, but took early retirement after the 1964 season because of illness (the nature of which was never specified by the writers of the time).

Murtaugh returned in the middle of the '67 season, but the Pirates didn't improve and he quit again after the season (again citing ill health). This time his replacement was Larry Shepard, who'd managed in the minor leagues for eighteen seasons.

In the middle of Shepard's first season, with the Pirates in seventh place, he said, "I never saw a team so helpless. We can't do anything right. We can't hit, can't run, can't do anything." According to Willie Stargell, Shepard "was often quick to praise but also quick to discredit and . . . had already lost twenty-six pounds because of worry." [11]

The Pirates got off to a good start in '69, but by the All-Star break they were just 47–48. Around the same time, Shepard suffered chest pains and was sent to the hospital, where he spent three days. The Pirates did play better down the stretch, but not well enough to save Shepard's job; the morning after his club swept a doubleheader from the Phillies, he was fired with only five games left in the season.

Shepard landed on his feet, serving as Sparky Anderson's pitching coach in Cincinnati throughout Anderson's tenure there.

Ted Williams (1969–1972)

In Williams's first season as manager, his Washington Senators made a Great Leap Forward: after going 65–96 in 1968, in '69 they jumped to 86–76, easily the best record in franchise history (which began in 1961) and the best for a Washington team since World War II. And Ted Williams, less than a decade removed from his playing days and still very much in the national baseball consciousness, got a great deal of the credit.

In particular, he got a great deal of credit for the improvement of Washington's hitters. And the hitters certainly did improve. Hitting stats in general were up in '69 (because the pitcher's mound was lowered by five inches) and the strike zone was shrunk. But even taking that into account, nearly all the regulars were better after Williams arrived. The following lists each regular's adjusted OPS—like ERA+, OPS+ places a hitter's OPS in the context of league and home ballpark, with 100 being average—and whether or not it went up or down from '68 to '69 . . .

		1968	1969	+/-
c	Paul Casanova	41	54	+
1b	Mike Epstein	117	175	+
2b	Bernie Allen	98	108	+

ss	Ed Brinkman	44	88	+
3b	Ken McMullen	117	121	+
lf	Frank Howard	170	177	+
cf	Del Unser	73	110	+
rf	Hank Allen	70	87	+

That's right: all nine regulars in 1969 were more productive than they'd been the year before. Statistically, the pitching improved just a tiny bit, but that can be partially (and perhaps completely) explained by the entry of two lousy expansion teams that season. So what happened in 1970?

		1969	1970	+/-
c	Paul Casanova	54	69	+
1b	Mike Epstein	175	129	-
2b	Bernie Allen	108	99	-
ss	Ed Brinkman	88	80	-
3b	Ken McMullen	121	43	-
lf	Frank Howard	177	170	-
cf	Del Unser	110	83	-
rf	Hank Allen	87	59	-

McMullen batted .203 in April, and the Senators traded him to the Angels. Hank Allen batted .211 early in the season, and the Senators traded him to the Brewers. Only Casanova improved in 1970 (and he had a great deal of room for improvement). Granted, anything like an across-the-board improvement would have been practically impossible, because so many Senators had already improved so much in 1969. But with the exception of Brinkman, most of these guys simply returned in 1970 to their 1968, pre–Teddy Ballgame performances. Even though Teddy Ballgame was still their manager.

Williams hung around for two more seasons, even accompanying the Senators as they became Rangers. By all accounts, he hated every minute of that first—and last, for him—season in Texas. As Rangers catcher Rich Billings later said, "Ted was just angry all the time. He didn't want to be in Texas. He let everybody know."[12]

Karl Kuehl (1976)

Things didn't start well for Karl Kuehl, who managed for eight seasons in the minor leagues before taking over in 1976 as manager of the Expos. By the end of May, the club was 16–23, thirteen games out of first place. Right around the same time, shortstop Tim Foli called an impromptu press conference and said of Kuehl, "He's a rookie. He's got some complex or something that won't let him manage the team and learn with the rest of the guys."[13]

Kuehl told Foli to keep his mouth shut and play shortstop. Foli told Kuehl to get bent. Kuehl benched Foli. Three games into Foli's benching, his replacement, Pepe Frias, made three errors in a 6–2 loss. The next night, Foli was back in the lineup, apparently at the behest of club president John McHale. At which point everybody knew who was really running things.

In mid September, the following item appeared in *The Sporting News:*

> Manager Karl Kuehl of the Expos responded to an incident involving Montreal writer Ian McDonald and righthander Clay Kirby with a meeting during which he told his players that too many of his rules were being abused and that fines would be levied for future infractions. McDonald and Kirby emerged with minor bruises after trading punches in a Los Angeles bar. Kirby took exception to remarks McDonald made about Kirby's current statistics.

A few days later the Expos were swept by the Pirates in a doubleheader. That gave the Expos eighty-five losses—tops in the majors—and got Kuehl fired. No, it probably wasn't all his fault. But the Expos lost eight-seven games in 1975, they lost eighty-seven games in 1977 . . . and in 1976, they lost 107.

Vern Rapp (1977–1978, 1984)

In 1981, the Reds posted the best record (66–42) in the major leagues. In 1982, they posted the worst record (61–101) in the National League. During that season they fired John McNamara (good move) and hired Russ Nixon (bad move). The Reds improved some in 1983, but not enough to save Nixon, who was replaced by Vern Rapp.

Bad move.

Rapp first managed in 1977 and was, according to the record books, successful. He took a St. Louis team that finished 72–90 in '76 and brought them home at 83–79. In late August the Cardinals were still in the thick of the pennant race. But as Bill James has written, "You would have had to read the papers carefully to detect the positive elements in this. The *story* about the Cardinals that year was 'Rapp fighting with his team.' "

Fortunately, the owner was on Rapp's side, and after a particularly intense stretch of disharmony, the manager was rewarded with a contract extension. That was a good thing for Rapp, who was fired shortly into the '78 season after broadcaster Jack Buck reported that Rapp had called superstar Ted Simmons "a loser." According to *The Sporting News*, in St. Louis that "was like calling Stan Musial a Polish joke."

Okay, so Rapp wasn't the right man for the job. He wasn't the first and wouldn't be the last. What's amazing is that the Reds, four years later, would give Rapp another shot. What's more amazing is that when he got fired— roughly five months into a two-year contract—Tony Perez, finishing up his career as a reserve with the Reds, said he thought Rapp had been "too soft."[14]

The Reds were 51–70 when Rapp got canned, but went 19–22 the rest of the season under Pete Rose, and finished second in the NL West in each of the next four seasons.

Terry Bevington (1995–1997)

During the '97 season, White Sox batting coach Bill Buckner was fired, and said it was because he didn't get along with his manager. During the season, Tony Phillips was traded to the Angels, supposedly because he didn't get along with his manager.

According to the Associated Press account of Terry Bevington's firing, near the end "the fans turned on the manager, booing him loudly at home when he went to the mound to change pitchers."[15]

According to the *Sporting News Baseball Guide*, "Many fans openly wondered why it took so long for G.M. Ron Schueler to pull the trigger. In his 2½-year stay as manager, Bevington failed to gain the respect of his players or coaching staff, and he was pummeled by the media. New manager Jerry Manuel hardly has big shoes to fill."[16]

1. Harold Kaese, *The Boston Braves* (New York: G. P. Putnam's Sons, 1948).
2. *Boston Daily Globe*, July 17, 1909.
3. Rick Huhn, *The Sizzler: George Sisler, Baseball's Forgotten Great* (Columbia: University of Missouri Press, 2004).

Tim Johnson (1998)

Tim Johnson, who managed the Blue Jays, doesn't really belong with the others in this Interlude, because by most accounts he was a decent enough manager. In 1998, Johnson's first (and, as it turned out, only) season, the Blue Jays moved from 76–86 and fifth place to 88–74 and third place, falling only four games short of a tie for the wild card.

This guy was *going* places. Until, that is, everyone discovered that he'd been telling everyone he'd been someplace he actually hadn't.

Johnson's success as a rookie manager was sometimes attributed to the inspiring stories he told about his combat experiences as a U.S. Marine in Vietnam.

But Johnson had never set foot in Vietnam. He'd been in the Marine Corps reserves, and taught prospective mortarmen at Camp Pendleton in California when he wasn't playing baseball; at the same time, Johnson was in the Dodgers' farm system. Johnson also had been claiming for twenty years that he'd been an All-American basketball player in high school, and turned down a scholarship to attend UCLA. Also not true.[17]

This news broke in late November, apparently after reporters in Toronto did their jobs (if only political reporters in the U.S. could be as diligent).

When Johnson arrived in training camp the next spring, he met with his players and apologized, and apparently believed the whole thing would be forgotten. But the players who didn't like Johnson didn't forget, and baseball writers never forget anything. On March 17, Johnson was fired. His presence was simply a distraction. As Blue Jays general manager Gord Ash said, "Each day brought a new revelation from a new source. The media would go to players and say what do you think about what this guy said."[18]

4. Ibid.

5. Fred Lieb, *The Baltimore Orioles: An Informal History of a Great Baseball Club* (New York: G. P. Putnam's Sons, 1955).

6. Franklin Lewis, *The Cleveland Indians* (New York: G. P. Putnam's Sons, 1949).

7. Bill Veeck and Ed Linn, *Veeck—As in Wreck* (New York: G. P. Putnam's Sons, 1962).

8. Donald Dewey and Nicholas Acocella, *Total Ballclubs: The Ultimate Book of Baseball Teams* (Toronto: SPORT Media Publishing, 2005).

9. Bill James, *The Baseball Book 1990* (New York: Villard, 1990).

10. Terry Pluto, *The Curse of Rocky Colavito* (New York: Simon & Schuster, 1994).

11. Willie Stargell and Tom Bird, *Willie Stargell: An Autobiography* (New York: Harper & Row, 1984).

12. Leigh Montville, *Ted Williams: The Biography of an American Hero* (New York: Doubleday, 2004).

13. Bob Dunn, "Kuehl, Foli Fire from Lips in Expo Shootout," *Sporting News*, June 19, 1976, p. 19.

14. Earl Lawson, *Sporting News*, Aug. 27, 1984.

15. Associated Press, "Bevington Dismissed; Thomas Re-Signs," *New York Times*, Oct. 1, 1997, p. C6.

16. *Baseball Guide*, 1988 Edition (St. Louis: Sporting News, 1988).

17. Jason Diamos, "Jays' Manager is Hounded by War Tales," *New York Times*, Dec. 15, 1998, p. D4.

18. Murray Chass, "False War Tales Lead Jays to Drop Johnson," *New York Times*, March 18, 1999, p. D3.

THE GENERAL PANICS

Future generations will be told this incredible horror story September after September . . . Children will shriek, adults will shiver, managers will faint. The legend will take its place alongside such classics as the Dodgers of '51 and Frankenstein and the Wolfman.

—Larry Merchant, *Philadelphia Daily News*

On the morning of September 21, 1964, here's how things stood at the top of the National League:

Phillies	90–60	–
Cardinals	83–66	6½
Reds	83–66	6½
Giants	83–67	7

The Phillies and Giants had twelve games left to play; the Cardinals and Reds, thirteen. The Phillies were a mortal lock to win their third National League pennant in franchise history, dating back to 1883. (Well, maybe not *mortal*; as manager Gene Mauch told his charges, "Just remember, the 1950 Phillies had a seven-and-a-half-game lead with only eleven games to play. But they lost eight of their next ten and had to win the last game to save the pennant.")

Three days later, on the 24th, the standings looked like this:

Phillies	90–63	–
Reds	86–66	3½
Cardinals	84–67	5
Giants	85–68	5

The Phillies had lost three straight to the Reds; the Cardinals and Giants picked up some ground, too. Things got worse on the 24th, when the Phillies lost to the Braves and the Cardinals swept a doubleheader from the Pirates (the Reds and Giants were both idle), leaving the standings like this:

Phillies	90–62	–
Reds	86–66	3
Cardinals	86–67	3½
Giants	85–68	4½

The Phillies had eight games left, in ten days. Like this (where G = game and X = day off):

GGGGGGXGXG

Gene Mauch has just seen the Phillies lose their
tenth straight game. (Where's Jimmy Dugan
when you need him?)

And they were still sitting in the catbird seat. The great majority of teams that hold three-game leads with eight to play do win.

Nevertheless, Mauch chose this point to get creative. Only eight games left, beginning on the 25th . . . but who would start them?

Ray Culp (8–7, 4.13) had pitched well during the first few months of the season, but hadn't pitched at all since September 12 (Mauch said that Culp didn't want the ball; Culp would deny that, but admitted he wasn't completely healthy). So Mauch had five options when looking for starting pitchers in those last ten days; other than Culp, these are the only Phillies who'd started more than three games through September 24, along with their numbers at that point:

	Starts	Innings	W–L	ERA
Jim Bunning	36	269	18–6	2.38
Dennis Bennett	31	207	12–13	3.57
Chris Short	28	202	17–8	2.14
Art Mahaffey	28	157	12–9	4.58
Rick Wise	8	65	5–3	4.15

Just looking at the 25th, Mauch's options were Short (who'd started on the 22nd), Mahaffey, and Wise (Bennett, who was suffering from a shoulder injury, had started on the 23rd, Bunning on the 24th). Mauch clearly had little confidence in Wise, a nineteen-year-old rookie, leaving only Short on two days rest or Mahaffey on three.

Mauch started Short.

Why not Mahaffey? According to one account, Mauch was still sore at Mahaffey for letting Chico Ruiz steal home, a few days earlier, in a 1–0 loss to the Reds.[1]

Short pitched well, but the Phillies lost 7–5 in twelve innings.

Mahaffey did start on the 26th and he too pitched well. But the bullpen gave up four runs in the last two innings and the Phillies suffered another crushing loss. Now their lead was just a half-game over the Reds (who had won three games while the Phils were losing two). And the Cardinals were just a game behind the Reds.

Bunning started on the 27th—he asked Mauch for the assignment—and got knocked out in the fourth inning of a 14–8 loss. The Reds swept another doubleheader from the Mets to grab first place, and the Cardinals won again.

The Phillies lost their next three games, behind Short, Bennett, and Bunning, and with only two games to play they were two-and-a-half games out of first place. They'd blown it.

What Mauch did with his starting pitchers didn't work. But did he have an attractive alternative?

Beginning on the 25th, if Mauch pitched both Short and Bunning on short rest twice, he could get six starts out of them (three apiece), with Bennett and Mahaffey each starting once. If he did *not* pitch anybody on short rest, he would get five starts out of his two aces, with Mahaffey going twice rather than once. Mahaffey was the Phillies' worst starter, and since tossing a two-hit shutout on August 20 he'd been knocked out of two starts in the first inning. On the other hand, in his three other starts he'd been moderately effective, pitching into the seventh inning in each of them. In hindsight, Bunning argued that Mahaffey should have been given more work.

"All I know is," Bunning told his biographer, "the reason he started us with two days rest was because, first of all, he wouldn't give Mahaffey the ball. There was no reason for him not to. Art should have been starting right along with Shortie and myself because he was sound and willing. Some of the others weren't. They were kind of glad Short and Bunning were pitching every third day."

A Bitchy Payback

Among the Phillies' many tormen-tors in 1964—Lady Luck, their own manager, etc.—was Cardinals right-hander Curt Simmons.

Simmons went 18–9 for St. Louis that season, and they certainly wouldn't have won the pennant without him. Three of Simmons's wins came against the Phillies, including one on Septem-ber 30 that dropped the Phillies two-and-one-half games behind the Cardinals.

And the hell of it all? Simmons had, until a few years earlier, always been a Philly.

At only eighteen, back in 1947, Simmons debuted with the Phillies and pitched a five-hitter to beat the Giants on the last day of the season. It took him a few seasons to establish himself, but from 1950 through '57 he was one of the better pitchers in the National League, going 96–73 over the eight seasons (and he spent all of 1951 in the service). All for the Phils.

But he struggled some in '58, missed most of '59 with a sore arm, and in May 1960 the Phillies re-leased him. The Cardinals signed him . . . and he went right back to pitching like Curt Simmons, and continued to pitch like Curt Sim-mons until (roughly) the middle of 1965, winning seventy-seven games after the Phils dumped him.

Of course, you never know how things would have worked out. If the Phillies had kept Simmons, maybe he wouldn't have come around. If they'd kept him, maybe they wouldn't have traded for Bun-

Here are two schedules, Mauch's actual and my hypothetical, beginning on the 25th and running through the end of the season:

Mauch's		Neyer's
Short		Mahaffey
Mahaffey		Short
Bunning		Bennett
Short		Bunning
Bennett		Mahaffey
Bunning		Short
	(off day)	
Short		Bunning
	(off day)	
Bunning		Short

In my scheme the same pitchers are starting the same number of games, except Bunning loses one start to Mahaffey. What would this have meant, practically? Of course we can't really know. But if we assume the pitchers would have done, in those starts, what they'd done previously in the season, then starting Bunning rather than Mahaffey in one game should have saved roughly two runs. Of course, in the context of one game that's a significant number of runs; in 1964, seventy-seven of the Phillies' 154 games were de-cided by one or two runs.

But the prospect of saving those two runs has to be weighed against the prospect of losing two (or more) runs because Bunning and/or Short won't be as effective as usual, because they're working on two days rest. In fact, roughly a week earlier Bunning had worked on two days rest, with ugly re-sults. On September 13 he pitched ten innings and beat San Francisco, 4–1. Three days later he started against Houston and got knocked out in the fifth. (Short had started once on short rest, but that was a special case, com-ing three days after the Pirates kayoed him in the second inning.)

In other words, Mauch had little reason to think that Short and Bunning could, at the end of a tough month at the end of a long season, pitch effec-tively on less rest than normal.

And of course it didn't work. On September 27 the Phillies scored eight runs but lost because Bunning gave up seven in three innings. On September 30 the Phillies scored five runs but lost because Bunning gave up eight in three-plus. The Phillies lost all four games started by Bunning and Short in that stretch, and they also lost Mahaffey's and Bennett's starts (Mahaffey pitched well, Bennett didn't).

The Phillies did win their last two games, with first Short and then Bunning pitching on three days rest (thanks to the Phils' days off). On the last day of the season, Bunning shut out the Reds; if the Cardinals had lost to the Mets that afternoon, then St. Louis, Philadelphia, and Cincinnati would have finished in a three-way tie for the National League pennant (which had never happened in either major league, and still hasn't).

The Cardinals did not lose to the Mets. The Phillies and Reds both finished one game out of first place. The Phillies wouldn't come close to another pennant until 1976, long after Mauch had been sent elsewhere.

ning prior to the '64 season. Still, as things played out, releasing Curt Simmons looks an awful lot like a blunder.

---

1. B. G. Kelley, "The Boys of Bummer," *Inside Sports*, October 1994.

INDIANS TRADE THE ROCK

and

INDIANS DIG UP THE ROCK

They say I'm out of my mind. But I say I swapped a hamburger for a steak.
—Frank Lane (after trading Rocky Colavito for Harvey Kuenn)

We hated to give up on Romano, but when you get a chance to get someone like Colavito, you don't muff it.
—Gabe Paul (after giving up not only Johnny Romano, but also Tommie Agee and Tommy John, to reacquire Rocky Colavito)

It's one thing to make a lousy trade. It's quite another to compensate for the first lousy trade by making another lousy trade to get back the player you gave away in the first lousy trade. But that's exactly what the Cleveland Indians did with Rocky Colavito.

In the late 1950s, the Cleveland Indians were run by Frank Lane, who so loved trading, that's what they called him: "Trader" Frank Lane. For a couple of years in the mid-'50s, Lane ran the Cardinals and wanted to trade Stan Musial (he didn't). The Indians lured Lane away from St. Louis. He was hired on November 12, 1957, and three weeks later he engineered a block-buster deal, sending Al Smith and future Hall of Famer Early Wynn to the White Sox for Fred Hatfield and Minnie Minoso. In the first calendar year that Lane was running the Indians—November 12 through November 11—he made ten trades involving thirty-two players.*

By most accounts, Lane wasn't a particularly likable sort of fellow, and the annual contract negotiations between him and Colavito were not friendly.† When spring training began in 1960, Colavito was a holdout. So was Tigers right fielder Harvey Kuenn. In '59, Colavito had tied for the American League lead with forty-two home runs. Kuenn had hit .353 to win the batting title. Colavito wanted a big raise,

---

* In those twelve months, Lane traded Roger Maris to Kansas City and sold future Hall of Famer Hoyt Wilhelm to the Orioles for $75,000. Rocky Colavito wasn't one of those thirty-two, but it wasn't for lack of Lane's trying. He had a couple of trades worked out to move Colavito, but both deals fell through.
† Onetime Indians manager Bobby Bragan reported in his autobiography with a decided lack of surprise that when Lane died in 1981, there were eight people at the funeral. Including the minister.

from $28,000 to $45,000. Kuenn wanted a big raise, from $35,000 to $50,000.

Lane suggested to anybody within earshot that he wouldn't mind trading Colavito for Kuenn. My headache for yours. Kuenn liked Detroit, and signed a new contract for $42,000. Colavito liked Cleveland, and signed a new contract for $35,000 (with a bizarre clause: he would receive a $1,000 bonus if he hit *fewer* than thirty-five home runs; Lane wanted more singles and fewer strikeouts).[1]

Signed or not, Lane couldn't get Colavito and Kuenn out of his head. And on the day before the Indians' first game—against Detroit, coincidentally enough—Lane pulled the trigger, sending Colavito to the Tigers for Kuenn, straight up.

Here's columnist (and Colavito biographer) Gordon Cobbledick, writing in the *Cleveland Plain Dealer*:

> In Lane's critical mind, Colavito became expendable when he went into a batting slump last September that cost the Indians the pennant. He did himself no good when he waged a winter-long holdout fight for a salary many thousands greater than Lane considered him worth.[2]

Colavito had struggled terribly in September of '59, batting .207 with three home runs in twenty-four games. He hardly cost the Indians the pennant, though. They finished five games behind the White Sox, and even if Colavito had been at his best, it's highly unlikely the Indians would have gone 19–5 in September rather than 14–10.

The truth is that Lane didn't know what the hell he was doing. He just wanted to do *something*. Had to do something.*

Based purely on performance, the deal didn't help either club in 1960. Kuenn's batting average dropped to .308, and he still didn't have any power. Colavito's numbers dropped across the board. And little more than a year after trading for Kuenn, Lane sent Kuenn to the Giants for pitcher Johnny Antonelli (who was finished) and Willie Kirkland (who was sort of a poor man's Colavito).

As Terry Pluto puts it, "Colavito was traded because the Indians didn't need his power as much as they needed Kuenn's singles. Then Kuenn was moved on because he didn't hit enough homers. Add it up, and the Indians traded a guy who had averaged forty homers a year from 1959 to 1963 for a guy who averaged twenty-two."[3]

---

* With the trade of Colavito, Lane completely turned over the forty-man roster he'd started with, just two-and-a-half years earlier.

Transcendental Graphics

Colavito surveying Tiger Stadium.

Lane resigned early in 1961, in favor of a lucrative four-year deal with the Kansas City A's. His replacement in Cleveland: Gabe Paul.

In 1959, Colavito's last season in Cleveland, the Indians drew more than 1.5 million fans, just a hair behind the Yankees. In 1964, with a 79–83 club, the Indians barely drew 650,000 fans, more than only the terrible clubs in Washington and Kansas City.

Gabe Paul, then running the Indians as co-owner and president, would later explain, "We were in a real financial bind. We had opportunities to move the club, and we knew if we didn't draw more people, we were going to have to move. It seemed like a lot of the fans just lost interest after Rocky was traded."

Attendance *had* dropped precipitously—down thirty-seven percent—in the first season after the Indians traded Colavito. Then again, the Indians hadn't attracted many fans in 1957 or 1958, when Colavito was establishing himself as a big star. The Indians drew well in 1959 not because fans loved "The Rock," but rather because the Tribe spent all but a few days of the season in first or second place.

Paul, however, apparently did not understand the strong correlation between wins and attendance. So he brought Colavito back to Cleveland, via a three-team trade . . . and probably felt like a genius when attendance did go up in '65 . . . but then, so did the Indians' record. When they dropped below .500 in '67, back down went the attendance, to almost exactly the 1964 level.

Anyway, the Indians got two good years from Colavito. In 1965, he played 162 games and led the American League with ninety-three walks and 108 runs batted in. In '66, he hit thirty homers and drove in seventy-two runs, not bad at all for that pitcher's season.

He got off to a poor start in 1967, though, and on July 29 the Indians traded Colavito again, this time to the White Sox. In exchange, Cleveland received outfielder Jim King (who got twenty-one at-bats with the Indians, and was never seen in the major leagues again) and second baseman Marv Staehle (who never played for the Tribe and later finished his career with a .207 batting average in 145 major-league games).

Essentially, the Indians got exactly two good seasons and nothing else in return for Tommy John, Johnny Romano, and Tommie Agee, who'd been sent to the White Sox in the three-team deal for Colavito.

And what of those three? Let's start with Romano, because he's easy to dismiss . . . until you actually check. Romano played for the White Sox for two seasons, and those seasons were about as similar as any two consecutive seasons you'll ever find. Romano played 122 games in both, and rapped out twenty-seven long hits in both. In 1965, he drove in forty-eight runs and walked fifty-nine times; in '66 he drove in forty-seven runs and walked fifty-eight times.

And of course Romano was by far the least valuable player the Indians gave up.

Following the trade, Colavito earned sixty-two Win Shares (all but eleven of those with Cleveland). Romano, whose career ended abruptly in 1967, earned thirty-seven Win Shares after the Indians traded him. So far, advantage Cleveland.

But then there's Tommie Agee. He earned 139 Win Shares after the trade, and from 1966 through 1971 he ranked as one of the better center fielders in the game. And there's Tommy John, too. When the Indians traded John, he'd won two games in the major leagues. He would win 286 more.

In fairness to Gabe Paul, it's apparent that the White Sox didn't know how good their new players were, either. According to *The Sporting News*, "Colavito and catcher John Romano were the key men in an eight-player transaction."[4] As Sox manager Al Lopez said, "We've needed a power-hitting

(Not) Catching Butterflies

At the risk of seeming to pile on, I'd like to point out a Frank Lane move that was arguably stupider than trading Colavito for Kuenn. How do you get dumber than brain dead? It's not easy, but say what you will about Colavito for Kuenn, it did not cost the Tribe a pennant. The one I'm talking about probably did.

Just months before Lane took over in Cleveland, the Indians purchased Hoyt Wilhelm, in the midst of a subpar season, from the Cardinals. The seller? Then-Cardinals general manager Frank Lane. This probably did not auger well for Wilhelm's future in Cleveland, but as the '58 season unfolded there was no getting around the fact that he was pitching well, his 2–7 record balanced by a 2.49 ERA, best on the staff. But there was a problem: none of the Indians' three catchers could handle Wilhelm's baffling knuckleball. And when there was a problem on a Frank Lane team, he had only one way of solving it—make a move. On August 23, Wilhelm was claimed off waivers by the Orioles (who did pay Cleveland $75,000 for the privilege).

In Baltimore, Paul Richards had other methods of problem-solving. He put Wilhelm in the rotation, and on September 20 was rewarded with a no-hit victory over the pennant-bound Yankees. Worried about his catchers' inability to contain the flutterball, Richards devised a larger mitt with a gigantic pocket. Hoyt Wilhelm was about to enter his prime. It might not have mattered so much, except that in 1959, opportunity unexpectedly knocked for the Indians. The Yankees had a bad year and never got into the race. The Tribe offense, meanwhile, was hitting on all cylinders; it led the league in home runs, batting average, slugging percentage, and runs scored. What more did they need?

Pitching. Their only competitors for the pennant, the White Sox, had a far less potent offense, but better pitching. Which brings us back to Wilhelm, who in '59 went 15–11 with a league-leading 2.19 ERA in his only full season as a starter. This, for a sixth-place team that scored 194 fewer runs than the Indians. The Tribe lost the pennant by five games. Would Wilhelm have been worth that much to them? By the time Colavito was traded, in 1960, nothing he could have done would have put the Indians over the top.

So which was the bigger blunder?—*Mike Kopf*

catcher for some time. In Agee we got a young, fast outfielder who can back up Ken Berry. We have good reports on Tommy John." He also said that Romano "could make the difference for us in the pennant race this year."[5]

It didn't take long for the White Sox to realize what they'd done, though. In 1965, John went 14–7 for the White Sox.

In 1966, Agee took over from Berry in center field and won a Gold Glove and a Rookie of the Year Award.

In 1967, *with* Colavito—at least until they traded him on July 29—the Indians finished tenth (and last) in American League attendance.

In 1968, *without* Colavito, the Indians—who jumped from eighth place to third place in the standings—finished fifth in American League attendance.

The fans might have loved The Rock, but what they really wanted was a winning ball club. There have been a few players who fans would pay to see. Babe Ruth. Jackie Robinson. Mark McGwire. But while Rocky Colavito was a fine player, he certainly wasn't worth the price of a ticket.

Frank Lane made a bad trade because he didn't understand baseball. And Gabe Paul made a bad trade because he didn't understand the *business* of baseball.

1. Terry Pluto, *The Curse of Rocky Colavito: A Loving Look at a Thirty-Year Slump* (New York: Simon & Schuster, 1994).

2. Gordon Cobbledick, *Don't Knock the Rock: The Rocky Colavito Story* (Cleveland: World, 1966).

3. Pluto, *Curse.*

4. Russell Schneider, "Cleveland's Cup Runneth Over—Fans Toast the Return of Rocky," *Sporting News,* Jan. 30, 1965, p. 13.

5. Edgar Munzel, "Fluttering on Wings of Deal for Romano," *Sporting News,* Jan. 30, 1965, p. 15.

REDS TRADE ROBINSON FOR PAPPAS

I make them feel confident, and they make me feel safe. And pretty. Of course what I give them lasts a lifetime. What they give me lasts a hundred and forty-two games. Sometimes it seems like a bad trade. But bad trades are a part of baseball. I mean, who can forget Frank Robinson for Milt Pappas, for God's sake?

—Annie Savoy in *Bull Durham*

First, let's be very clear about something: this deal was *not* Robinson for Pappas. It was Robinson for Pappas and Jack Baldschun and Dick Simpson.

So who were all those guys?

Over the three previous seasons, Pappas had won forty-five games, lost twenty-five, and posted ERAs significantly better than league average while averaging 230 innings per season. Oh, and he was twenty-six. By almost any measure, Pappas ranked as one of the best young pitchers in the game.

Jack Baldschun—acquired by the Orioles three days before they traded him to the Reds—was no star, but from 1961 through '65 he'd been one of the better relief pitchers in the National League.

Dick Simpson, little more than a footnote now, was a pretty hot prospect in 1965. Despite not turning twenty-two until midway through the season, Simpson, a speedy center fielder, had batted .301, hit twenty-four home runs, and led the Pacific Coast League with twelve triples. (Like Baldschun, Simp-

son had just joined the Orioles a few days earlier, coming over in a trade that sent Norm Siebern to the Angels.)

In fact, initially the Orioles balked at trading three players for one. According to then-Orioles general manager Harry Dalton—who had *just* been promoted, and handed the prospective trade by outgoing GM Lee MacPhail—he tried to get a minor-league pitcher from the Reds, was offered Roger Craig, said no thanks, and eventually accepted "just" Robinson.

Purely in terms of performance, the trade was a disaster for Cincinnati.

Simpson spent all of 1966 and '67 with the Reds, but apparently got most of his action as a late-innings defensive replacement for Tommy Harper. Simpson did get a pretty good shot with the Astros in '68, but batted .197 and struck out in nearly a third of his plate appearances. After brief stints with the

Yankees and Pilots in '69, Simpson's career in the majors was over. He was still only twenty-six, but faded from professional baseball two years later.

Baldschun was awful in the season after the trade, going 1–5 with a 5.49 ERA in forty-two games, and he spent nearly all of '67 and '68 in the minors.

There's a famous quote of Reds owner-operator Bill DeWitt saying he'd made the deal because Robinson was "an old thirty," but that's not precisely what DeWitt said. What he said, in the spring of '66, was this: "Nothing personal at all. Robinson is not a young thirty. If he had been twenty-six, we might not have traded him." To which Robinson quickly responded, "I can't argue with DeWitt if he says he traded me to strengthen his ball club, but that comment about me being an old thirty is hitting below the belt. It was uncalled for."[1]

Later that season, Dewitt said, "We had Robinson here ten years. We won one pennant with him. But to follow the Branch Rickey theory, we'd rather trade a player too soon than a year too late. And Pappas is winning for us now."[2]

On June 13—the date of the *Sports Illustrated* article in which DeWitt was quoted—Pappas was 4–5 with a 4.04 ERA; Robinson was hitting .344 with a .682 slugging percentage.

Pappas finished the season with twelve wins. Robinson was the American League's Most Valuable Player, and the Orioles won the World Series. DeWitt took the wrong lesson from Rickey. You certainly don't want to trade a player a year too late; but when you're talking about a player like Frank Robinson, you don't start worrying about that until he's closer to forty than thirty. And when the Reds traded Robinson, he was still a long ways from forty.

Then again, all that stuff about Branch Rickey might have been a smokescreen. This was the 1960s, Robinson was black, and a few years earlier he'd been busted for carrying a concealed, unlicensed pistol. According to DeWitt's obituary in *The Sporting News*, whatever he might (or might not) have said about Robinson's age, "It was more likely that growing differences between Robinson, whom DeWitt regarded as a troublemaker, and the owner led to the trade."[3]

Obviously, the trade worked out well for the Orioles, who won four pennants in Robinson's six seasons in Baltimore.

But how badly did it hurt the Reds?

There are two ways to approach this question. Obviously, knowing what we now know, the Reds could have done a lot better than they did. The deal essentially wound up being Frank Robinson for Milt Pappas (for God's sake), and that's nothing like a fair deal. The bottom line is the standings, though. Here's how the Reds fared, relative to first place, in the eight more seasons in which Robinson was a premier player:

1966	−18
1967	−14½
1968	−14
1969	−4
1970	+14½
1971	−11
1972	+10½
1973	+3½

As much as the Reds missed him, Robinson wouldn't have made any difference from 1966 through '68, or in 1971. The Reds won their division in 1970, '72, and '73; they lost the '70 World Series to Robinson and the Orioles; they lost the '72 World Series to the A's; and they lost the '73 National League Championship Series to the Mets. The '72 World Series was exceptionally close, and perhaps Robinson would have made a difference for the Reds. But by then he was thirty-seven, and didn't play particularly well (for the Dodgers) during the regular season.

So let's focus on 1969, when the Reds finished four games behind the first-place Braves in the shiny new National League West. Robinson wasn't at his *best* that season . . . but he wasn't far off, and finished third in the MVP balloting.

If Robinson were with the Reds in the '69 season, he could have played either of the outfield corner spots, and first base. Here are the Reds at each of those positions, and one other guy:

		Win Shares
1B	Lee May	26
LF	Alex Johnson	19
RF	Pete Rose	37
??	F. Robby	32

Here's where things get tricky. You know how the Reds got Alex Johnson? They traded Dick Simpson to the Cardinals. What happened to Milt Pappas? In June 1968, the Reds traded Pappas and a couple of scrubs to the

It's sort of a shame that Bill DeWitt is so often remembered for trading away Frank Robinson, because his career as a baseball executive is one of the more distinguished in the game's history.

DeWitt got his start in baseball in 1916, when Browns general manager Branch Rickey hired DeWitt, then fourteen, as his office boy. When Rickey went to work for the Cardinals the next year, he took DeWitt with him, and eventually DeWitt became Rickey's secretary, and later the Cardinals' treasurer while earning a law degree.

By 1936, DeWitt was running Rickey's vast farm system. According to *The Sporting News*, "That same year, Rickey was asked to help find a buyer for the Cardinals' poor relations, the Browns. He convinced loan tycoon Don Barnes of St. Louis to buy the club—and to hire DeWitt as his general manager."

It took some time, but DeWitt built a solid farm system for the Browns, and in 1944 the franchise won its first (and as it turned out, only) American League championship (most of DeWitt's young prospects were in the service, of course, but the Browns would have finished third without ex-farmhands Vern Stephens and Jack Kramer). After buying and then selling the Browns, DeWitt spent a few years with the Yankees, but left when it became apparent he wouldn't get a chance to run the front office. He spent a few years with the Tigers, but left under a cloud of acrimony, then took over as Reds general manager shortly after

the 1960 season. Soon he purchased the franchise for
$4,625,000.

DeWitt's new team was not a
good one, and had little apparent
chance of becoming one. The Reds
had finished under .500 for three
straight seasons, and in 1960 they
were twenty-eight games out of
first place. DeWitt made some
moves over the winter, but it's not
like he could go out and sign a
bunch of free agents. As Bill James
has noted, "Among the 232 writers
polled by *The Sporting News* in the
spring of 1961, not one picked the
Reds to win."

Well, they did win the National
League pennant in 1961. At the
time, it was one of the biggest
turnarounds in major-league history. And it wouldn't have happened without Bill DeWitt.

Braves for shortstop Woody Woodward and pitchers Clay Carroll and Tony Cloninger.

In 1969, Woodward split time at shortstop with Darrel Chaney. Wood-ward was a poor hitter, Chaney much poorer. Carroll went 12–7, pitching mostly out of the bullpen. Cloninger, though, killed the Reds. He started thirty-four games, and went 11–13 with a 5.03 ERA.

If the Reds hadn't traded Frank Robinson, in 1969 *he* probably would have been in the outfield instead of Alex Johnson, and Tony Cloninger almost certainly would not have been in the rotation. We don't know who would have been in Cloninger's place, but considering how poorly Cloninger pitched that season, we can guess this unknown starter would have been at least somewhat better. And this combination—Robinson instead of John-son, somebody instead of Cloninger—would quite likely have been worth at least four games. Perhaps five or six.

Ah, but that's only part of the equation. Woodward was the best short-stop the Reds had in 1969, and Carroll was exceptionally useful. Those two must have been worth, what, two or three games?

Yes, all this is something of a fool's game. We're talking about more than a butterfly flapping its wings on the other side of the world. This was a big trade, and if you erase it from the record, who knows what other things would have happened? Based on the evidence we've got and just a reason-able measure of speculation, though, I think we can say two things.

> One: trading Frank Robinson *might* have cost the Reds a divi-sion title in 1969 and *perhaps* the World Series in 1972 (though by then, Robinson wasn't much of an outfielder, and the Reds had Tony Perez at first base).
> Two: this trade deserves to be remembered for the uneven swap that it was, but the negative impact on Cincinnati's fortunes wasn't nearly as great as we might have guessed.

---

1. "Robbie, DeWitt Feuding," *San Francisco Chronicle*, April 4, 1966.

2. Robert H. Boyle, "Cincinnati's Brain-Picker," *Sports Illustrated*, June 13, 1966, p. 40.

3. *Sporting News*, March 20, 1982, p. 34.

LORDS ADOPT SPIKE

My God, they've elected the Unknown Soldier!

—Larry Fox, *New York World-Telegram*

Major League Baseball's first commissioner, Kenesaw Mountain Landis, died while in office. The second, Happy Chandler, was fired six years into his seven-year term, largely because he behaved more like an ex-United States senator (which he was) than an employee of sixteen wealthy white men (which he also was). In his autobiography, Chandler wrote, "Many of the owners were greedy. They were cruel to the players and umpires. They abused the fans. They tried to dominate me. But I fought them. I took charge."[1] The third, Ford Frick, was an ex-sportswriter who knew how to get along. Frick, famous for responding to various sticky issues with the proclamation, "That's a league matter," resigned in good standing after serving two seven-year terms.

The first list of candidates to replace Frick was a large one: one hundred and fifty-six names. "By discreet investigation,"[2] that list was whittled all the way down to fifty names. At a meeting in July 1965, the owners further whittled, this time to fifteen. And finally they met again, in October, after which the following item appeared in the *Sporting News*:

CHICAGO, Ill.—Not ten, not five, not four, but seven candidates continue in the race for the commissionership of baseball, according to the Chicago Daily News.

George Vass, a Daily News sports writer who secreted himself in an adjoining room during the major moguls' meetings, October 19–20, and overheard the conversations through a thin-panelled door, reported that the candidates consist of:

Stephen Ailes, former Secretary of the Army; Eugene Zuckert, former Secretary of the Air Force; General Curtis LeMay, retired Air Force Chief of Staff; Joe Cronin, American League president; Gabe Paul, Cleveland president; Bing Devine, assistant to the president of the Mets; and Lou Carroll, National league attorney.[3]

(By the way, if anybody's interested in playing a game of *What if?* here's a perfect chance. One of the candidates on an earlier list was "Richard Nixon, former Vice-President of the United States." And since we're on the subject, before the owners settled on Bud Selig as Commissioner-for-Life in the 1990s, they supposedly considered fellow owner George W. Bush.)

After reviewing that list, it shouldn't be a big surprise that the owners, a month later, chose a military man to succeed Frick. The big surprise was the name of the military man: William D. "Spike" Eckert, whose name had appeared exactly zero times in the *Sporting News*—then known as "the Bible of Baseball"—prior to his selection by the owners.

How did Eckert get the job? Nobody seemed to know for sure, though there was talk that he and Tigers owner John Fetzer shared the same p.r. guy. One thing everybody soon agreed about, though, was that Eckert had been terribly miscast.

Like a lot of career military men, Eckert often fell back on his professional experience, whatever the situation. During his first tour of spring-training camps, he felt compelled to list the similarities between baseball

© Bettmann-CORBIS

That's Eckert on the left. He's just been introduced to the press, and already has the thousand-yard stare. That's Ford Frick on the right, telling reporters, "Let's give the man a chance. He was elected only an hour and a half ago. He should not be subjected to such questions."

and the Air Force: "First, you have highly competitive units—the different teams, just as you have squadrons. Then you have rules and regulations in both, rules to be made and interpreted and changed. And third, you have franchises, like Air Force bases, being opened and moved to fill needs."[4]

At a time when Major League Baseball desperately needed credibility—the NFL was making great inroads in the public consciousness, the Players Association was just beginning to flex its muscle—the owners had hired a commissioner who couldn't be taken seriously, because he knew little about baseball and perhaps even less about big business (and despite what the owners liked to tell their employees and their patrons, they certainly did consider baseball a big business).

So Eckert had to go. It was just a question of when.

When the owners fired Eckert, slightly more than three years after they'd hired him, he still had four years left on his contract. Still ridiculously naïve in the ways of big business, Eckert moved out of his office . . . and into an adjoining office, right next door to his successor, Bowie Kuhn. Officially, Eckert still held a position as "consultant," and he expected to actually work for the rest of his money. After a few days, Kuhn finally leveled with Eckert: "Spike, I really don't think it will work having you here in the office . . . I know I can call on you and get your advice but I can do that wherever you are. I'm sorry, but I really think this will be the best."[5]

Eckert moved out that same day. Two years later he died in the Bahamas, while playing tennis. "He was buried in Arlington National Cemetery, not far from the Tomb of the Unknown Soldier."[6]

1. Albert B. Chandler with Vance Trible, *Heroes, Plain Folks, and Skunks: The Life and Times of Happy Chandler* (Chicago: Bonus Books, 1989).

2. *The 1966 Official Baseball Guide* (St. Louis: Sporting News, 1966).

3. "7 Candidates Still in Race for Post of Commissioner," *Sporting News*, Nov. 6, 1965, p. 6.

4. Jerome Holtzman, *The Commissioners: Baseball's Midlife Crisis* (New York: Total Sports, 1998).

5. Bowie Kuhn, *Hardball: The Education of a Baseball Commissioner* (New York: Times Books, 1987).

6. Holtzman, *Commissioners*.

A.O. FOR JOE FOY

The Mets came south with one goal . . . to fortify themselves at third base, where forty-one men have appeared in eight seasons. They reached the goal Wednesday by trading Amos Otis and Bob Johnson to Kansas City for Joe Foy, who batted in 71 runs last season and stole 37 bases.

Many people felt they got Foy cheaply. But Kansas City was gambling that Otis would develop into a long-term centerfielder, a young player who also could hit and run.

—Joe Durso, *The New York Times*

When the Red Sox drafted Amos Otis in 1965, he was a shortstop. That summer he played third base for the Harlan (Kentucky) Red Sox and learned two lessons. The first?

For a guy who had never been more than twenty miles away from home by himself, Harlan—those mountains and those people in the hills with the jugs slung over their shoulder with the shotguns—was frightening, but I survived it.

When I went away my father and mother said, "Make sure when you go into your hotel room check behind the shower curtains, in the closet, under the beds," and I did. I checked the room, under the bed, and there were a pair of shoes standing straight up. And there was a guy lying under the bed—dead. So I left the hotel! I was frightened, but I survived.[1]

And the second? Otis didn't much like third base. In 1966, he played some third, but he also played in the outfield, and spent more time at first base than anywhere. That November the Mets drafted Otis out of the Red Sox organization, and in the spring of '67 they jumped him all the way to the International League, with Jacksonville. There, Otis mostly played in the outfield, but also got into thirty-three games at third base. Still barely twenty, Otis debuted with the Mets that September.

In 1968, at the end of spring training, the last outfield slot on the roster came down to Otis and Don Bosch, a young switch-hitting outfielder with a .155 career batting average in ninety-seven major-league games.[2] Bosch stayed, and Otis returned to the minors.

He did join the Mets in 1969 . . . and ran into trouble.

Gil Hodges was the manager. I wanted to play the outfield, and he wanted to keep me at third base.

He was stubborn and I was, too. He didn't get his way. I wouldn't play no third base. I only played about four games there and I was considered one of the failures of the Mets' hundred-and-something third basemen. But he wanted me at third and I wanted to play the outfield. I could outplay all their outfielders, out-throw them, out-run them, but I didn't have the experience, so they kept me on the bench until they got mad enough, and they sent me to the minor leagues for a month.

They called me back September 1, just in time to go into the record books when Steve Carlton struck out nineteen. I was something like numbers three, seven, twelve, and nineteen!

Then on December third, my father's birthday, I got traded to Kansas City along with Bob Johnson for Joe Foy. And my career took off from there.

Gil was the boss, and so he got his way, and I got traded.[3]

The *moment* the Royals got Otis, they put him in center field, and there wasn't a better center fielder in the American League in the 1970s. Meanwhile, the Mets' center fielders during the '70s were Tommie Agee (three seasons), Don Hahn (two), Del Unser (two), and Lee Mazzilli (three). Agee was actually quite good in '71 and '72, but Hahn (with Willie Mays, in 1973)

University of Kansas Library

Amos Otis scoring one of his 1,080 post-Mets runs.

Who Needs Nolan?

Everybody knows the Mets traded Nolan Ryan to the Angels, and all they got back was Jim Fregosi. At the time, though, a one-for-one swap would have been considered one-sided . . . in the Mets' favor. In addition to Ryan, they sent along three other players, one of whom, outfielder Leroy Stanton, was considered a pretty solid prospect (over the two previous seasons with the Mets' Tidewater farm club, he'd batted .314 with forty-two home runs).

The plum, though, was Fregosi.

How good was he? Jim Fregosi and Derek Jeter both became every-day shortstops in the majors when they were twenty-one. In Fregosi's first eight seasons, he earned 207 Win Shares. In Jeter's first eight seasons, he totaled 192 Win Shares.

This is *not* a knock on Jeter. Cal Ripken also was twenty-one when he won a regular job; in his first eight seasons, he earned 219 Win Shares. The point is that Fregosi obviously had Hall of Fame talent and, for eight seasons, he also had Hall of Fame performance. Fregosi was a good hitter and—because he played a decent shortstop—a great player.

Until 1971. Fregosi didn't hit his first home run of the season until May 7. On July 12, then hitting .191, Fregosi went on the disabled list. On July 14, he entered the Mayo Clinic for surgery to remove a tumor on his right foot. Fregosi did return to the lineup on August 10, and through the end of the season he batted .288/.371/.366. Not a lot of power, but fine numbers for a shortstop.

Two problems for the Mets, though. First, they turned Fregosi into a third baseman. And then he got hurt again.

According to Peter Golenbock, "when Fregosi came to camp to learn his new position, he was chunky and out of shape. At third base, balls rocketed past him."

Gil Hodges decided he would personally see to Fregosi's training, and hit hundreds of ground balls to his new third baseman every day. On March 5, one of Hodges's sharp grounders skipped up and smashed Fregosi's right thumb. He spent the rest of spring training in a cast.

Golenbock blames Fregosi's disappointing season on this injury, but here's a fact: he entered the Mets lineup on April 15, and after going 3 for 4 on May 17, Fregosi was batting .306/.376/.510. He was *exactly* what the Mets thought he'd be (and more). From that point, though, Fregosi's numbers went down the toilet, and as the season progressed he suffered from various injuries to his back, his knees, and at least one of his hamstrings.

And that was essentially the story of the rest of Fregosi's career. He hung around through 1978 and occasionally showed flashes of the old ability, but after 1972 he would never again play in more than ninety games in a season.

(One other thing about this deal: according to various sources, the Angels would have been happy with either Nolan Ryan or Gary Gentry. The Mets, and Gil Hodges in particular, believed that Ryan was the more dispensable of the two.

wasn't so hot, nor was Unser. It wasn't until 1978, Mazzilli's second season as a regular (and Otis's ninth as a star), that the Mets were set in center.

The moment the Mets got Joe Foy, he became the forty-second third baseman in their relatively brief history. Foy was still fairly young—not quite twenty-seven—and he could hit and he could run and he could walk. The Mets expected, reasonably enough, that Foy would rank as one of the better third basemen in the National League.

He didn't. Foy entered the season with these career percentages: .250/.346/.383, and of course his numbers would have been better if not for 1968 (when he hit .225, like everybody else in the American League except Yastrzemski). But with the Mets, he struggled. What happened? In Peter Golenbock's *Amazin'*—the primary source for this chapter—Jerry Koosman tells this story:

> Joe Foy was from the Bronx, so now he was back in town with his old cronies, and pretty soon he started walking down the wrong sidewalk again.
>
> We saw it gradually coming on. I remember a doubleheader in New York. The first game Hodges didn't play Foy, and you could tell in the dugout he was high on something. One thing you didn't do was walk in front of Gil Hodges during a pitch. Foy not only walked in front of him, he stood in front of him, cheering. We could see right away this was a no-no. Here was a disaster about to happen. We could see he really wasn't in his right mind.
>
> Well, Gil put him in to play third base for the second game. And we knew he wasn't capable of playing that day. I remember the first batter hit a hard ground ball by Foy, and after the ball went by him, he was still patting his glove and saying, "Hit it to me. Hit it to me." He never even saw it.
>
> We were looking at each other and saying, "Oh, my God, you gotta get him out of there." But Gil left him in a little longer just to let everyone see that he didn't fit on that ball club.
>
> And it was not long after that that Joe was gone.

Golenbock claims flat-out that Foy, after joining the Mets, "almost immediately [got] hooked on drugs, destroying his career." After the 1970 season, the Mets left Foy off their forty-man roster, and he was grabbed by the Senators in the Rule 5 draft. A couple of years later, Senators broadcaster Shelby Whitfield wrote an incisive book about the franchise's last few seasons in Washington, and mentioned in passing that Foy "came to the Senators with a marijuana history."[4]

Of course, if Foy was smoking pot in the early '70s, he was far from alone among professional baseball players (who were, by the way, also regularly popping amphetamines and occasionally injecting steroids). But perhaps Foy was more than a recreational user. Though his statistics with the Senators weren't all that bad, in late May they sent him to their farm club in Denver. There, Foy batted .191 in fifteen games, and the Senators released him. He was twenty-eight years old, and never played again. He died in 1989.

After the Mets traded Ryan, he won 295 games. Gentry won twelve. And for all the talk about Gil Hodges's baseball acumen—and I'm sure he possessed considerable of it—he seems to have believed that Amos Otis was a third baseman and Gary Gentry was better than Nolan Ryan.)

1. Peter Golenbock, *Amazin': The Miraculous History of New York's Most Beloved Baseball Team* (New York: St. Martin's Press, 2002).

2. Ibid.

3. Ibid.

4. Shelby Whitfield, *Kiss It Goodbye* (New York: Abelard-Schuman, 1973).

BAD DRAFTS

or

"HEY, IT LOOKED GOOD IN THE BROCHURE."

How beautiful is youth! how bright it gleams
With its illusions, aspirations, dreams!
—Longfellow

In 2005, my friend Rany Jazayerli conducted a comprehensive study of the June draft—officially known as the "Rule 4 draft"—from 1984 through 1999, and wrote up the results in a series of indispensable articles for BaseballProspectus.com. Here's one of the many things I took home with me . . .

> Draft Rule #1: The greatest difference in value between consecutive draft picks is the difference between the first and second picks in the draft.

Furthermore, once you get past the first four picks, there's not a discernible pattern of value during the rest of the first round. Players chosen with the thirteenth pick were, on the whole, just as valuable as those taken with the seventh pick. Twenty-second picks were nearly as valuable as sixth picks. Et cetera.

I bring all this up as a way of explaining why, when we're looking at busted draft picks—the subject of these next few pages—it's essentially pointless to look past the first few picks in each draft. That No. 13 pick never did make it to the majors? Hey, most of them don't. For every Manny Ramirez (1991) and Paul Konerko (1994), there's a Chad McConnell (1992) and a Robert Stratton (1996).

And anybody can make a bad pick. Anybody can make a *lot* of bad picks.

In 2001, the Royals' draft was an absolute disaster. With the ninth pick in the draft, they chose a pitcher named Colt Griffin, who shall forever be remembered as the first schoolboy in history to hit 100 on the radar gun. The Royals gave him $2.4 million to sign, and five years later they were still waiting for him to reach Class AAA.

Same draft, the Royals used their second-round pick on a high-school outfielder named Roscoe Crosby. His *tools* were off the charts, so they offered him $1.75 million to sign, even though he was committed to playing football at Clemson. Well, Crosby didn't actually play much football, and—due in part to a serious elbow injury—he didn't actually play much baseball, either. The Royals eventually paid $1.25 million of the bonus before Crosby finally and officially abandoned them (saving the club $500,000).

None of the Royals' other draft picks of 2001 have panned out, either. Rough draft, and enough to make one wonder if they had any idea what they were doing.

But look at the Indians in the same draft. Because they'd lost Manny Ramirez, Sandy Alomar, and David Segui to free agency—and by the way, kudos to the brilliant general managers who signed Alomar and Segui—the Indians owned five of the first fifty-one picks in the draft. With those picks, they drafted Dan Denham, Alan Horne, J. D. Martin, Michael Conroy, and Jake Dittler. Conroy was a high-school outfielder; the other four were schoolboy right-handed pitchers.

Haven't heard of any of them? That's my point.

So take what comes below not as indictments of the drafters, but rather as simply stories about the draftees. These are the guys who really, *really* didn't do what almost everybody thought they would do.

The first truly lousy draft pick came in 1966—just the second year of the amateur draft—when the Mets owned the first pick and used it to select . . . high-school catcher Steve Chilcott. The A's had the next pick, and happily selected Reggie Jackson. Chilcott, plagued by injuries in his seven years as a professional, never reached the majors. Jackson got a candy bar named after himself.

Joe McDonald, then a low-level Mets functionary, later said, "It was a position pick. We did not feel that we had an adequate catching prospect in the organization." Of course that's a lousy rationale, and today most teams draft for "talent" rather than "need."

According to Jackson, the Mets didn't draft him because they thought he had a "white" girlfriend (whatever that meant; her parents were from Mexico).

There are any number of lessons that may be learned from studying the draft, and one of the most important is: "Don't base draft decisions on the current state of your major-league roster."

In 1967, the Senators owned the fifth pick in the draft. One of the top talents available was John Mayberry, a big first baseman out of Detroit. But a week before the draft, the Senators acquired first baseman Mike Epstein from the Orioles. And with Epstein in the fold, the Senators passed on Mayberry and instead chose a high-school catcher named John Jones.

Mayberry played in the big leagues for fifteen seasons. Jones batted .150 in a four-year pro career that didn't take him past Class A. And Mike Epstein? He was fantastic in 1969, but otherwise was just a warm body at first base. And shortly after the Senators traded Epstein in 1971, John Mayberry became a star.

Some sort of special award should be reserved for Danny Goodwin, on whom *two* teams wasted the first overall pick. In 1971, the White Sox had the first pick and drafted Goodwin, a catcher who'd batted .494 at Peoria Central High School. Goodwin didn't sign with the White Sox—in fact, they signed only fourteen of their thirty-four picks that year—and instead attended Southern University.

Four years later, Goodwin was again the first player chosen, this time by the California Angels, who got their man for $125,000. Drafted as a catcher, Goodwin did spend portions of seven seasons in the majors, but never as a catcher; when he played, he DH'd or played first base. And he didn't hit enough to fill those slots in a meaningful way.

In defense of the Angels, it's worth noting that the first round of the '75 draft was almost a complete bust. Among the twenty-four picks, the *best* major leaguers were Rick Cerone (Indians, seventh pick), Clint Hurdle (Royals, ninth), and Dale Berra (Pirates, twentieth). And eventually the Goodwin pick actually worked out nicely for the Angels, because at the end of 1978, they included Goodwin in a package that netted Disco Dan Ford from the Twins. And three years later, they traded Ford to the Orioles for Doug DeCinces.

And there's another lesson: "Even if your draft pick doesn't work out, you'll often be able to find a trading partner who places a high value on the potential that you once saw."

(Postscript: Goodwin always argued that he'd never received the chance to play that he deserved, and he might have been right, as his minor-league numbers were, superficially at least, pretty impressive. But when he showed big-time power, he was in hitter's leagues, and in 636 major-league at-bats he hit thirteen homers.)

In 1979, the Mariners got their first real chance to come up with a great player. They certainly didn't have that opportunity in the expansion draft, two years earlier. While they did well with their first pick in their first amateur draft, grabbing Dave Henderson with the thirtieth overall pick, he didn't have superstar potential. In the '78 draft, the M's had the sixth pick, and selected Tito Nanni, who never reached the majors.

In '78, though, the Mariners finished with the worst record in the American League, which meant they would have the very first pick in the 1979 draft. This was the first truly important choice in the franchise's history . . . and they blew it (we can say, retrospectively). The M's drafted a huge high-school first baseman named Al Chambers, who was perhaps as well known in Pennsylvania for his football talents as his baseball skills. Chambers did reach the majors but, like Goodwin, he probably didn't get the chance to play that he deserved. After the draft, Chambers made his professional debut in the Northwest League, and hit only two home runs while batting .247. A lot of guys don't show power in their first pro season, though. In 1980, Chambers batted .300 with nine homers, and in 1981 he hit twenty homers in the pitcher-friendly Eastern League. He was only twenty, and still looked like a potential star. But from there his career just sort of petered out. He'd go to the Pacific Coast League, hit decently (or better), get a few at-bats with the big club, not hit, and head back to the PCL. Chambers didn't play at all in 1986—I'm assuming he was hurt, but he might have just been sick of the minor leagues—and when he returned in '87 with the Astros' Southern League farm club, he wasn't the same hitter he'd been. (That summer the M's had another No. 1 pick, and this time they got it right, selecting Ken Griffey Jr. In fairness, though, if there'd been a Ken Griffey Jr. available in 1979, the Mariners certainly would have drafted him. Most years there just isn't a talent like that available.)

In 1983, the Twins owned the first pick in the draft, and selected Tim Belcher, who became a pretty good major-league pitcher. Problem: he wouldn't sign with the Twins. It wasn't a bad risk, though, because the talent was pretty thin that year. The Reds had the second pick and chose Kurt Stillwell, who wound up as probably the best hitter in the entire round. One caveat, though: the Twins—and seventeen other teams—left on the board a big Texas right-hander named Roger Clemens. Eleven months later, Clemens was pitching for the Red Sox, and two years after that he was in the middle of his first Cy Young season.

I have, over the years, spent some considerable amount of keystrokes attacking the use of valuable draft picks on high-school players. At the moment, though, there's little evidence that picks used on high-schoolers are worse than picks used on collegians.

The 1989 draft is wonderful to look at, though.

The Phillies, Rangers, and Cardinals owned the fourth, fifth, and sixth picks, and each club selected "toolsy" high-school outfielders: Jeff Jackson, Donald Harris, and Paul Coleman. Only Harris eventually reached the majors, and if not for his draft status he wouldn't have made it, either.

The White Sox had the seventh pick. They drafted a college player. First baseman named Frank Thomas.

The Cubs had the eighth pick. They drafted a high-school outfielder named Earl Cunningham. Big strong guy from South Carolina, could hit the ball over the parking lot. I don't mean to make fun of Cunningham, because I'm sure he was doing his best. But when you talk about busted draft picks, you have to talk about Earl Cunningham. He spent eight seasons in the minor leagues, all eight in Class A. Here are the interesting numbers from those eight seasons:

	Games	Ks	Ws	Avg	HR
1989	49	40	12	.258	7
1990	78	108	13	.216	5
1991	101	145	10	.239	19
1992	97	152	19	.196	10
1993	43	38	10	.194	5
1994	76	93	12	.217	13
1995	78	97	15	.239	15
1996	64	66	16	.223	10
Totals	586	739	107	.224	84

My favorite line actually doesn't show up here (because when he played for two teams in a season, I combined the numbers). In 1992, the Cubs promoted Cunningham to Winston-Salem in the Carolina League (still Class A, but a better class of Class A). In twenty-five games, Cunningham totaled three walks and fifty-four strikeouts (and batted .108).

I don't know anything about Cunningham, other than what we all can see in the numbers. I don't know whether he was terribly stubborn, or admirably persistent.

Postscript: Drafted later in the first round, after Earl Cunningham: Cal Eldred, Mo Vaughn, and Chuck Knoblauch.

Here's another thing about the draft . . . sometimes, even when you make exactly the right decision you can't take a whole lot of credit for it.

Prior to the 1990 draft, Texas schoolboy pitcher Todd Van Poppel was widely regarded as the premier prospect. But he said he wanted to attend the University of Texas, and wasn't going to sign if he was drafted. Still, the Braves—who held the first pick—"met frequently with Van Poppel to determine if they would be able to sign him. Convinced they couldn't the Braves took . . . *Chipper Jones as their fallback pick."*

Ellipses and italics mine.

The Athletics took Van Poppel with the fourteenth pick in the first round, and signed him to a $1.2 million contract. The A's also owned the twenty-sixth, thirty-fourth, and thirty-sixth picks in that draft, and used them to select three college pitchers: Don Peters, David Zancanero, and Kirk Dressendorfer. This quartet, known by *Baseball America* readers as "The Four Aces," wound up winning forty-three games in the major leagues. Van Poppel accounted for nearly all of them, though at 40–58 with a 5.58 ERA, he didn't exactly justify his draft status, either. (Van Poppel did have one fine season, as a reliever with the Cubs in 2001, but of course that was little consolation for the A's; they'd waived him five years earlier.)

What happened in 1991 was the result of a sort of fluke.

It's hard to remember now (and hard to believe if you can't remember it), but in 1990 the New York Yankees finished with the worst record (67–95) in the American League. It wasn't the worst record in the major leagues—the Braves "topped" the Yankees by two games—but at that time, the two leagues alternated getting the No. 1 pick in the draft.

With that No. 1 pick, the Yankees chose a schoolboy lefty named Brien Taylor. Initially, the Yankees offered Taylor $350,000 to sign. They were dealing with a couple of tough cookies, though: Taylor's mother Bettie *and* Scott Boras. Summer came and went without a deal, but Taylor finally signed, just hours before he was scheduled to start classes in college, for a record bonus: $1.55 million.

For two years, the Yankees looked smart. In 1992, his first professional season, Taylor blew through the Florida State League: 2.57 ERA, 187 strikeouts and 66 walks in 161 innings. In 1993, he moved up a level and struggled a bit with his control, but the Yankees must have been pleased with his K-rate—150 strikeouts in 163 innings—and his 3.48 ERA. He threw ninety-eight miles an hour.

That December, Taylor's career essentially ended. Back home in North Carolina for the winter, Taylor got into a fight and landed on his left shoulder. Ten days later, Frank Jobe performed surgery for a torn labrum and a torn capsule. Boras said that Jobe said that Taylor would, after a year or so, throw as hard as ever.

Bleeding Dodger Blue

For many years—since the 1940s, really—the Dodgers have been famous for an organizational ability to fairly judge young talent. That's how the Boys of Summer were built, and forty years later (1992–1996) the franchise could boast five straight National League Rookies of the Year.

From 1983 through 1990, the Dodgers owned nine first-round picks, and used six of them on pitchers. Not only did none of the six reach the majors, but all six flamed out spectacularly.

In 1983, the Dodgers used the No. 18 pick on Wichita State left-hander Erik Sonberg. He pitched well that summer in the Florida State League, and in '84 was skipped past Class AA to the Pacific Coast League. In two seasons with Albuquerque—a tough place for a young pitcher—Sonberg went 7–19 with a 7.37 ERA. Afterward he never pitched higher than Class AA.

(Oh, and the No. 19 pick in the '83 draft? Roger Clemens.)

In 1984, the Dodgers used the No. 23 pick on Oklahoma State left-hander Dennis Livingston. He spent much of his pro career in doctors' offices, and never reached the majors.

(The No. 24 pick? Terry Mulholland.)

In 1987, the Dodgers used the No. 8 pick on Las Vegas schoolboy right-hander Dan Opperman. But he didn't make his professional debut until 1989, and his career was killed in 1992 by an elbow injury.

(The No. 9 pick? Kevin Appier.)

Taylor rehabbed in 1994, then returned to the mound in 1995, going 2–5 with a 6.08 ERA at the lowest level of the minor leagues. That was as good as it got. Over the next two seasons, Taylor pitched in seventeen games in the South Atlantic League. In forty-three innings, he walked ninety-five batters and compiled at 15.99 ERA.

According to Buster Olney in a 1998 *New York Times* column, that summer Taylor was occasionally throwing his fastball at ninety-four. "But his inconsistency is chronic. In a game May 14"—in extended spring training—"Taylor allowed seven runs, five hits and six walks in one and two-thirds innings." He did pitch in the minors that season: in twenty-five innings with Class A Greensboro, Taylor walked twenty-six batters.

His contract with the Yankees expired the following January. The Mariners signed him, but Taylor couldn't earn a roster spot on one of their farm teams. In 2000, he hooked up with the Indians, and pitched for the Columbus RedStixx. In two and two-thirds innings, he walked nine batters.

(By the way, Taylor aside, the draft's first round was particularly productive. Among those the Yankees passed up: Dmitri Young, Manny Ramirez, Cliff Floyd, and Shawn Green).

I just realized why I wanted to write this book: it's all for yet another excuse to write about Josh Booty.

In 1992 and '93, the Florida Marlins and Colorado Rockies, despite their status as brand-new franchises, weren't allowed to draft until the last two slots in the first round. In '92, the Rockies drafted twenty-seventh and the Marlins twenty-eighth, and in '93 they swapped spots. Nevertheless, both clubs did well. The Rockies drafted John Burke and Jamey Wright, both of whom later pitched in the majors. The Marlins drafted Charles Johnson and Marc Valdes; the latter also pitched in the majors, and of course the former enjoyed a long and productive career.

In 1993, their first season, the Marlins finished with the third-worst record in the National League, which earned them the fifth pick in the '94 draft.

They blew it. They drafted a shortstop named Josh Booty. According to *Baseball America Draft Almanac* (published in 2003, with the benefit of hindsight), "The Louisiana high school star was arguably the nation's best high school player in both baseball and football. He would have been a shortstop and quarterback at Louisiana State had he not signed."

He did sign, though . . . for $1.6 million, breaking Brien Taylor's three-year-old record for largest bonus ever.

As it happened, Josh Booty could not hit. Just could not do it. Nevertheless, well into Booty's pro career, the following note appeared in the September 19, 1997, edition of *USA Today*:

> **What we've heard:** . . . That the critics of Florida third base prospect Josh Booty (.210, 20 homers, 60 RBI at Class AA) have no sense of history. Booty, once the nation's top college quarterback recruit, is a great fielder with power. Buddy Bell, Steve Buechele and Graig Nettles had long careers with Booty-esque skills . . .

I submitted then, and continue to maintain now, that anybody who could get something so spectacularly wrong has no business making a living as a baseball writer. It's not that Booty did not enjoy a long career in the major leagues, or that I did not, at the time, think that he would. It's that anybody who *writes* so condescendingly about a "sense of history" should actually *have* a sense of history. And the first three seasons of Josh Booty's professional career bore virtually no relation to those of Bell, Buechele, and Nettles.

In Nettles' first three minor-league seasons, he batted .269 (with twenty-eight home runs), .323, and .297. His fourth pro season was in the American League.

In Bell's first three minor-league seasons, he batted .229, .269, and .289. His fourth pro season was in the American League.

In Buechele's first three minor-league seasons, he batted .296, .276, and .264.

Now let's look at young Master Booty's first three seasons (plus a bonus season!):

Year	Level	Games	HR	W	K	Avg
1995	A	105	7	30	130	.187
1996	A	128	21	46	195	.206
1997	AA	122	20	27	166	.210
1998	AA/AAA	109	13	27	118	.182

Graig Nettles, my ass.

Roughly a year after *USA Today*'s Rod Beaton displayed his stunning sense of history, Josh Booty turned in his bat and his glove and finally went to Louisiana State, where he spent two seasons throwing passes to his kid brother (among others).

What did Josh Booty cost the Marlins? Well, they gave him $1.6 million, but they would have spent at least half that no matter who they picked. And of course that's what we don't know: *who* they'd have picked, if not Booty.

In 1988, the Dodgers used the No. 5 pick on right-hander Bill Bene. He's one of my all-time favorites, sort of the pitching version of Earl Cunningham. In his first pro season, Bene did all right: 5–0 in the Pioneer League, with fifty-six strikeouts in sixty-five innings.

Then things got ugly. In 1989, fifty-six walks in twenty-seven innings. In 1990, ninety-six walks in fifty-seven innings. In 1991 the Dodgers shifted Bene to the bullpen, and his control did improve some. But not nearly enough. He did reach Class AAA in 1994 . . . and posted a 10.13 ERA in thirteen innings.

(Later in the first round? Jim Abbott, Robin Ventura, Tino Martinez, and Royce Clayton.)

In 1989, the Dodgers used the No. 15 pick on high-school righty Kiki Jones. In his pro debut that summer, Jones blew away the Pioneer League: in twelve starts, 8–0 with a 1.58 ERA. Then came the shoulder injuries, and Jones would pitch only 100 more professional innings.

(Later in the first round? As we saw earlier, Eldred, Vaughn, and Knoblauch.)

In 1990, the Dodgers used the No. 9 pick on high-school lefty Ron Walden. Like Jones, Walden came out like gangbusters in the Pioneer League: in four starts, Walden went 3–0 with a 0.42 ERA and twenty strikeouts in twenty-two innings. After which he hurt his elbow and then his shoulder, and pitched exactly nine more professional innings.

(The No. 10 pick? Carl Everett. Later in the first round? Mike Mussina.)

Passing Hitting

I wonder it maybe teams should get over this fascination they've got with quarterbacks.

In 1979, the Blue Jays used the No. 3 pick to draft Jay Schroeder. He batted .213 in four minor-league seasons, enjoyed whatever bonus money the Jays had given him, then played in the NFL for ten years. With the No. 13 pick in that same draft, the Tigers chose Rick Leach, more famous as the University of Michigan's star quarterback than as a baseball player. The Tigers rushed Leach because of who he was, and he did wind up playing in the major leagues for ten seasons (or parts thereof). But his decent years came after the Tigers released him in 1984; as a Tiger, Leach batted .237/.306/.335 (and should have reminded everybody that local talent can sometimes be blinding).

In 1981, the Yankees didn't have a first-round pick—they'd forfeited it when they signed free agent Dave Winfield—and they used their second-round pick to select Stanford quarterback John Elway. As I recall, George Steinbrenner was personally involved, and convinced Elway to sign a contract that would pay him $150,000 to play baseball for six weeks in the summer of 1982. Perhaps it was a smart gamble, as he batted .318 in the New York–Penn League. But of course he saw a brighter future in the other sport, and never played baseball again (he did use his theoretical baseball career as leverage when trying to convince the Colts to trade him to the Broncos).

In 1998, the Yankees used their third-round pick—the ninety-

He was drafted fifth. The next two picks were washouts. The eighth, ninth, and tenth picks were Todd Walker, C. J. Nitkowski, and Jaret Wright. The twelfth, thirteenth, and fourteenth picks were used on Nomar Garciaparra, Paul Konerko, and Jason Varitek. The Marlins could have done a lot better than they did.

In 1996, everybody learned just how much top amateurs might really be worth, if they were available to the highest bidder. Due to a loophole in the draft rules that was first exploited by Scott Boras, four first-round picks—No. 2 Travis Lee (Twins), No. 5 John Patterson (Expos), No. 7 Matt White (Giants), and No. 12 Bobby Seay (White Sox)—were declared free agents.* Lee and Patterson signed with the Diamondbacks, White and Seay with the Devil Rays. Lee and White both got around $10 million.

Perhaps those numbers were artificially high, with the two expansion franchises particularly desperate for young talent. But as far as Scott Boras was concerned, $10 million was now the going rate for the very best amateur baseball players.

A year later, Florida State outfielder J. D. Drew was considered the best player available in the draft. Represented by Boras, Drew declared he would not sign for less than $10 million. The Tigers, with the No. 1 pick, had no intention of paying Drew that sort of money, and selected Matt Anderson. The Phillies, with the No. 2 pick, also had no intention of spending $10 million, but they drafted Drew anyway.

As promised, he refused to sign. The Phillies did receive "compensation": the forty-second pick in the 1998 draft, with which they selected UCLA outfielder Eric Valent. Some compensation.

And if the Phillies hadn't drafted J. D. Drew? With the next pick, the Angels drafted Troy Glaus. I don't know if the Phillies had Glaus so high on their board. But if the Phillies had drafted Troy Glaus, they probably wouldn't have signed David Bell in 2002. And if they hadn't signed David Bell in 2002, they probably would have won the Wild Card in 2005.

(Also drafted fairly early in the first round: Vernon Wells, Jon Garland, and Lance Berkman.)

As I write this, early in 2006, I'm optimistic about the Tampa Bay Devil Rays. Their organization is loaded with young hitters who, though still struggling to control the strike zone, should enjoy long and productive careers.

---

* The rules say a team must make a formal contract offer within fifteen days of the draft, but many teams hadn't been taking the rule seriously.

It should have happened sooner. In 1998, their first season, the Devil Rays did not have a first-round draft pick. Or a second-round draft pick. Or a third-round draft pick. Why? Because the previous winter they'd signed free agents Roberto Hernandez, Wilson Alvarez, and Dave Martinez (none of whom ever participated in a meaningful game for the franchise). Otherwise it was a pretty good draft—the Rays snagged Aubrey Huff, Ryan Rupe, Joe Kennedy, and Brandon Backe—which only leaves one to wonder how well they'd have done with those three foregone picks.

In fairness to the Devil Rays, though, their first-round pick would have been the twenty-ninth, and of course the twenty-ninth is far from a sure thing. In 1999, the Devil Rays retained their first-round pick. The *first* pick, of course, is as sure as sure gets.

The Rays selected a high-school player from Raleigh named Josh Hamilton. He had a middle-nineties fastball, but could do so many other things so well that the Devil Rays immediately tabbed him an outfielder, and signed him for nearly $4 million.

Hamilton began his professional career that summer, in the Appalachian League, and batted .347 with power. He moved up a level in 2000 and batted .302 (albeit with somewhat less impressive power), but missed much of the second half of the season with a knee injury. Nevertheless, *Baseball America* rated Hamilton the organization's No. 1 prospect heading into 2001.

Hamilton got into a car accident that spring. Throw in various back and leg injuries suffered during the season, and he managed to play only twenty-three games. But again *Baseball America* rated Hamilton the organization's No. 1 prospect.

2002? Another lost season, with three trips to the disabled list and surgeries to repair his left shoulder and his left elbow. Given Hamilton's now-extensive list of injuries, after the season *Baseball America* dropped Hamilton all the way down to . . . No. 2 on the organizational list (behind Rocco Baldelli).

That was three years ago, and Hamilton hasn't played since. In 2003, he left the Devil Rays "to address certain private non-baseball matters." Early in 2004, Hamilton was suspended by Major League Baseball for one month for failing at least two drug tests. A month later, having failed at least two more drug tests, Hamilton was suspended for one year.

He went to rehab (for the sixth time, according to one report). Got married. Faithfully attended AA meetings. Spoke at Fellowship of Christian Athletes meetings. Was arrested after smashing the windshield of a friend's truck.

seventh overall—to draft Michigan quarterback Drew Henson. Not much of a risk, at that point in the draft. Ah, but they also paid Henson a $2 million signing bonus.* Two years later, with Henson reluctant to make a full-time commitment to baseball, the Yankees traded him to the Reds in a deal for Denny Neagle. Less than a year later—with Henson promising to focus on baseball—the Yankees got him back. All they had to do was 1) give the Reds a big player (Wily Mo Pena) and a big check ($1.9 million), and 2) give Henson a six-year contract for *$17 million*. The result? Josh Booty all over again. Henson spent the better part of three seasons in Class AAA, and batted .234 with 358 strikeouts in 332 games. After the 2003 season, Henson returned more than $10 million to the Yankees, and began his career as a guy who stands on the sidelines of NFL games, wearing a baseball cap and holding a clipboard.

* It should be said that some longtime observers of George Steinbrenner—a big Ohio State fan—suspected he paid Henson all that money mostly in hopes that Henson wouldn't suit up for the Wolverines.

Oops.

On November 15, 2005, the following item appeared in the newspapers:

Tampa Bay—Reinstated OF Josh Hamilton from the restricted list.

It was just a paper move. A few days later, Major League Baseball suspended Hamilton for the entire 2006 season. In 2007, he'll turn twenty-six.

(The Marlins had the No. 2 pick in the 1999 draft. They chose Josh Beckett. The A's and Brewers were Nos. 9 and 10. Barry Zito and Ben Sheets.)

(The primary source for this chapter was the wonderful *Baseball America Draft Almanac*, published by Baseball America in 2003.)

SHORT SHORTS HIMSELF

McLain is the greatest pitcher in baseball. This is *my* trade.

—Senators owner Bob Short[1]

Which of these pitchers would you like to have in Year 4? For each pitcher, the numbers in the last column represent his runs saved above average . . .

	Dennis			Joseph		
	Innings	ERA	RSAA	Innings	ERA	RSAA
Year 1	336	1.96	33	223	3.27	7
Year 2	325	2.80	29	248	3.27	13
Year 3	91	4.63	3	219	3.58	10

When Dennis is good, he's really, really good. And when he's bad, he's really, really bad (at least for one season). Joseph is just okay; durable, sure, but otherwise he's nothing special (yes, the ERAs look pretty good, but this was a pitcher-friendly era).

So do you want to take a chance on Dennis, or instead enjoy Joseph's clearly established level of performance? Wait, don't answer; a few more pieces of information:

Joseph is only twenty-three (so he's probably thrown a lot of pitches at a tender age), while Dennis is twenty-six years old, a sometime nightclub singer, and was recently suspended for associating with gamblers.

Had enough of this game? I don't blame you.

These two pitchers are Denny McLain and Joe Coleman, it's shortly after the 1970 season, and, based on the facts I've provided, it's a tough call. You probably know that McLain won thirty-one games in 1968 (nobody's won more than twenty-seven since), but did you know he also led the American League with twenty-four wins in 1969?

Of course, 1970 didn't go as well for McLain. On April 1, Commissioner Bowie Kuhn suspended him until July 1 for investing in a bookmaking operation that might (or might not) have been tied to the Detroit mob, and might not (or might) have taken bets on baseball games. Upon his return to the mound, McLain pitched poorly for a couple of months, then earned another suspension for dousing a couple of Detroit writers with buckets of ice water. And finally, before the second suspension had been completed, Kuhn suspended McLain a third time, for the rest of the season, after learning that McLain had been routinely carrying a handgun, including on a commercial airline flight (which was then, and probably still is, a federal crime). Kuhn also "suggested" to the Tigers that McLain undergo a psychiatric examination. The results? McLain was "not mentally ill and not in need of much service."

So that was Denny McLain, circa 1970.

Shortly afterward, during the World Series, Tigers general manager Jim Campbell asked to see Kuhn and American League prexy Joe Cronin. Campbell had worked out a big trade with Senators owner Bob Short, but there was a problem: a suspended player can't be traded, and Campbell wanted to trade Denny McLain. So he needed Kuhn's approval.

Kuhn wrote in his autobiography:

> Cronin and I looked at each other. We had Campbell repeat the names of the players. We were flabbergasted. We could not believe that Short would make such a deal. Campbell was trying not to smile but did so in spite of himself. He hoped we would not share our evaluation with Short.
>
> The Tigers were getting the excellent starting left side of the Washington infield in Brinkman and Rodriguez and a fine starting pitcher in Coleman in return for much less. Short was gambling that McLain could come back. As an old Senator fan, I was appalled by Short's foolish gamble, but I decided to let the trade go through, since McLain was due to have his suspension lifted.[2]

Given McLain's troubles in 1970, along with Coleman's youth and consistency, you could make a pretty reasonable case that trading Coleman for McLain wasn't a great move. But this deal, when it was made, wasn't nearly so simple. When it was announced, with Kuhn in attendance, there were eight players involved. Coming to the Senators: McLain, young outfielder Elliott Maddox, washed-up third baseman Don Wert, and minor-league pitcher Norm McRae. Going to the Tigers: Coleman, pitcher Jim Hannan, young third baseman Aurelio Rodriguez, and shortstop Ed Brinkman. Maddox and Rodriguez were both young defensive specialists with severe limitations as hitters. Brinkman was a middle-aged defensive specialist with severe limitations as a hitter.

In the long term—and maybe I'm just engaging in blatant hindsight, but

I hope you'll indulge me—this deal figured to come down to four players: McLain and Maddox versus Coleman and Rodriguez.

And for a month, at least, it looked pretty good for Washington. In April, McLain went 3–2 with a 2.79 ERA. Writers were writing about the "Denny McLain Comeback," with a capital C. And in August he went 4–2, 2.95.

The problem was the other four months: 3–18, 5.12 ERA.

Do you remember the original question, about Year 4? Here's the next set of rows in the progression:

	Denny			Joe		
	Innings	ERA	RSAA	Innings	ERA	RSAA
Year 4	217	4.28	−25	286	3.15	5
Year 5	76	6.37	− 8	280	2.80	21
Year 6	0	–	–	288	3.53	10

There was no Year 7 for McLain; he didn't pitch after 1972. Coleman kept pitching after 1973 (Year 6), but he was no longer an effective starter; perhaps his young right arm simply couldn't handle all the innings he'd pitched. He'd given the Tigers two good years and one great one, though.

In addition to his lousy pitching, McLain was also a malcontented reprobate. When five Senators gathered one day in 1971 to convene the first meeting of the "Underminers Club"—devoted to getting Ted Williams fired—McLain was one of the five.[3]

McLain and Williams spent much of the season in a public pissing match over McLain's dissatisfaction with pitching in a five-day rotation. And here's my favorite story. According to then-Senators broadcaster Shelby Whitfield, when Williams yanked McLain early from a July 5 start against the Indians—by this point, he'd essentially stopped throwing fastballs—McLain walked past the rest of the Senators on his way to the locker room and said, "I'm going to call Short and get rid of this fucker."

Williams had a rule about playing golf the same day as a ball game: don't. McLain did, regularly. The list just goes on and on. When McLain pitched like he did in 1968 and '69, he was worth having around. But when he wasn't pitching well, he might have been the worst guy in the world. And in 1971 he wasn't pitching well. And in 1972 the Rangers—thanks in part to McLain's wonderful performance, the Washington Senators had become the Texas Rangers—traded McLain to the A's for a couple of bodies.

And what of the other guys in the deal? Maddox never did hit much, with the exception of a big season with the Yankees in '74 (immediately after the

Dumb Thing #37 (Chronologically, not Qualitatively)

Speaking of dumb things that Bob Short did, his handling of David Clyde has to rank somewhere near the top of the long list.

In 1973, the Rangers owned the No. 1 pick in the amateur draft, and they used it to select a Houston schoolboy pitcher named David Clyde, who'd gone 18–0 with five no-hitters in his senior season.

Short was desperate. In 1972, their first season in Texas after moving from Washington, the Rangers drew only 663,000 fans, next-to-last in the American League (the Indians fared even worse). Clyde said he would sign a contract, but only if he could make two starts for the big club before heading to the minors.

Short agreed. In Clyde's first start—in Arlington, of course—nearly 37,000 fannies were in the seats and Clyde pitched well. He pitched well in his second start, too, and thoughts of demoting him to Class A were gone. Clyde eventually started six home games, and the average attendance for those games was 27,000. In the home games he didn't start, the average was just 6,000.

Clyde finished the season with a 5.01 ERA, returned in 1974 and went 3–9 (but with a decent ERA), and finally headed to the minors in '75 (probably because Short had sold the Rangers to somebody who wasn't insane). He did pitch well in 1978 with the Indians, but essentially his career was destroyed by various injuries and perhaps too much drinking (though Clyde says he was never actually an alcoholic). Like most eighteen-year-olds, he couldn't handle the big time. And the (supposed) adults didn't do him any favors.

Rangers sold him to the Yanks). Aurelio Rodriguez never learned to hit, either. But his defense was so impressive that he spent nine seasons as Detroit's regular third baseman, and was still in the majors at thirty-five.

Bob Short did a lot of dumb things during his six-year tenure as owner of the Senators/Rangers. But this trade might have been the dumbest.

1. Shelby Whitfield, *Kiss It Goodbye* (New York: Abelard-Schuman, 1973).

2. Bowie Kuhn, *Hardball: The Education of a Baseball Commissioner* (New York: Times Books, 1987).

3. Whitfield, *Kiss It Goodbye*.

SOX MAKE SPARKY A YANKEE

I dream at night of playing eighty-one games in Fenway.

—Danny Cater (1970)[1]

It's dumb, is what it is. They've got Cecil Cooper, who can play, or they could play Yaz at first and Ben Oglivie in the outfield. Both Oglivie and Cooper are better than Cater.

—Bill Lee (1972)[2]

On March 22, 1972, the Red Sox made their worst deal with the Yankees since they sold Babe Ruth. On March 22, they traded one of the league's best relief pitchers for an over-the-hill first baseman even though they had a number of talented young first basemen and outfielders on hand.

Why did they do it? Chalk it up to a personality conflict between Sparky Lyle (the reliever) and Eddie Kasko (the manager), and a trade the previous autumn that cost the Red Sox (among other things) first baseman George Scott, and management's lack of confidence in prospects Cecil Cooper, Ben Oglivie, and Dwight Evans.

First, the personality conflict, as later related by Lyle:

> But what really burned me was a meeting Kasko held in spring training in '72. He said, "If you have anything to say to me, come to my office and say it to my face. Don't talk be-

hind my back." A couple of days later, Kasko fined me for being overweight and gave the clubhouse boy the message to give to me. The clubhouse boy was having drinking problems and forgot to give it to me, so when I went into the clubhouse the next day, he said, "I forgot to give you this." It was the message from Kasko that he had fined me. I went bananas. I stormed into Kasko's office yelling and carrying on, and I reminded him of his speech about saying things to guys' faces. I said, "You don't have enough respect for me to tell me about this fine to my face? I have to find out from the clubhouse boy?"[3]

According to Lyle, the blow-up with Kasko—who was, by the way, well liked by most of Lyle's teammates—happened on March 21. That date is notable because the very next day the Red Sox traded Lyle to the Yankees for first baseman Danny

National Baseball Hall of Fame, Cooperstown, New York

How could the Red Sox trade such a happy
handsome fellow?

Cater and a player to be named later, who turned out to be named Mario
Guerrero (and who also, as it unfortunately turned out, *was* Mario Guerrero).

Next, the previous autumn's trade. On October 11, 1971—that afternoon, the Orioles blew out the Pirates in Game 2 of the World Series—the
Red Sox made a huge deal with the Brewers. Coming to Boston: pitchers
Marty Pattin and Lew Krausse, outfielder/infielder Tommy Harper, and
minor-league outfielder Pat Skrable. Going to Milwaukee: pitchers Jim Lonborg and Ken Brett, outfielders Billy Conigliaro and Joe Lahoud, catcher
Don Pavletich . . . and first baseman George Scott.

About half of these guys were essentially finished, so long-term the deal
essentially became Pattin and Harper for Lonborg, Brett, and Scott. In the
short term, the Red Sox gained an outfielder (Harper) and lost a first baseman (Scott). This wasn't so awful in terms of performance, as Harper was
just as productive in '72 as Scott had been in '71. But it left a hole at first base.
And instead of filling that hole with one of their many talented youngsters—Cooper, Oglivie, and Dwight Evans would all wind up with fine careers—the Red Sox decided to trade for Danny Cater.

Why Cater? Cater had been a decent hitter with a number of teams since
reaching the majors in 1964. But he'd been particularly successful in Fenway
Park; in fifty-four games, Cater had batted .347 with power. I don't know if

Red Sox management had the exact numbers, but they must have known that Cater'd enjoyed himself at Fenway, and they quite probably assumed he would continue to enjoy himself. So they made the deal.

And the impact? You want impact? In 1972 alone,

- Lyle pitched 108 innings, saved thirty-five games, and went 9–5 with a 1.92 ERA.
- Cater was awful. He showed good power, but his combination of low batting average (.237) and few walks (15) led to a crippling .270 on-base percentage. On May 7, he was batting .130 and got benched for a week. Cater's hitting improved from there—he was hot from mid July through early August—but he finally lost his job for good in late August, and didn't play even once after September 4.
- And the Red Sox . . . if there's only one thing you take from this page, it should be this . . . the Red Sox finished one half-game behind the first-place Tigers.

In the season immediately following one of the worst trades in Red Sox history, they lost a division title by the thinnest of possible margins. And why just a half-game? Believe it or not, in 1972 every team didn't play, wasn't *scheduled to play*, the same number of games. That was the season of the first player strike, which began on April 1, the last day of spring training. The two sides settled things on April 13.

But what about the schedule? The American League favored cutting back to 156 games for everybody. The Nationals favored playing all 162, by eliminating some off-days and scheduling extra doubleheaders.

The owners, in a typical masterstroke of compromise, came up with the worst of all solutions: the season would simply begin on April 15 with the old schedule, and none of the missed games would be played. This, of course, led to the absurdity of competing teams playing different numbers of games. Some teams lost six games, and some lost nine. The Red Sox lost seven games, the Tigers only six . . . which proved to make a big difference.

As it happened, the Red Sox and Tigers were scheduled to finish the season with a three-game series against each other, in Detroit. The Red Sox entered with a half-game lead, but Monday night they lost to Mickey Lolich. They lost again Tuesday night, this time to Woodie Fryman, and the pennant race was over. Even if the Sox won on Wednesday afternoon—which they did, with both teams fielding skeleton lineups—they couldn't catch the Tigers.

It should be said, there wasn't any easy solution. Yes, it would have been

III Conclusions

In three divisions, the uneven 1972 schedule didn't make a lick of difference. In the National League, the Pirates finished eleven games ahead of the second-place Cubs, the Reds ten-and-a-half games ahead of the second-place Astros and Dodgers. In the American League West, the A's aced the second-place White Sox by five-and-a-half games.

Still, the Lords should have known that something bad might happen. Because in 1905 *and* 1907 *and* 1908, the gap between first and second place in the American League *could* have been made up if both teams had played the same number of games. In '05 the Athletics and White Sox both won ninety-two games, but the A's lost fifty-six, the Sox sixty. In 1907 the Tigers won four more games than the second-place A's . . . but they also *lost* one more; the Tigers *played* five more games than the A's and finished one-and-a-half games up.

The National League changed its rule that winter, henceforth requiring every contending team to play as many games as it took to determine an undisputed champion. Meanwhile, in the American League the following season, *three* teams finished within the margin of "schedule error." The Tigers played 153 games and finished a half-game ahead of the Indians (who played 154) and one-and-a-half ahead of the White Sox (who played 152). And that winter, finally, the American League changed its rule, too.

good if the Red Sox had played one of the seven games that got excised by the strike. But which one? Four of those seven games were supposed to be against the Tigers. So just playing one of those wouldn't address the problem. The other three were supposed to be against the Indians, but an additional Red Sox–Indians game would have left the Indians with more games than anybody else in the league.

Still, it could have been done. A few smart people could have sat down with the schedules and a few legal pads, ordered out for pizza, and got the damn job done. Instead the Lords left the potential for a travesty, and that's just what they got.

Getting back to Lyle and Cater: the damage, of course, extended far beyond 1972. Lyle ranked as one of the game's top relievers through 1979. He might have made a difference in the 1975 World Series and in the 1978 pennant race (assuming, of course, that he wouldn't have signed elsewhere as a free agent, or been traded). And the most obvious impact is in 1977, when Lyle won the Cy Young Award and the Red Sox finished only two-and-a-half games behind the first-place Yankees. Aside from Bill Campbell, the Red Sox bullpen that season was shaky, and there's simply no doubt that if Lyle had been around the Red Sox would have finished ahead of the Yankees. (Then again, if the Red Sox still had Lyle in 1977, they probably wouldn't have signed Campbell as a free agent after the 1976 season. Presumably, though, they would have spent that money on some other fine player.)

So this trade—consummated by Red Sox general manager Dick O'Connell and Yankees general manager Lee MacPhail—significantly changed the course of American League history. It cost the Red Sox one division title and perhaps two or three, and possibly a World Series (or two). And on the other side of the equation, the Yankees probably would not have won division titles in 1977 and '78, nor won the World Series in '77, without Sparky.

---

1. Peter Gammons, *Boston Globe*, March 23, 1972.

2. Ibid.

3. Sparky Lyle and Peter Golenbock, *The Bronx Zoo* (Crown: 1979).

CARDINALS TRADE CARLTON
(AND JERRY REUSS, TOO!)

Wise was a reliable pitcher, but Carlton was obviously a great one and delivering him to Philadelphia was a matter of depositing another two hundred-something victories into the account of one of our division rivals. Before the strike was settled—the 1972 season was shortened by six or seven games—the Cardinals also packaged off a promising lefthander from St. Louis, Jerry Reuss . . . It is virtually impossible to count the pennants that were kissed goodbye.[1]

—Bob Gibson

Steve Carlton, as I'm sure you know, was considered to be a cantankerous sort, but a lot of his reputation was due to his disdain for the writers (and you can hardly blame him for that). He really wasn't *that* hard to get along with. Not long before Carlton was traded, early in 1972, *The Sporting News* reported that he was one of the few Cardinals to attend the franchise's annual Christmas party, and in early January he was one of five Cardinals who participated in the "Cardinals' caravan," which visited twenty-five Missouri cities in the interest of drumming up ticket sales and such. So there wasn't any obvious reason to think Carlton planned on holding out. He was simply tough at contract time. Two years earlier, negotiations had become so acrimonious that Cardinals owner Gussie Busch said of Carlton, "I don't care if he throws another damn ball for us." But Carlton wound up signing a two-year contract for roughly $90,000.[2]

According to *The Sporting News*, he started negotiations for 1972 at $75,000; the club countered by offering $57,500. According to Carlton, further talks left the parties slightly less than $10,000 apart.

But the Cardinals had had enough. According to general manager Bing Devine, "Many times Mr. Busch gave me a little leeway in the budget, but in the case of Carlton, Mr. Busch developed the feeling that Carlton was a 'smart-aleck' young guy, 'and I'm not used to having smart-alecks tell me what to do.' "

Busch kept pressuring Dick Meyer, his right-hand man, to pressure Devine to trade Carlton, and so finally Devine did just that. On February 25, 1972, the Cardinals sent Carlton to the Phillies for Rick Wise (who also was going through some tough contract talks).

Shortly thereafter, both pitchers signed new contracts with their new teams: Wise, for close to $60,000; Carlton, for $65,000 (which was about what Wise had been asking for). Those numbers seem ridiculously trivial today, of course, but in the early 1970s a few thousand dollars one way or the other still seemed like a lot of money to both the players (for whom it could make an actual difference in their financial situation) and their employers (who didn't like smart-alecks taking any more of their money than absolutely necessary).

Was the deal, at the time, considered terribly unbalanced? Those 1972 salaries are a good indication that it wasn't. Most people thought Carlton was more valuable because he had better stuff—he threw hard, and had the killer breaking ball—but not *much* more valuable. Wise was nine months younger. He'd won seventy-five games in the majors; Carlton had won seventy-seven. And while Wise's 3.61 career ERA didn't compare favorably with Carlton's 3.10, he'd been the better pitcher in 1971. As Tim McCarver—who'd caught Carlton in St. Louis but by then was a Phillie—said shortly after the deal, "It was a real good one for a real good one . . . Rick might have a little more poise and mound savvy. Steve has an edge in raw ability and stuff. Both are excellent pitchers."

This was a classic "challenge trade": my pitcher for your pitcher (or my shortstop for your shortstop, etc.) and we'll see who comes out on top.

The Phillies won the challenge. After the trade, Wise enjoyed some good seasons, started an All-Star Game, and won 113 games. Carlton won 252.

A couple of months later, the Cardinals made another questionable deal, trading twenty-two-year-old Jerry Reuss to the Astros for Scipio Spinks, a right-handed power pitcher (and Lance Clemons, a somewhat less promising young left-hander). It's not clear why Reuss was dealt, but apparently it was a combination of 1) Busch's distaste for Reuss's new mustache, and 2) Busch's distaste for Reuss's request for $25,000 in his new contract; Busch wanted to hold firm at $20,000 (Reuss had earned $17,000 in 1971, while going 14–14 with a bloated ERA).

In truth, this was a trade that could easily have worked out in the Cardinals' favor. Reuss was young, of course, but his 4.43 ERA in the majors wasn't impressive, and in '71 he'd walked 109 batters in 211 innings. Spinks, two years older than Reuss, had been piling up huge numbers of strikeouts in the American Association over the previous two seasons. And for a few months in 1972, Spinks seriously out-pitched Reuss.

In sixteen starts for the Cardinals, Spinks went 5–5 with a 2.67 ERA. In thirty-three starts (and three relief outings) for the Astros, Reuss went 9–13 with a 4.17 ERA. That June, umpire Ed Sudol told *The Sporting News*, "I've been in baseball thirty years, and I've seen a lot come and go, but this guy Spinks is one of the greatest I've seen break in. Besides that fastball, he has a snapping curve. All that kid seems to need is some experience."[3]

He wouldn't get it. On July 4, Spinks tore ligaments in his right knee, in a collision at the plate with Johnny Bench. Fast enough that he'd been used as a pinch-runner several times during the season, Spinks ran through a stop sign at third base. He said he was just going too fast to stop. At the time, he ranked third in the National League with ninety-three strikeouts, behind only Carlton and Seaver.

Spinks came back in 1973, struggled in eight starts, and never pitched in the majors again.

Reuss won 198 games after the Cardinals traded him.

Even if Spinks hadn't suffered the knee injury, of course it's highly unlikely that he'd have won two hundred games in the major leagues. The Cardinals weren't going to "win" that trade, based on career value. I wouldn't call it a "blunder," though. They traded an unproven young pitcher with good stuff for an unproven young pitcher with *really* good stuff. It just didn't work out.

In *The Spirit of St. Louis*, Peter Golenbock wrote, "The trades of 'Lefty' Carlton and Jerry Reuss may have cost the Cardinals at least four division championships. As a result of withholding the $10,000 that Carlton had wanted, Gussie Busch probably lost many millions of dollars from lost attendance and World Series revenues."

Four division championships? That seems like a lot.

Steve Carlton's last good season was 1984; Reuss's was 1988. But let's stop with 1981, because Reuss pitched well that season, and anyway it's highly problematic, assuming that a player would have been with a particular team for a long time, considering that free agency became a big part of the game in the late 1970s. The table below lists the difference between the Cardinals and first place in each season from 1972 through 1980, and the Win Shares for each of the three key pitchers in these two trades.

		Win Shares		
	Behind	Carlton	Reuss	Wise
1972	21½	40	5	20
1973	1½	14	15	13
1974	1½	22	13	3
1975	10½	14	20	17
1976	29	18	13	14
1977	18	26	9	8
1978	21	20	2	6
1979	12	18	7	17
1980	17	29	21	6
1981	½*	16	13	3

* The Cardinals finished with the best overall record in the National League East, but didn't win either half of the split season, and finished a half-game out of first place in the second half.

More than Lefty

In the passage that leads off this chapter, Gibson wasn't just talking about Carlton and Reuss. He was also talking about Fred Norman and Mike Torrez, who both were traded in June 1971, and would between them win 266 games with other teams.

Torrez went to the Expos for right-hander Bob Reynolds (who, six months later, was sent, *with* Jose Cardenal, to the Brewers in another terrible trade for the Cardinals). Norman was traded, with Leron Lee, to the Padres for Al Santorini, who would win eight games in 1972 before disappearing forever.

So in the span of eleven months—June 1971 through April 1972—the Cardinals traded four pitchers who would, afterward, win 716 games. In return, the Cardinals essentially wound up with Rick Wise and not much of anything else. It might be among the worst eleven months any GM ever had.

As good as Carlton was in 1972—twenty-seven wins for a Phillies team that lost ninety-seven games—he couldn't have made up, all by himself, the huge gap between the Cardinals and first place (and by the way, Wise was damn good that season). As good as Carlton and Reuss were in 1975 and '76, they wouldn't have been enough to put the Cardinals atop the standings. Not without Wise.

Reuss didn't do a whole lot from '77 through '79, and Carlton certainly couldn't have made up those huge deficits by himself.

So that leaves four seasons: 1973, 1974, 1980, and 1981.

In 1973, Carlton and Wise were equally effective, but if the Cardinals hadn't traded Reuss, they certainly would have finished ahead of the first-place Mets.

In 1974, Wise missed most of the season with a shoulder injury. Either Carlton *or* Reuss would have been enough to put the Cardinals over the top; with both of them, the Cards win the East by a dozen games.

In 1981, the Cardinals actually had two shots at the postseason. In the first half of the strike-punctuated season, they finished three games behind the Phillies. In the second half, they finished one half-game behind the Expos. Overall, the Cardinals finished with the best record in the division, but didn't qualify for the postseason derby (and in the West, the same thing happened to the Reds). Carlton that season went 13–4 with a 2.42 ERA and finished third in the Cy Young balloting. Clearly, if the Cardinals had him they'd have won one of the season-halves and perhaps both of them. Reuss was also excellent that season, with an ERA (2.30) even lower than Carlton's.

That's three. Golenbock said maybe four. To reach four, you almost have to assume the Cardinals would have been seventeen or eighteen games better than they actually were in 1980. And even though 1980 was Carlton's second-greatest season and perhaps Reuss's best, it's hard to see them making up that seventeen-game difference between the Cardinals and first place. True, it's the Phillies who finished in first place, and they wouldn't have been as good without Carlton, but the Expos finished just one game behind the Phillies.

Sure, if you replace the starts of Silvio Martinez (4–10, 4.75 as a starter) and Bob Sykes (6–7, 4.08) and Jim Otten (0–3, 7.16) and Roy Thomas (1–2, 5.87), you're going to add some wins. But here's the problem with playing a game so speculative: while Carlton and Reuss would certainly have replaced some of the lousy starts, they would have replaced some of the good ones, too. St. Louis rookies Al Olmsted and Andy Rincon combined for nine starts and a 2.74 ERA that season. You start playing around with this stuff, so many seasons removed from the original transactions, and the evidence has to be overwhelming.

Trading Carlton and Reuss probably cost the Cardinals three division titles. I don't believe that trading Reuss was actually a blunder, though. It could easily have worked out, but didn't. The real blunder was trading Carlton because of a few thousand dollars and a personality conflict. I'm sure that Gussie Busch had his good points. But in this case, his bad points cost his Cardinals a playoff berth in 1973, 1974, and 1981.

---

1. Bob Gibson and Lonnie Wheeler, *Stranger to the Game* (New York: Viking, 1974).

2. Neal Russo, *Sporting News*, March 11, 1972.

3. *Sporting News*, June 24, 1972, p. 26.

STROH'S 9, INDIANS 0

Imagine what a buck's worth of beer would mean. Imagine drinking ten beers in an hour. Imagine the lines at the rest rooms. Imagine selling the beer behind the stadium fence during the game, the fans lining up, some of them simply unzipping and relieving themselves right there, not wanting to lose a place in line to buy ten more beers.

—Terry Pluto, *The Curse of Rocky Colavito*[1]

On June 4, 1974, the Cleveland Indians decided to sell beer for ten cents per cup. And as Bob Costas noted on HBO last year, it was "a very bad idea, executed very poorly." One of the running themes, in the 2005 *Costas NOW* segment, was that the Indians in '74 were a lousy club and couldn't attract paying customers without resorting to crazy stunts.

Not true. At least not for the entire season. As June dawned, the Indians were 22–25 and in fifth place in the American League East (though only three-and-one-half games behind the first-place Red Sox). But beginning on June 1—and including the forfeit loss on June 4—the Tribe ripped off twenty-three wins in their next thirty-three games. On the morning of July 9, the Indians had played exactly half their schedule and owned a one-game lead over the *second*-place Red Sox.

Cleveland soon pitched into a slump and, after a so-so August, fell completely out of the running in September, dropping six of eight against the Orioles and eight of eight against the Yankees. Fourth-place finish aside, the Indians drew more than 1.1 million fans, which represented an improvement of eighty-one percent over 1973 and was the first time the franchise had drawn a million since 1959.

Nineteen seventy-four was a *good* baseball season in Cleveland. There was just this one bad night . . .

On June 4, the Indians sold cups of beer for ten cents apiece. No limit. As you might imagine, this promotion—cleverly called "Beer Night"—was fairly popular, with more than 25,000 fans showing up for a Tuesday-night game against the Rangers. As you might also imagine, a significant percentage of those more than 25,000 fans spent more than a few dimes on beer.

Almost from the beginning, things were going amiss in Municipal Stadium. The start of nearly every half-inning was delayed by one thing or another. A young woman tries to kiss umpire Larry

McCoy. A fine young man strips in right field, then prances back and forth across the outfield. And so forth. According to *The Sporting News*, nine were arrested, "but many, many more could have been, and should have been."[2]

In the bottom of the ninth, the dam finally busted open. With one out and the Indians trailing the Rangers 5–3, George Hendrick doubled. The next three batters singled, pushing Hendrick across the plate and loading the bases. John Lowenstein followed with a sacrifice fly that tied the game. The fans went nuts. And two of them "jumped out of the right field stands and raced toward Texas outfielder Jeff Burroughs, intent on stealing his cap."[3]

Burroughs fought them off but more crazies streamed out of the stands, and momentarily players from both clubs were on the field. Initially they were going to the aid of Burroughs, but before long they were aiding themselves, as roughly fifty "fans" engaged in a general sort of melee. Somebody threw a metal folding chair onto the field, "landing on the head and shoulders of Indians pitcher Tom Hilgendorf" (he wasn't badly hurt, but the photo of him leaving the field, his hands covering the top of his head, wasn't pretty).[4] An umpire was slightly injured, as were a few players and one coach.

Ten minutes after all this tomfoolery began, the field was clear and the game was apparently about to resume. But as the Rangers were headed back to their dugout, another fight broke out near the mound, and this time umpire Nestor Chylak, the crew chief, had seen enough. Once everybody was safely off the field, Chylak declared the game a forfeit.

The following editorial appeared in the next issue of *The Sporting News*:

BEER BUST OR BALL GAME?

The mob action which endangered players at 10-cent beer night in Cleveland should have created some somber reflection on the wisdom of such promotions. Indeed, there was every indication that major league executives were taking a second look at beer night as an attendance lure.

But post-game statements by Cleveland General Manager Phil Seghi and Vice-President Ted Bonda left some doubt as to their paramount concern. Their remarks suggested the No. 1 priority was to shift the blame for the riotous behavior of spectators which resulted in a forfeit to the Texas Rangers.

Seghi rapped Nestor Chylak's umpiring crew for "losing control" of the game. "The umpires should have made a more concerted effort to have policemen clear the field so the game could be resumed," Seghi

Dyn-o-mite!

Today, Mike Veeck is baseball's top impresario. But history will remember him for his national debut, a notorious foul-up called "Disco Demolition."

In 1979, Veeck, as promotions director, was helping his dad run the White Sox. Mike hated disco music, and in Chicago he had a kindred soul: twenty-four-year-old disc jockey Steve Dahl, who was using the airwaves to foment a "Disco sucks!" revolution (his followers were known as the "Insane Coho Lips Army").

On July 12, the Sox were scheduled to play a doubleheader against the Tigers. At Mike's suggestion, and with no oversight from his father, the Sox offered admission for ninety-eight cents—the frequency of Dahl's station, WLUP, was 97.9—to anyone who brought a disco record to Comiskey Park. With Dahl as emcee, the records would be gathered and, between games, blown up. Disco Demolition.

As a promotion, Mike's idea was a smash. The official attendance was 47,795—plenty good for a fifth-place team—and thousands more climbed walls and fences to gain entry (many more were left outside the ballpark, and traffic on the highways leading to Comiskey was backed up for miles).

Trouble began early. With so little spent on admission, the rowdies had more money for beer, and clouds of marijuana smoke hung over sections in the upper deck. During the first game, fans used records as Frisbees. Afterward, Dahl, wearing a helmet and military-style uniform, rode out to center field in a jeep. Disco records were piled into a crate. Dahl led the crowd in a chant of "Disco Sucks!" before setting off the explosive.

Moments later, a riot broke out. Thousands of fans dropped over the walls and rushed the field. They tore up the grass, which was littered with shards of black record vinyl. Even though the rioters were eventually cleared from the field, the Sox had to forfeit the second game of the doubleheader.

The next day, Disco Demolition made headlines around the world. Mike Veeck's debut as a baseball promoter had made him famous—his old man must have been proud—but it also got him blackballed from baseball for ten years, beginning the moment his father sold the White Sox.* In *Slouching Towards Fargo*, Neal Karlen's account of Veeck's comeback, Karlen wrote, "Not since Frank Sinatra, Jr. had one fucked up so magnificently in his father's profession."

—*Keith Scherer*

---

* Veeck spent his years in exile drinking himself silly while hanging drywall and dabbling in advertising. But after nearly ten years, a minor-league owner named Marvin Goldklang decided he wanted to hire "somebody like Bill Veeck," tracked Mike Veeck down, and hired him. Veeck's been coming up with wild promotional ideas for Goldklang—at this writing, the Goldklang Group owns four teams—ever since.

said in a wire to American League President Lee MacPhail. Seghi's perspective might have been different had he been in Chylak's shoes, in the midst of knife-wielding, bottle-throwing, chair-tossing, fist-swinging drunks. Chylak described the hundreds who invaded the field in the ninth inning as "uncontrollable beasts."

Confirming Chylak's view was Frank Ferrone, chief of stadium security, who reported, "They were drunk all over the place. We would have needed 25,000 cops to handle it."

Despite such testimony, Bonda cited Texas Manager Billy Martin for contributing to the explosive incident by leading his players on the field armed with bats. Players on both teams said they left the dugouts to rescue Texas right fielder Jeff Burroughs from fans who roughed him up when he tried to regain the cap they'd snatched from his head.

Hindsight tells us the Indians' beer promotion was unwise on at least two counts. First, it was held with the Rangers as the opposition. Just a week previously, the Indians and Rangers had engaged in a donnybrook on the Rangers' field. Cleveland officials would have been smart to reschedule beer night against a foe less likely to trigger an excuse for a fan uprising.

Second, the Indians put no limit on the amount of beer each customer could buy. The Twins employ a more realistic approach to their beer-night promotion, giving each adult two chips, each one good for one five-cent beer. The Brewers follow a similar policy. If the Indians hold another beer bust, they'd better adopt such a restraint. Meanwhile, blaming the umps and the Rangers changes nothing.

Was Beer Night a true blunder? Many were arrested, a few were slightly injured, and the Indians quite possibly lost a game they might otherwise have won. But attendance, which was lagging badly before Beer Night, took off afterward. Of course that wasn't *because* of Beer Night; it was because the Indians played so well in June, giving fans real hope throughout the summer. But Beer Night didn't hurt the Indians nearly as much as the franchise's general inability to develop good young players.

1. Terry Pluto, *The Curse of Rocky Colavito: A Loving Look at a Thirty-Year Slump* (New York: Simon & Schuster, 1994).
2. Russell Schneider, "Incident or Riot? That Depends on Who's Talking," *Sporting News*, June 22, 1974, p. 5.
3. Ibid.
4. Ibid.

MLB OWNERS REJECT THE "FINLEY SOLUTION"

In the wake of the Messersmith decision it dawned on me, as a terrifying possibility, that the owners might suddenly wake up one day and realize that yearly free agency was the best possible thing for them; that is, if all players became free agents at the end of each year, the market would be flooded, and salaries would be held down. It wouldn't so much be a matter of the teams bidding against one another as of players competing against *each other.* I realized that it would be in the interests of the players to "stagger" free agency so that every year there would be, say, three or four players available at a particular position and many teams to compete for their services. What would we do, I wondered, if just *one* of the owners was smart enough to figure out the money they would save if all players became free agents every year? One owner *was* smart enough: Charlie Finley.

—Marvin Miller[1]

Imagine for a moment, the baseball universe reconfigured. Imagine a world where the buyers, and not the sellers, dominate the annual free-agent market. A world where players traipse from door to door, baseball caps in hand, begging owners to sign them. The top salaries do rise from season to season, but quickly crash into a low ceiling. Midrange salaries plateau or, in some years, even plummet. Players no longer win whopping pay hikes in arbitration, because arbitration no longer exists.

It is a world that very nearly existed.

October 1975. The Major League Baseball Players Association, led by Marvin Miller, files a joint grievance on behalf of two members, pitchers Andy Messersmith of the Los Angeles Dodgers and Dave McNally of the Montreal Expos. *John A. (Andy) Messersmith v. Los Angeles Dodgers* challenges baseball's "reserve clause," which essentially binds a player to the major-league club that currently employed him unless that club traded or released him. The clause is considered so ironclad that even after a player retires, his last employer can hold his "reserve" until his death.

Few expected Messersmith and McNally to win. The reserve system had been in place, in one form or another, since 1876, and had been upheld by the Supreme Court on various occasions, most recently in 1972, in *Flood v. Kuhn.* Owners and players alike had come to believe that Section 10(A) of the Uniform Player Contract granted clubs the rights to a player in perpetuity.

However, Miller interpreted the clause differently. As he told this writer in 2005, "It required clubs to tender contracts to their players on or before January 15 of each year and said that if the player and the club could not agree to terms, the club had the right to renew the contract for one year.

"The owners believed this renewal applied to the entire contract including the reserve clause, so that every time they renewed the contract, they extended the option on the player. This meant that once a player signed a contract with a team he was, in effect, bound to that team for life. But I believed that the clause only granted the club an option on a player's services for one additional year. When Messersmith and McNally both played entire seasons without signing their contracts, the union took the position that their ties to the Dodgers and Expos had been severed and they were free to seek employment with any of the other major-league teams."

After hearing arguments from both sides, veteran arbitrator and labor mediator Peter Seitz took aside John Gaherin, the representative for the owners' Players Relations Committee, and said, "Look, take this case out of my hands. Negotiate with the players and settle your differences."[2]

It was a subtle caveat. Seitz was, in effect, telling the owners that the case would go against them and that they should cut the best deal they could before he rendered a decision that would give the players an overwhelming advantage at the bargaining table. The warning went unheeded. On December 23, 1975, Seitz handed Miller and Gaherin a sixty-four-page document, replete with footnotes, that concluded with these devastating words:

> The grievances of Messersmith and McNally are sustained. There is no contractual bond between these players and the Los Angeles and Montreal clubs, respectively.

The reserve clause was dead. All that remained was for the players and owners to agree on the logistics of a system that would allow the players to sell their services to the highest bidders.

When the two sides next met, they weren't working from the same volume, much less the same page.

"At first, the owners claimed the decision applied only to Messersmith and McNally, which was, of course, absurd," says Miller. "Once they understood we had to negotiate a modified reserve system for everyone, the central point was how much service time would be required before a player became a free agent. They wanted to restrict that right only to those players who completed ten years of service and who were earning salaries below the major-league average."

The union rejected that generous offer, and Miller came back with a system that would grant players free agency after six years of major-league service. It was a framework that would limit the number of free agents—thus maximizing their value, according to the principles of supply and demand—in any particular off-season.

When the owners met to consider their response, most of them were prepared to accept something close to Miller's proposal. However, Charlie Finley, the owner of the Oakland A's, suggested a counterproposal:

"Make them all free agents. Every one of them. Every year."

Finley would repeat those words like a mantra, throughout the meeting. Afterward, he cornered several owners and tried to sell them on the plan. Then he reiterated the proposal for a national audience during a press conference. His words made an immediate impact on at least one interested party.

"The moment I heard Charlie's proposal," says Marvin Miller, "I was worried the owners would agree to it. Finley knew more about baseball than anybody in that room. He could see a player in high school or on some local team in the Dominican Republic and recognize a budding star. Few owners could do that. And he also understood Economics 101. If you made all the players free agents, every year, they would be competing against each other for a limited number of jobs. It would not have been in the players' interest."

Finley understood that, but his colleagues did not. To them, the proposal was just another madcap scheme from a rogue owner who didn't believe in pushing the envelope when you could rip it to shreds. Orange baseballs, designated runners, three-ball walks, and interleague play were just some of the "outlandish" ideas this baseball innovator had proposed in the past. Not one of Baseball's Lords took his latest brainstorm seriously.

They would pay an enormous price for their shortsightedness. As Miller explains, "The owners could have pitted the players against each other. If the Yankees didn't want to pay Reggie Jackson what he wanted, they could turn to Dave Parker or Jim Rice. These were superstars and would still command top dollar, of course, but not as much as they could without that competition."

"However, the system Finley proposed would have been particularly disastrous for the average player. You would have hundreds of players competing for a finite number of positions on teams. And keep in mind that if every player became a free agent every year, you would eliminate arbitration. The owners would have been in the driver's seat."

So why didn't they adopt the Finley Solution?

Miller says, "I'm guessing—I've never asked one of them—but I think that they just couldn't envision an environment in which they no longer controlled the players. It was not just about the money. They were so accus-

The Big One That Got Away

Charlie Finley certainly owned one of the sharper minds in the game, but he could also be incredibly stupid. The A's won the World Series in both 1972 and '73, and their best pitcher in those years was Catfish Hunter. He won forty-two games in the regular seasons, plus five more in the postseasons. As a result, Hunter was able to wangle a pretty good contract from Finley: two years at $100,000 per, with $50,000 the first year deferred—sort of. Instead of paying Hunter the $50,000 at some point in the distant future, Finley was supposed to deposit the money with an insurance company, in the form of an annuity. Charlie didn't like this, because not only would he be spending the money just as soon as if it were simply salary, but this particular payment, he was informed, would not be tax-deductible.

So Finley hemmed and he hawed, and finally, on the eve of the 1974 ALCS between the A's and the O's, Finley offered Hunter a check for $50,000. Hunter refused to accept it. He won a couple of postseason games, the A's won another World Series, and shortly afterward the Players Association claimed that because Finley was in breach of contract, Hunter should be ruled a free agent.

In the old days, the dispute would have been decided by the commissioner (and if Commissioner Kuhn were doing the deciding, he'd have let Finley off with a stern warning and a small penalty). But thanks to Marvin Miller, by 1974 such matters were decided by an arbitrator. And arbitrator Peter

Seitz, to the surprise of many, made Catfish Hunter a free agent. And like so many free-agent pitchers in the years to come, Hunter, after an intense bidding war, got a lot more money—in his case, from the Yankees—than he wound up earning.—*R.N.*

tomed to saying, 'You must play for me or you can't play professional baseball for anyone anywhere in the world.' That was a tremendous power and I suspect they didn't want to relinquish it so abruptly. What we eventually negotiated, the six years of service time, left them with some control and that was what mattered to them. Charlie was able to take the long view and they couldn't. It was a costly mistake. They didn't realize that Finley's proposal would have put me in a box. I couldn't figure out how to explain to players that we had to reject free agency for everyone.

"And fortunately, I didn't have to."

—*Richard Lally*

We thank Marvin Miller for speaking with Richard Lally on December 5, 2005.

---

1. Marvin Miller, *A Whole Different Ball Game: The Sport and Business of Baseball* (New York: Birch Lane Press, 1991).

2. John Helyar, *Lords of the Realm: The Real History of Baseball* (New York: Villard, 1994).

THE BALLAD OF ZIM THE GERBIL

During the off-season I had joined the California Angels . . . From my perspective, Zimmer single-handedly cost the Red Sox the pennant in 1978. Zim played the same nine guys every day that year, no matter what. Take a look at their roster and see how many bench players got one hundred or more at-bats. If a guy was ill or injured Zim would say, "You can play today, right?" and stick him in the lineup. By the end of August those guys were so tired they would have lost a 25-game lead. Smart managers use their bench so that the subs don't go stale and the regulars stay fresh through the pennant stretch . . . Ballplayers need rest. Zimmer didn't seem to understand that and it cost him and the Red Sox.

—Rick Miller[1]

Today's Top 5 List, from the home office in Wauwatosa . . .

Top 5 Mistakes made by Don Zimmer in 1978

5. Not getting along with Bernie Carbo.
4. Not getting along with Bill Lee.
3. Sticking with Torrez too long in the divisional playoff.
2. Running Butch Hobson out to third base every day.
1. Letting Dwight Evans play in September.

5. Not getting along with Bernie Carbo

Actually, I don't really hold this against Zimmer. By all accounts, Carbo spent much of his time as a disinterested observer of the general proceedings. Worthless in the field and on the bases, Carbo was just a decent hitter. Which would have been useful. But Carbo was often late for various pregame practices, when he didn't skip them altogether. Finally, Zimmer said enough was enough and the Red Sox sold Carbo to the Indians for $15,000 (i.e., nothing).

According to Bill Lee—who probably was under the influence of some substance or another, and thus shouldn't be completely trusted—after returning from a one-day protest strike, he told Zimmer, "You are going to rue the day you got rid of Carbo. The day will come when you are going to need him. There will be a crucial spot in a crucial game when only his bat can save us. Only he won't be here."[2]

As it turned out, there were some spots exactly like that.

4. Not getting along with Bill Lee

I'm glad there are people like Bill Lee in the world, but I sure as hell wouldn't want to manage one of them.

"Don't worry, boys. I've got everything under control."

In 1977, Lee was a charter member of the Loyal Order of the Buffalo Heads, named in honor of Don Zimmer, because—as fellow member Fergie Jenkins observed, and Lee reported in *The Wrong Stuff*—"the buffalo was generally considered to be the dumbest animal in creation."

Also in 1977, Lee gave Zimmer the nickname for which he's still remembered. According to Lee, though, it was sort of a compliment. A reporter asked him what Billy Martin was. "Billy Martin is a no-good dirty rat." What about Don Zimmer? "He's a gerbil. He has fat, pudgy cheeks and kids like him."[3]

As you might imagine, Bill Lee wasn't one of Zimmer's all-time favorites.* Throw in the fact that Lee didn't start a game after August 19, and didn't pitch at all after September 10, and you might think that Zimmer buried Lee simply because he didn't like him.

Not according to Zimmer, though. In September when he needed a starter, he went with rookie Bobby Sprowl.† "There was a hue and cry from Lee and his supporters for me to start him, and when Sprowl failed to get out of the first inning, I was blamed for letting personalities get in the way of

---

* Zimmer would later write of Lee, "He's the only man I've ever known in baseball who I wouldn't let in my house, and I don't care who knows it."

† For more on Bobby "Ice Water" Sprowl, see sidebar.

winning. Believe me, my decision to start Sprowl had nothing to do with personalities."[4]

Perhaps. Lee *had* been struggling. From July 20 through August 19, Lee went 0–7 with a 5.18 ERA, and only nine strikeouts in forty-one innings. At which point Zimmer yanked him from the rotation. In *The Wrong Stuff*, Lee admits that by late August his pitching shoulder "had gotten . . . unraveled," but also claims that after receiving a huge supply of vitamins and supplements from Dick Gregory, his arm healed up. And though Lee did pitch somewhat effectively in his four bullpen outings, Zimmer didn't summon him from the bullpen even once in the season's final three weeks.

3. Sticking with Mike Torrez too long in the playoff game

You don't need me to tell you that the Red Sox held a huge lead over the Yankees in the middle of the season, fell behind the Yankees in early September, then fought back and forged a tie for first place on the last scheduled day of the season.

Mike Torrez started for the Red Sox in their playoff game against the Yankees. After six innings, he (and the Sox) were ahead, 2–0. Torrez had given up only two hits and two walks, and struck out four Yankees. He was cruising.

That's not what Bill Lee remembered, though. "I could see he was tiring in the fifth," Lee wrote. "I wanted to run in and give him a rest. When Bucky Dent hit a three-run homer in the seventh, I flew into a rage. Not at Mike, who had pitched a gutsy game. My anger was directed at my favorite manager for not getting Torrez out of there when he was obviously spent."[5]

Sorry, but I just don't see it. Lee probably should have pitched at some point after September 10 (in case you missed it, see Mistake No. 4). But just before Torrez gave up the fluke homer to Dent, he'd given up a couple of singles (a soft liner to left and a shot up the middle) and there were two outs (both coming on routine fly balls). Torrez had thrown seventy-seven pitches. In 1978, there probably wasn't a manager in the world who would have lifted Torrez in that situation. Particularly considering that Torrez was a right-hander with a fine slider and Bucky Dent was a right-handed hitter with a .308 slugging percentage. Zimmer did have a couple of guys warming up in the bullpen, in case Torrez got into serious trouble. But he wasn't in serious trouble.

Letting Torrez face Dent was a mistake only in the mind of Bill Lee (and remember, this is the guy who liked to sprinkle hashish on his pancakes).

"Is that ice water? Or just ice?"

Oddly enough, among all the mistakes Zimmer might have made in 1978, the one for which he's best remembered—pitching rookie Bobby Sprowl against the Yankees in the fourth game of the "Boston Massacre"—was not a mistake. Or at least it wasn't Zimmer's mistake.

As the story goes, when explaining why he'd selected Sprowl to start against the Yankees, he said something like, "The kid's got ice water in his veins." Sprowl walked four batters in the first inning and got yanked. The Red Sox wound up losing 7–4, their fourth straight loss to the Yankees, which made the two clubs dead even in first place.

But Zimmer didn't say that Sprowl had ice water in his veins. Not exactly. According to a 1983 Peter Gammons column, Zimmer said, "The minor league people say Bobby Sprowl has ice water in his veins." That's a distinction worth making, I think.

Sprowl started three games, but the only one anybody remembers is the start against the Yankees. In his debut, though, he'd turned in a quality start—seven innings, three earned runs—against the Orioles, but the Red Sox lost to Jim Palmer. In his third start, he didn't pitch particularly well, giving up three runs in five innings, but the Red Sox beat the Tigers on Jerry Remy's RBI single in the eleventh.

And that was it. Sprowl didn't pitch again that season, not even in garbage relief. He opened the '79

2. Running Hobson out to third base every day

Butch Hobson had bone chips in his right elbow. Between pitches, he would adjust them. When he threw the ball, the fans behind first base were in mortal danger.

Hobson was particularly bad in the last two months of the season, when the Red Sox were busy blowing their big lead. From August 5 through September 22, Hobson was charged with twenty-three errors, leading to uncounted (because I don't want to count them) unearned runs.

It wasn't until the last few days of the season that Zimmer finally figured out that Hobson should be in the lineup at DH, with banjo-hitting Jack Brohamer at third base. (And by the way, if Brohamer's bat was so weak—which it was—why was *he* Zimmer's starting DH in twenty-two games earlier in the season?)

1. Letting Dwight Evans play in September

This is the most obvious mistake that Zimmer made in 1978.

On August 28 in Boston, Evans was beaned by Seattle rookie Mike Parrott. Evans was knocked out of both the game—Parrott threw hard, and Evans's batting helmet was smashed—and, for nearly a week, the lineup. But Evans did return on September 3, and was in Zimmer's lineup in every game through September 22, except two.

Evans obviously wasn't right. On the 4th, he made two errors (matching his total for the season to that point), and on the 8th he made two more, and took himself out of the game, because he was dizzy (after which Zimmer gave him a couple of days off). It wasn't just his fielding, either. In twenty September games, Evans batted .164 with one double, one triple, and one home run. Baseball's a hard enough game without dizzy spells.

When the Red Sox sold Bernie Carbo to the Indians, they called up Garry Hancock, a twenty-four-year-old outfielder, from Pawtucket. There, he'd batted .303 in eighty-four games. That wasn't a fluke; in 1979, he would win the International League batting title. Not that Hancock was a great hitter. He hardly ever struck out and he had some power, but he rarely walked and didn't run particularly well. Hancock eventually played in parts of six major-league seasons, and his career stats—.262 on-base percentage, .358 slugging—were decidedly underwhelming. But I've little doubt that if the Red Sox had simply handed him Evans's job (or at least half of it), Hancock would have been more productive in September than Evans was.

Actually, just as Zimmer figured out in the season's last days that Hobson didn't belong at third base, he also figured out that Evans didn't belong in the outfield. Jim Rice went to right field, Yastrzemski took Rice's spot in left, Hobson took Yaz's DH slot, and the Red Sox finally had the lineup they should have had all month (prior to the playoff, the Sox lost six games in September by just one run). They didn't need Hancock. They just needed Brohamer at third base, with everybody else shifting as necessary.

Tellingly, in Zimmer's autobiography he devoted nine pages to the 1978 season, yet Dwight Evans makes not a single appearance in those nine pages. Nothing in Bill Lee's book, either. The season hinged, as much as anything, on Mike Parrott's errant fastball and management's unwillingness to replace Evans in the lineup. And yet nobody seems to remember just how badly that hurt them.

1. Richard Lally, *Bombers: An Oral History of the New York Yankees* (New York: Crown, 2002).

2. Bill Lee with Dick Lally, *The Wrong Stuff* (New York: Viking, 1984).

3. Peter Golenbock, *Fenway: An Unexpurgated History of the Boston Red Sox* (New York: Putnam, 1992).

4. Don Zimmer with Bill Madden, *Zim: A Baseball Life* (Kingston, N.Y.: Total/Sports Illustrated, 2001).

5. Lee, *Wrong Stuff*.

season in the minors, and was traded to Houston in June.

Sprowl *was* an odd choice. The Red Sox's farm team in Pawtucket had the best pitching in the International League (park effects notwithstanding). Sprowl posted a 4.15 ERA in fifteen games. Meanwhile, the Pawtucket staff included Chuck Rainey (13–7, 2.91), Joel Finch (11–8, 3.18), Burke Suter (11–6, 3.24) and (most interestingly, considering the future) John Tudor (7–4, 3.09). Yet none of these guys pitched at all for the Sox in '78.

Pitching Sprowl might have cost the Red Sox the pennant. But 1) he pitched poorly just once, 2) in that game the Red Sox scored only four runs, and 3) either way, it was hardly Don Zimmer's fault. Bobby Sprowl was the best that he had.

BILLY MARTIN:
"YES, WE HAVE NO TOMORROWS."

Managers, like anyone else, tend to be shaped by their experiences. Billy
Martin probably manages as if there were no future because he has never
had a future with any organization, only a string of todays here and
there.

—Bill James, 1981

Here are some hard, cold facts about the five men who comprised the Oakland A's pitching rotation in 1980 and 1981 (and if you're squeamish about the destruction of promising careers, you might want to turn your head away from the page while you're reading).

- In 1980 and '81, Mike Norris went 34–18 with a 2.99 ERA; in '82 and '83, he went 11–16 with a 4.41 ERA.
- In 1980 and '81, Rick Langford went 31–22 with a 3.15 ERA; in '82 and '83, he went 11–20 with a 4.83 ERA.
- In 1980 and '81, Matt Keough went 26–19 with a 3.09 ERA; in '82 and '83, he went 16–25 with a 5.59 ERA.
- In 1980 and '81, Steve McCatty went 28–21 with a 3.16 ERA; in '82 and '83, he went 12–12 with a 3.99 ERA.
- In 1980 and '81, Brian Kingman went just

11–26, but with a decent 3.87 ERA; in '82 and '83, he went 4–12 with a 4.59 ERA.

(And remember, the 1981 season was interrupted for a couple of months.)

In 1980, those five pitchers won seventy-nine games. In 1983, they won fifteen games. I don't know if this was the most precipitous decline ever for a good pitching rotation, but it must be close. On the first day of the '83 season, Norris was twenty-eight, Langford thirty-one, Keough twenty-seven, McCatty twenty-nine, and Kingman twenty-eight. They were all, by the standards of almost any other profession in the world, still young men. And they would, as a group, win twenty-two more games in the majors.

So what happened? We'll never know for sure, but one reasonable theory is that Billy Martin worked them to death.

◆　◆　◆

By 1979, the Oakland A's were a basket case. Only five seasons removed from a World's Championship, the A's went 54–108 in '79 and drew only 300,000 fans, the worst attendance for a major-league team since the A's did even worse in 1954 (their last season in Philadelphia). In 1978 the franchise very nearly moved to Denver, and for a while New Orleans looked like the franchise's future home; in the end, only the A's lease on the Coliseum kept them in Oakland.

But then Charlie Finley did something smart: he hired Billy Martin, who seemed to have finally worn out his welcome with the Yankees and was deemed a reprobate by every other club.

Of course Martin was a reprobate. He was also a miracle worker.

In 1979, the A's had finished with the second-worst ERA in the league.

In 1980, Martin's first season, they finished with the best ERA in the league (they also moved up in scoring, from last to tenth) and improved their record by twenty-nine wins; they went from 54–108 to 83–79.

It was an amazing turnaround. What's more, the pitching staff in 1980 was essentially the same as it had been in 1979. So how did they do it?

In 1979, Milwaukee's pitching staff led the American League with sixty-one complete games; the A's ranked eighth with forty-one.

In 1980, Milwaukee's starters completed forty-eight games . . . which was good for second place in the league, and was barely *half* Oakland's total of ninety-four. No American League team had finished with as many complete games since 1946, when the Tigers hit ninety-four exactly.

In 1981, the season was abbreviated, so Oakland's starters completed only sixty games—twenty-seven more than anybody else. Also in 1981, the A's sported the best record (64–45) in the American League and swept the Royals in their Division Series.

After the season—which ended, for the A's, with a sweep by the Yankees in the ALCS—the club ran ads in Bay Area newspapers that read, in part, "Thanks, to the greatest fans in all of baseball, for a year we'll never forget. Spring training begins February 15th and, frankly, we can hardly wait."[1]

Indeed, the future looked awfully bright for the A's. But as so many of Martin's teams had done before, this one wasn't able to maintain its recent success. By the All-Star break in 1982, the A's were 28–50, their season essentially finished.

What happened? They didn't hit and they didn't pitch, and here's what happened to that fine rotation:

- ◆ Steve McCatty left spring training with a sore shoulder, spent some time on the Disabled List, and pitched only 129 innings

- Mike Norris suffered from tendonitis, also landed on the DL, and went 7–11 with a 4.76 ERA while pitching only 166 innings
- Rick Langford came down with a sore elbow, supposedly late in the season, but his statistics—11–16, 4.32 ERA, lousy peripherals—suggest that he might have been suffering all season
- Matt Keough was healthy, supposedly, but went 11–18 with a 5.72 ERA

Oakland's starters, all of them, looked like they were pitching hurt, and as things turned out, they probably were. In 1983, Keough pitched only 100 innings; Norris eighty-nine; Langford twenty; Kingman pitched five innings. McCatty wasn't *healthy* in 1983, but he led the way with 167 innings and a decent ERA.

After 1983, none of them ever won more than five games in a season again.

Was it all those complete games, all those *innings* in 1980 and '81, that killed all those careers? I don't know. But I do know that innings aren't the same as pitches. One can reasonably argue that throwing 100 pitches in nine innings results in less fatigue that throwing 120 in eight innings. I believe that's true. Maybe all those complete games were accomplished with a great deal of efficiency. If so, then why worry?

As Martin's biographer David Falkner argued, "The charge"—that Martin overworked his starters—"probably carried more weight than substance."

Though it was true A's pitchers led the league in complete games and innings pitched for two years, they were breaking-ball pitchers who normally got balls in play before going deep into the count. Their low pitch count per game (often in the 90–100 range) was better than average and a better barometer of their actual work load.

Except there's no reason to think Oakland's starters actually were efficient. In 1980, the A's ranked fifth-best in the American League in strikeouts, and seventh-worst in walks. In 1981, they were fifth-best in strikeouts and fourth-worst in walks. They were *not* particularly efficient. Falkner's book is a good one, but his claim about low pitch counts is utterly preposterous, essentially a claim that an entire rotation was more efficient than Greg Maddux at his best.

Nobody in the media was counting pitches twenty-five years ago, and the A's don't have that information (I asked). But we can, with a fair degree of accuracy, estimate the number of pitches thrown by a starting pitcher, thanks to a tool devised by a sabermetrician who goes by "Tangotiger."*

And as I said, the notion that these guys were routinely throwing between ninety and one hundred pitches is preposterous. Here are their estimated pitches for those two seasons, broken down in groups of ten:

	GS	90–99	100–109	110–119	120–129	130–139	140–149	150+
Langford	57	2	6	11	11	11	10	3
Norris	56	4	4	12	11	7	10	4
McCatty	53	2	5	12	9	13	3	2
Keough	51	4	4	9	6	13	3	4
Kingman	45	2	8	9	8	5	2	0

The numbers in the pitches column don't match exactly the games started, because of course occasionally these guys were knocked out before they got a chance to throw ninety pitches. But there were *zero* complete games of fewer than ninety (estimated) pitches, and in fact these five combined for only *two* complete games of fewer than one hundred (estimated) pitches.

There's still another way to look at this. In their complete games—and of course there were a lot of them—how many pitches did these guys average?

	CG	Pitches/CG
Langford	46	129
Norris	36	131
Keough	30	131
McCatty	27	131
Kingman	13	126

They did not routinely throw in the "90–100 range" as Falkner claims. They routinely threw in the 120–140 range. There are certainly pitchers who can survive, or even thrive, under the yoke of such workloads. Most cannot.

It's often said that the pitchers themselves never blamed Martin for what

---

* Here's the formula: Estimated Pitches = 3.3 x (Batters Faced - Strikeouts - Walks) + (4.8 x Strikeouts) + (5.5 x Walks)

"Hey, don't blame *me.*"

Like Charlie Dressen, Billy Martin never made a mistake that he couldn't blame on somebody else. In one of his autobiographies—and I swear on a stack of *Baseball Encyclopedias* this is true—Martin said he never started a fight in his life.

In another of his books, he explained all the injuries to his Oakland pitchers this way: "For two months, I wasn't there and my pitching coach, Art Fowler, wasn't there to see that my pitchers did their work, warmed up properly, did their running, wore a jacket when they were sweating, threw with the proper motion—all the things that managers and pitching coaches have to watch to baby their pitchers. And I'm convinced the sore arms that came later were the result of improper training during the strike, not overwork."

Of course anything's possible. But if Martin's theory was correct, wouldn't there have been a rash of injuries to pitchers all around the majors? And I don't recall that there was.

Fun with Statistics!

Here's a strange one for you. In 1981—shortened because of the strike, of course—Steve McCatty and Baltimore's Sammy Stewart both pitched enough innings to qualify for the American League ERA title. McCatty finished at 2.33, Stewart just a hair better, at 2.32.

McCatty was awarded the title. Why? Because (as had long

been the case) when figuring the official ERAs, partial innings were rounded. So instead of McCatty allowing 48 earned runs in 185⅔ innings for a 2.33 ERA (as he actually did), MLB in their great wisdom gave McCatty a 2.32 ERA (48 earnies in 186 innings). Meanwhile, Stewart took a hit in the opposite direction, as his 112⅓ innings were rounded down to 112, resulting in the "official" 2.33 ERA instead of the actual 2.32 that Stewart posted.

It's hard to feel too sorry for Stewart, who, ERA aside, didn't actually pitch all that well, and wouldn't have qualified for the title anyway if he'd pitched eight fewer innings. Still, McCatty's title exposed the foolishness of the old rule, which was changed shortly thereafter.

happened to them. As Steve McCatty told Peter Golenbock (another of Billy's biographers),

> My God, look back a long time ago. Walter Johnson and those guys were throwing five hundred innings a year. I threw two hundred and forty-something, which isn't any big amount.
>
> I didn't know what my problem was, what happened in my particular case. The doctors didn't know what it was, and it took eight years to figure it out. I had belaborments inside the shoulder, a muscle on top of the cartilage that was torn, bad tissue in the front and the back. I had some frayed tendons, scar tissue, but then I had a big bone spur under my biceps that nobody ever knew about for eight years.
>
> Mike Norris got hurt after we had a fight with Seattle that year. He threw at somebody and got knocked down, and later in the game he said he had lost some feeling in his hand, and then he had a nerve problem, and he had surgery on it.
>
> Rick Langford, one day, threw a pitch and his elbow popped, and Matt Keough hurt his shoulder pitching on a wet day in Baltimore. I remember he came in, slipped, and said, "Something happened to my shoulder." It ended up he had a slight tear in there.
>
> All in the same year. So how could they have blamed Billy for that? Personally I would run through a brick wall for the guy . . .[2]

There's nothing McCatty says here that really conflicts with the notion that Martin worked his pitchers awfully hard. Couldn't McCatty's and Norris's and Langford's and Keough's problems all have been related to fatigue?

Without Billy Martin, the A's would not have made the huge improvement they made in 1980, and without Billy Martin the A's would not have won a postseason series in 1981. Matt Keough went 2–17 in 1979, before Martin arrived. But the next spring, Martin told him, "Matt, you're going to be one of my top three guys in my rotation. Don't worry about it. I'm going to get some guys that catch the ball for you, and we're going to score some runs, and you're going to be fine. You'll win."[3] Martin's success with so many teams was due to far more than just x's and o's. He somehow convinced grown men that they were better than they actually were.

So I'm not going to suggest that Martin shouldn't have been hired in the first place. What I will suggest is that Martin could have achieved very nearly the same dramatic results without destroying the futures of his starting pitchers.

1. *Official Baseball Guide—1982* (St. Louis: Sporting News, 1982).

2. Peter Golenbock, *Wild, High and Tight: The Life and Death of Billy Martin* (New York: St. Martin's, 1994).

3. Michael DeMarco, *Dugout Days: Untold Tales and Leadership Tales from the Extraordinary Career of Billy Martin* (New York: Amacom, 2001).

BAD TRADES (PART 2)

There is no crime in the cynical American calendar more humiliating than to be a sucker.

—Max Lerner, *Actions and Passions* (1949)

Continuing the discussion of trades that in retrospect seem a tad questionable . . .

May 29, 1971: Giants trade George Foster (266 Win Shares after the trade) to Reds for Frank Duffy (54) and Vern Geishert (0).
   and

November 29, 1971: Giants trade Frank Duffy (54) and Gaylord Perry (215) to the Indians for Sam McDowell (12).

The immediate impact of the first trade was nil. Duffy hardly played after the deal, and Foster did very little for the Reds in '71. Meanwhile, the Giants wound up winning their first division title; with Willie Mays, Ken Henderson, and Bobby Bonds in the outfield, they didn't miss Foster at all. But the Giants probably could have used him in 1978, when they finished six-and-a-half games out of first place. That season, Terry Whitfield was in left field and

earned fourteen Win Shares. With the Reds, Foster hit forty home runs and earned thirty Win Shares. Of course we don't know that Foster would have become a star if he'd stayed with the Giants. But he'd almost certainly have been more valuable than Duffy and Geishert were.

After the season, the Giants traded Perry (and Duffy) for McDowell. Seems crazy now, but here's how they compared, at the time:

	Age	Career
Sudden Sam	29	122–109, 3.00
Gaylord	33	134–109, 2.96

Perry had pitched slightly better than McDowell in '71, but McDowell had pitched slightly better than Perry in '70. So knowing only these things, which would you have preferred? Me, too. McDowell was four years younger than Perry, his career numbers were every bit as good, and you've probably heard about his stuff. That's why the Giants had to throw in Frank Duffy.

So who could guess that McDowell had almost nothing left? He won ten games for the Giants in '72 but with a poor ERA, and crashed after that. He won nineteen games after the Giants traded for him.

Perry didn't last a long time in Cleveland, but when the Indians traded him to the Rangers in 1975 they did well, picking up Jim Bibby, Rick Waits, and a hundred grand. He won 180 games after the Giants traded him away.

November 29, 1971: Astros trade Joe Morgan (357), Cesar Geronimo (103), Jack Billingham (75), Denis Menke (22), and Ed Armbrister (5) to Reds for Lee May (127), Tommy Helms (47), and Jimmy Stewart (1).

Here's something I didn't know: this would have been a bum deal for the Astros even if they had *kept* Joe Morgan. Remove Little Joe from the deal, and it's still 205 Win Shares for the Reds, 175 for the Astros. Of course, if you include Morgan—as the Astros so famously did—it's 562 to 175; at +387 for the Reds, this must rank as one of the more lopsided deals ever.

Despite all the players involved, the principals really were Morgan and May. Morgan, of course, was considered one of the league's top second basemen. But May enjoyed the same status among first basemen, having averaged thirty-seven home runs and 102 RBI per season over the previous three seasons. As correspondent John Wilson noted in *The Sporting News*, Astros general manager Spec Richardson and manager Harry Walker "felt it was more important to get the power hitting of May for a team that was a major disappointment at the plate last year."[1]

Meanwhile, the Reds seemed to know exactly what they were getting. When asked about Morgan's .256 batting average in '71, Reds manager Sparky Anderson said, "Here's a guy who gets on base an awful lot of times. His on-base ratio is unbelievable, like last year—149 hits and 88 walks."[2]

Cincinnati baseball writer Earl Lawson did note, in *The Sporting News*, that the big trade might negatively impact the Reds' team chemistry: "Helms and May, in particular, were greatly responsible for the good harmony that has existed among Reds' players in recent years."[3]

Everything worked out all right in the end. Funny how winning creates good harmony.

December 4, 1974: Expos trade Ken Singleton (224) and Mike Torrez (106) to Orioles for Dave McNally (1), Rich Coggins (2), and Bill Kirkpatrick (0).

A month before this deal, McNally—then the Orioles' all-time leader with 181 wins—said he wanted to be traded, "refusing to say exactly why, stating only that changing teams might have a salubrious effect on his pitching."[4]

As Bob Dunn wrote about the Expos' various off-season deals in *The Sporting News*, "The initial feeling, within a 100-mile radius of Jarry Park, is that the Expos have been attacked, stripped, raped and left for dead."[5]

Mike Torrez said, "I think the Expos might have given up too much. I think they could've gotten a little bit more. But they were so desperate for a lefthander that I guess they had to make the deal."[6]

(Here's a rhetorical question: Over the years, how many stupid things have been done in the interest of simply "getting a left-hander"? On the very same page in *The Sporting News* that contains Torrez's quote, there's this headline: INDIANS WHIFF IN BID FOR LEFTY PITCHER.)

Anyway, you probably know (or can guess) the rest of the story. McNally went 3–6 with a 5.24 ERA in 1975, then retired with a shoulder injury. Coggins, who'd done quite well as a rookie with the Orioles in 1973, never did hit again. Kirkpatrick never played in the majors. Torrez, among other things, won a bunch of games and helped give Bucky Dent a lasting nickname. And Singleton was one of the best hitters in the American League for nearly a decade.

December 10, 1980: Angels trade Carney Lansford (191), Mark Clear (51), and Rick Miller (26) to Red Sox for Rick Burleson (32) and Butch Hobson (6).

and

April 1, 1981: Angels trade Dickie Thon (142) to Astros for Ken Forsch (37).

and

May 12, 1982: Angels trade Tom Brunansky (174) *and* $400,000 to Twins for Doug Corbett (22) and Rob Wilfong (22).

In the space of less than two years, the Angels—specifically, Angels general manager Buzzie Bavasi—made three horrible trades.

In defense of Bavasi, Ken Forsch did play a key role when the Angels edged the Royals for a division title in '82. Otherwise, though, these were disastrous. In 1984, when the Angels finished three games behind the first-place Royals, Carney Lansford batted .300 and Tom Brunansky hit thirty-two home runs. In 1985, when they finished just one game behind the first-place Royals, Lansford and Brunansky weren't as good as they'd been, but might have been good enough. And if Dickie Thon hadn't been traded—and he was traded because Bavasi had traded for Burleson, another shortstop—he would have become a star with the Angels, he wouldn't have been hit in the face by a Mike Torrez fastball, and he might today be regarded as one of the very best shortstops of the 1980s.

January 27, 1982: Phillies trade Ryne Sandberg (346) and Larry Bowa (28) to Cubs for Ivan DeJesus (35).

Here's what you should take home from this one: Sandberg was roundly considered the *least* important component of this deal.

The trade never would have happened, if not for Larry Bowa's inability to keep his emotions in check (yeah, hard to believe). After the 1981 season—in which Bowa, thirty-five, had batted .283 with his customary lack of power and walks—there were acrimonious contract talks, and Bowa "had some nasty words in public for Phillies president Bill Giles. Paul Owens, the Phillies GM, was told to send Bowa packing."[7]

Bowa's contract ran through 1982, but he wanted a long-term extension. And if the Phillies wouldn't give him one—and considering his age and his lack of range at shortstop, an extension would have been incredibly foolish—he wanted to be traded. The Phillies agreed, and on January 27 the deal was made, with the Phillies getting Ivan DeJesus from the Cubs to play shortstop.

But DeJesus was seven years younger than Bowa. The Phillies would have to give up something else.

Enter Ryne Sandberg. In 1980, Sandberg, only twenty-one, had batted .310 with pop in the double-A Eastern League. In 1981, he moved up to the American Association and batted .293 while mostly playing shortstop (along with a few games at second). But the veteran-laden Phillies didn't have a place for Sandberg. They didn't think Sandberg could play shortstop in the majors (they were probably right), they had Manny Trillo at second base, they had Mike Schmidt at third, and they had defensive wiz Garry Maddox in center field.

Still, Owens didn't want to trade Sandberg. He would later say, "I offered everybody else in the organization. It went around and around and around. I tried all the young players."

According to Cubs general manager Dallas Green, he told Owens, "You're going to kill that kid . . . you're going to send him back to triple-A and you'll kill him because he's prepared and ready to come to the big leagues. And you're not going to be able to use him for a couple of years with the guys you've got."[8]

The New Jim Gantner?

Paul Owens wasn't the only general manager who fumbled Sandberg away. A few months before the Phillies sent Sandberg to the Cubs, Owens thought he had a deal with the Brewers: Sandberg and a couple of no-names to Milwaukee for starting pitcher Mike Caldwell. But Brewers general manager Harry Dalton called Owens and said he just couldn't make that deal.[9] Then again, maybe it was just as well, because Caldwell won seventeen games in '82, and without him the Brewers almost certainly wouldn't have won their first—and only—division title.

Owens went back to his scouts, who told him that Sandberg had little chance of becoming a star. Or so the story goes. If true, perhaps somebody should have looked at his minor-league statistics. It should be said, though, that the Cubs didn't know exactly what they had, either. On Opening Day in 1982, Sandberg played third base, because the Cubs had just traded for second baseman Bump Wills (and of course they had Bowa at shortstop). It wasn't until September, by which point the Cubs were disenchanted with Wills's defense, that Sandberg took over at second. In 1983 he won his first of nine straight Gold Gloves, and in 1984 he was the National League's MVP.

March 27, 1987: Royals trade David Cone (205) and Chris Jelic (0) to Mets for Ed Hearn (1!), Rick Anderson (2), and Mauro Gozzo (4).

and

April 6, 1995: Royals trade David Cone (83) to Blue Jays for Chris Stynes (55), David Sinnes (0), and Tony Medrano (0).

Let history recall that John Schuerholz, then running the Royals, happily traded David Cone for Ed Hearn (the other guys were throw-ins). At the time, Cone was twenty-four, and his major-league career consisted of twenty-three innings and a 5.56 ERA. His track record in the minors was exemplary, though, and Cone was generally considered the best pitching prospect in the organization. Hearn was twenty-six, and had spent 1986 backing up Gary Carter with the Mets. His minor-league stats suggested that he might hit .240 in the majors with a touch of power. Which is to say, at any one time there are thirty or forty catchers just like him, floating around professional baseball.

Almost immediately after joining the Royals, Hearn hurt his shoulder. His entire career with the Royals consisted of six games in 1987 and seven in '88, and then he was finished. Cone pitched sparingly (and just decently) with the Mets in '87, then went 20–3 in '88. And of course he was just getting started . . .

For the last fifteen years, the Royals have had a tendency to reacquire players they foolishly let get away earlier, and Cone was perhaps the first example. Roughly six years after trading Cone, the Royals signed him as a free agent, and he thrived: in 1994, he went 16–5 with a 2.94 ERA and was named the American League's Cy Young winner after the strike-shortened season. The Royals were successful that season, too.

But the players "won" the strike, so in the spring of '95 the watchword in Kansas City was "austerity." Just before Opening Day, the Royals—this time the perpetrator was general manager Herk Robinson, and by the way Herk Robinson was a blunder all by himself—traded Cone to the Blue Jays, and again the Royals didn't get much back (and before Stynes did anything worthwhile, the Royals traded him to Cincinnati for a couple of relievers).

January 10, 1991: Orioles trade Curt Schilling (222), Steve Finley (272), and Pete Harnisch (90) to Astros for Glenn Davis (12).

Is this the most lopsided trade of the last few decades? Did the Orioles have good reason to believe they'd be getting Glenn Davis, Astro Slugger rather than Glenn Davis, Oriole Washout?

The Astrodome was, during Davis's tenure with the Astros, certainly a pitcher's park, but nothing like the Death Valley it had been throughout most of the 1960s and '70s (the dimensions were shortened in 1985). From Davis's first full season (1985) through 1989, he hit sixty-seven home runs in the 'dome, and seventy-five in road games. In none of those seasons did his road home-run output exceed his home output by more than four.

Davis's 1990 season, though, was a strange one. His home/road splits were among the most extreme you'll ever see (and that includes Rockies):

	Games	HR	Batting	On-Base	Slugging
Home	50	4	.217	.315	.349
Road	43	18	.289	.403	.724

At home, Davis was a shortstop. On the road, he was Babe Ruth on steroids. Go figure. Prior to 1990, Davis had never hit fewer than twelve homers at home in a full season, or more than nineteen on the road. In a *full* season.

After that season, Houston baseball writer Joe Heiling wrote, "Unless the Astros get a bundle of talent in return, they are unlikely to trade Davis, despite the fact that they could lose him to free agency after the season. He remains the Big Bopper and the team's lone proven run producer in his five-and-a-half seasons as a regular."

The Astros got their bundle. On January 10, 1991—almost exactly ten years from the day Houston drafted Davis—they traded him to the Orioles for Curt Schilling. And Steve Finley. And Pete Harnisch.

I listed Harnisch last because some of you have probably already forgotten him. But Harnisch spent four seasons with the Astros and was outstanding in two of them; in 1991 his 2.70 ERA was fifth-best in the National League, and in '93 his 2.98 ERA was sixth-best. And of course he was the least of the players the Orioles gave up.

But you know what? *If* Davis was healthy when the Orioles got him or *if* he wasn't but they couldn't have known that he wasn't, then there's an argument to be made for the deal being a good one that just didn't work out. Because he *could* hit, and neither Schilling nor Finley had done anything noteworthy in the majors. Finley was nearly twenty-six, and at the time of the deal he'd batted .254/.302/.325 over 754 plate appearances with the O's. And Schilling had, to that point, showed a decided lack of interest in becoming a good major-league pitcher.

On the other hand, as Rany Jazayerli points out,

> As damaging as the trade was to the Orioles, it's aggravated by the fact that they didn't actually *need* Davis. Randy Milligan had batted .265/.408/.492 as the Orioles' first baseman in 1990, and Sam Horn batted .248/.332/.472 as the team's primary DH. When Davis flopped, Milligan kept playing first base, Horn kept hitting at DH, and the Orioles still couldn't find room for a young first baseman named David Segui.

So trading Schilling, Finley, and Harnisch was bad, but it was a calculated risk. The problem was that the Orioles were attempting to fill a need that didn't exist, when they had plenty that did.

March 27, 1992: Brewers trade Gary Sheffield (369) and Geoff Kellogg (0) to Padres for Ricky Bones (55), Jose Valentin (167), and Matt Mieske (32).

The season before the trade, Sheffield was limited to fifty games by various ailments, particularly a shoulder injury that necessitated surgery, and batted .194 with two home runs. The season after the trade, Sheffield batted .330 and hit thirty-three home runs. Go figure.

In 1989, Sheffield complained about being moved from shortstop to third base. In 1990, Sheffield accused Milwaukee's front office of racism. In 1991, Sheffield said that Brewers general manager Harry Dalton was ruining the franchise.[10] And at one point early in his career, Sheffield admitted to having intentionally made errors in the hopes that the Brewers would trade him. He finally got his wish, and his career took off.

Not that this wasn't fairly predictable. In 1991, when still only twenty-one, Sheffield batted .294/.350/.421 and walked (44) more often than he struck out (41). He had superstar written all over him. Performance aside, though, he was a terrible guy to have around the club. And the Brewers didn't do a lousy job in terms of who they got in the deal, as both Bones and Valentin would have their moments with the franchise.

Still, it's apparent that the Brewers didn't know what to do with Sheffield. They used the sixth overall pick in 1986 to draft him, presumably with absolutely no idea that he'd be such a problem child upon reaching the majors. And then, instead of figuring out a way to get along with Sheffield—assuming, of course, that there still was a way—they traded all that talent for three Grade B prospects.

November 13, 1996: Indians trade Jeff Kent (243), Julian Tavarez (55), Jose Vizcaino (63), and Joe Roa (9) to Giants for Matt Williams (82) and Trenidad Hubbard (12).

This one wasn't a "baseball deal"; it was a money deal. At the time, the Giants' roster included two superstars with big contracts: Matt Williams and Barry Bonds. General manager Brian Sabean couldn't afford both of them, and somehow concluded that if he could keep only one, it should be Barry Bonds. So he traded Matt Williams to Cleveland.

Oh, how the fans howled! As *Baseball Weekly* noted,

> The honeymoon is over for new general manager Brian Sabean, who drew non-stop criticism after trading superstar and crowd favorite Matt Williams to the Indians last week.
>
> Everywhere he turned—the newspapers, the talk shows, the voice mail—he was the villain.
>
> "All of a sudden I've gone from a golden boy to an idiot," Sabean said. "I didn't get to this point by being an idiot . . . I'm sitting here telling you there is a plan."[11]

The plan, essentially, was to concentrate a smaller percentage of the payroll on just two players. In 1996, the Giants had spent forty percent of their $37 million payroll on Bonds and Williams . . . and lost ninety-four games. Sabean came in with a mandate to make changes, and that's what he did.

The results couldn't have been more spectacular. Sabean traded a bag of peanuts for J. T. Snow, who enjoyed the best season of his career (before or since). Jose Vizcaino took over at shortstop, and played well. Julian Tavarez served as the Giants' top setup man in the bullpen. And Jeff Kent, whose career highs included twenty-one home runs and eighty runs batted in, finished 1997 with twenty-nine homers and 121 RBI.

Sabean knew what he was doing when he traded Williams, and in retrospect this should have been obvious. Nobody could have guessed that Kent would become the power hitter he became. But here's what nobody seemed to notice at the time: the Giants had a perfectly suitable, bargain-priced replacement for Williams on hand.

In 1996, Williams missed the last eight weeks of the season with a shoulder injury. A rookie switch-hitter named Bill Mueller stepped into the lineup, and batted .335 the rest of the way. Was Bill Meuller really a .335 hitter? Of course not. As I write these words, nine years later, Mueller's career batting average is .292. But he'd consistently batted .300-plus in the minor leagues, and Sabean figured Mueller would be good enough. Which he was. And so were the Giants, who won a division title in 1997, beating out the Dodgers by two games.

So in the end, it really was a baseball move. It's just that nobody in San Francisco except Brian Sabean knew it.

November 18, 1998: Indians trade Brian Giles (194) to Pirates for Ricardo Rincon (30).

Here's a list I'd like to see someday: Top 10 Silly Manifestations of Modern Baseball's Obsession with Lefty Relievers. I'll bet this trade is somewhere near the top of the list.

When Cleveland traded Giles, his career numbers included a .391 on-base percentage and a .485 slugging percentage. He was almost twenty-seven, but because the Indians had brought him along slowly, they still owned his rights for three more seasons.

They did have a lot of candidates for left field—Kenny Lofton was in center, Manny Ramirez was in right—including David Justice and Richie Sexson, both fine hitters themselves. But in 1999, the Indians were so desperate for a left-handed bat, they traded for forty-year-old Harold Baines (who'd been doing well in Baltimore but promptly went in the tank after joining the Tribe). And Ricardo Rincon? He pitched the grand total of forty-four and two-thirds innings, and racked up a 4.43 ERA.

In 2000, when the Indians fell just one game short in the Wild Card standings, they didn't really miss Giles much, as they ranked second in the league in scoring and their outfielders and DHs were generally productive. But Rincon spent most of the season on the disabled list.

And again, it's the same old story. It's not that trading Giles was the worst thing in the world. It's that they didn't get enough value in return.

---

1. John Wilson, "Astros See Home-Run Boom with May and Shorter Fences," *Sporting News*, Dec. 11, 1971.

2. Earl Lawson, "Red Hopes Take Off with Joe the Jet in Tow," *Sporting News*, Dec. 11, 1971.

3. Ibid.

4. Doug Brown, "Orioles Crowing Over Clout Supplied by May, Singleton," *Sporting News*, Dec. 21, 1974.

5. Bob Dunn, "Expos Get Southpaw, But Was Price Too Steep?" *Sporting News*, Dec. 21, 1974.

6. Ibid.

7. Fred Eisenhammer and Jim Binkley, *Baseball's Most Memorable Trades* (Jefferson, N.C.: McFarland, 1997).

8. Ibid.

9. Hal Bodley, "Phils Disgusted; Deals Collapse," *Sporting News*, Jan. 2, 1982, p. 38.

10. John Dewan, *The Scouting Report: 1992* (New York: STATS Inc., 1992).

11. *USA Today Baseball Weekly*, Nov. 20–26, 1996.

MARINERS HIRE MAURY WILLS

How qualified am I? I know I'm certainly as qualified as many of the people whose names have appeared in the paper as managerial material, either black or white . . . All are good men, yes, and as I compare our individual qualifications and backgrounds, I have to say I'm as good as any of them. I'd like to have the opportunity to prove it on the field.

If I were handed the reins of a big-league club, I would bring to the job the same maximum of self-confidence that I developed over a twenty-two-year playing career. As a manager I would be confident to issue a prediction right at the start.

—Maury Wills, *How to Steal a Pennant* (1976)

The Mariners were born in 1977. Darrell Johnson, who'd guided the Red Sox to the World Series only two seasons earlier, was hired to manage the shiny new club. When Johnson was fired on August 4, 1980, the M's were 39–65 and they'd lost nine straight games.

Enter Maury Wills, who just might have been the very worst manager ever.

In *How to Steal a Pennant*, which was essentially a book-length job application, Wills wrote, "Give me a last-place club, and after three years we would be strongly in contention, and by the fourth year we'd go all the way."[1]

The Mariners gave him a last-place club, and two years (at least according to his contract). Wills—the National League's MVP in 1962—had never managed in Organized Baseball, but he'd managed four winters in the Mexican Pacific League. In 1977, he'd been offered a one-year contract to manage the Giants, but turned them down.

Nobody considered the fired Darrell Johnson a genius, but he did get some sympathy from *Seattle Post-Intelligencer* columnist Steve Rudman:

His second baseman was hitting .229 and had batted in only 10 runs all season. His designated hitter had gone six for 62 and was hitting .223. His shortstop had plunged 50 points in batting average in five weeks and was hitting .254. His centerfielder was at .264. His first baseman had dropped 20 points in average from a year ago. One of his outfielders had tumbled 62 points in the last month. His catchers, three of them, had 27 runs batted in among them and couldn't hit a beach ball with an alder pole. His best reliever can tell you about the dynamics, physics and gravity of curveballs, but hasn't thrown a decent one in weeks. His best pitcher was corked in the family jewels by a one hopper, curled up like a helpless blob, and has been out to lunch ever since."[2]

After Wills's first game, he said about his new charges, "I think we have a lot of talent. It was on the field last night, but it didn't know how to get through. It was confused talent. My job will be to get that talent to get through and not be confused."[3]

Right. Confused talent. If nothing else, Wills had an original excuse.

Early on, he insisted that his players convene every day a half-hour before their normal pregame practice to work on bunting and baserunning, saying, "Everybody on this ballclub will become a good bunter except Willie Horton."[4]

On August 28, when Juan Beniquez—a thirty-year-old outfielder with a history of causing managerial hair loss—was pulled in favor of a pinch-hitter, he left the dugout, dressed, and spent the rest of the game in the stands. Wills did not discipline Beniquez.

A couple of games later, Beniquez dropped two fly balls, didn't run out a ground ball, and afterward was informed by Wills that he wouldn't be starting any more games the rest of the season. Two nights later, with one out and the tying run on second in the ninth inning against the Orioles, Wills ordered Beniquez to pinch-hit. Beniquez didn't move. Wills wanted Beniquez suspended without pay for the remainder of the season; instead, club president Dan O'Brien levied a five-day suspension (general manager Lou Gorman had very little power within the organization, and soon left the Mariners).

Around this time, Wills's frustration with his players came pouring out: "These kids need to grow up . . . They have been babied too long and it has been detrimental to them individually and as a team. I've been walking lightly since I took over the club, but I'm tired of having to talk to a player every time I make a strategic change in the lineup or don't start somebody . . . We don't have that mental toughness."[5]

Wills's high point as manager came on September 26, when the M's won their sixth straight game. Then they lost eight straight.

The following winter would not be a good one for Wills. For one thing, he developed an unhealthy fondness for cocaine.[6]

For another, at the winter meetings, Wills "told writers that his new center fielder was capable of covering ground and had great desire to play the position."

When asked who he was talking about, Wills replied, "Leon Roberts."

Maybe it was the coke talking. Roberts had recently been traded to the Rangers.[7]

At around the same time, George Argyros, a California real estate tycoon, purchased the Mariners for $13 million.[8] Argyros's personal slogan? "Patience is for losers," which was printed on a sign in his suite at the Kingdome.[9] Nevertheless, he decreed that the Mariners would pay their players the lowest average salaries in the major leagues.[10]

In spring training, Wills continued his attempts to implement his preferred style of baseball and turn up the disciplinary heat. Tommy Davis, Wills's teammate with the Dodgers back in the '60s, was hired as bench coach and batting guru, and Wills set a strict training schedule. The M's would often have practice sessions that lasted from nine in the morning until four in the afternoon. These, along with Wills-led evening lectures on the finer points of baserunning, surprised players accustomed to three- or four-hour workdays that left ample time for eighteen holes of golf.[11]

As training camp opened, Wills announced that his M's would play every game of the exhibition season to win. His M's did win eleven spring games. They also lost seventeen, including fourteen of their last seventeen.[12] In *Sport*, Peter Gammons predicted that Wills would be the first manager fired in 1981.

Gammons was right.

On April 25, a few minutes before game time, A's manager Billy Martin noticed something amiss around home plate, and asked the umpires to investigate. When crew chief Bill Kunkel laid down the batter's box template, he discovered that the box on both sides of the plate was one foot longer (later, Wills protested that it was no more than a couple of inches longer) than regulation.

Under questioning from Kunkel, the Mariners' head groundskeeper admitted that Wills had ordered the augmentation. Wills later admitted he did it for the benefit of his players, and specifically hot-hitting Tom Paciorek, whom the A's accused of stepping out of the box toward the mound in his previous game. Billy Martin believed that the move was made so the M's could catch the A's curveballs and sliders before they broke (Martin was a big fan of the breaking balls).

Although Wills argued that his cheating was "no big deal," the league disagreed, suspending him for two days and fining him $500. Observers quickly wondered how George Argyros, "on record with the comment that he will not tolerate anything that is not first class and done with integrity,"[13] would handle Wills's admitted cheating. Wills said, "they're not going to fire me for that. If they fire me, it will be for other reasons."[14]

Soon after the batter's box incident, Argyros said of his last place M's "We'll fix it. I'm not going to stand idly by . . . We are going to whip this problem one way or the other."[15] After twenty-four games, the M's were 6–18, the worst start in franchise history, and that's when Maury Wills finally got the axe. Rene Lachemann took over, and the M's went 38–47 the rest of the (strike-shortened) season. Not great, but fantastic compared to Wills's 26–56 record as skipper.

In Wills's autobiography—his third book, by the way*—he did accept some of the blame for his fate with the Mariners.

> Contrary to what I thought, I really needed managing experience below the major league level, to learn how to organize, how to delegate responsibility and how to deal with the press. Buzzy Bavasi had told me I should manage in the minor leagues. I said I didn't have any reason to go to the minors, but I really should have. They said managing in Mexico didn't count. I laughed at that, but maybe they had a point. I didn't have any problem with the press in Mexico because I didn't have any dealings with them.[16]

I'm being a tad simplistic here, but Wills's essential explanation for his failure was his inability to get along with the Seattle writers (particularly my old friend Tracy Ringolsby, then writing for the *Post-Intelligencer* and, along with his *P-I* colleague Steve Rudman, one of the top chroniclers of the Maury Wills Era). If only Wills were better at dealing with the media, things might have worked out differently.

That's fine. Whatever gets you through the night. But facts are facts, and in this case the fact is that Maury Wills would have been a horrible manager even if the newspaper writers had all been on the Mariners' payroll. He was just a lousy manager.

When Wills got fired, Steve Rudman came up with a long list of Wills's gaffes. I actually don't have the space for all of them, so instead here's just a representative sampling:

◆ Wills once made out a lineup card that listed two third basemen, but no center fielder.

---

* Wills's oeuvre: *It Pays to Steal* (1963), *How to Steal a Pennant* (1973), and *On the Run: The Never Dull and Often Shocking Life of Maury Wills* (1992); it's in the latter book that you can learn all about Wills's twin addictions to drugs and blond women who wanted him only for his money. Not for the faint of heart.

For want of a left fielder . . .

The Mariners' first decade was pretty tough. In their first ten seasons, the M's didn't reach .500 and never came all that close. But (as I wrote in another book) in 1987 good things started happening. In '87 they drafted Junior Griffey. In '88 they swindled Jay Buhner from the Yankees. In '89 they figured out that Edgar Martinez deserved an everyday job *and* they picked up a wild lefty named Randy Johnson. Teams have won World Series with fewer great players.

But the Mariners never could find a good left fielder, and in the space of two years they made two trades for left fielders that absolutely killed them.

On December 11, 1991, the Mariners traded Bill Swift, Mike Jackson, and Dave Burba—essentially, one-third of a solid major-league pitching staff, as things transpired—to the Giants for Mike Remlinger and Kevin Mitchell. Mitchell could still hit, but he couldn't stay healthy and he was sort of a thug, and after one season the M's traded him to the Reds for Norm Charlton (who was, it should be said, a good pickup). Remlinger never pitched for the Mariners in the majors.

On December 12, 1993, the Mariners traded Mike Felder and Mike Hampton to the Astros for Eric Anthony. Anthony batted .237 as a part-timer, and was released after one season. Hampton developed into a star (Felder didn't).

I don't think it's a big stretch to suggest that if the Mariners had ignored Mitchell and Anthony, and

- ◆ Wills once held up a game for ten minutes while he searched for a pinch-hitter.
- ◆ Wills once motioned to the bullpen for a relief pitcher, which would have been fine except he hadn't bothered telling anybody in the bullpen to warm up.
- ◆ Wills once told the writers he was going to bring outfielder Steve Stroughter to spring training as a non-roster player, which would have been fine, except Stroughter had been traded two weeks earlier.
- ◆ In the sixth inning of a spring-training game, Wills left the field without telling anyone and hopped a plane for California.
- ◆ Shortly before he was fired, Wills skipped most of batting practice three days in a row.[17]

There were a couple of other things that deserve a bit more detail. By his own admission, Wills treated young shortstop Jimmy Anderson terribly. In a spring-training game, for example, Anderson—who was "really eager to please and willing to work"—made a poor decision that cost the Mariners a run. Wills immediately yanked him from the game. And that wasn't the first time he'd humiliated his shortstop.

According to Wills he was so hung up on his on-again, off-again psycho girlfriend that he had trouble focusing on his job. He later wrote,

> I lost my patience with my team. I had thought I could do things with them, but it wasn't my kind of team. We had no speed. We were weak on fundamentals. It was a lousy team. It was the Mariners.
>
> I was talking to them as if they were a bunch of bums who couldn't play ball. A manager just can't do that. I knew I had a young expansion team. A lot of the guys weren't major league caliber. But I wasn't thinking clearly enough to treat them accordingly. I was just hard on them.[18]

What distinguished Wills wasn't that he made mistakes, or the nature of those mistakes. Rather, it was the *variety* and the *frequency* of his mistakes. Remember, 1) the above list really is just scratching the surface, and 2) he accomplished all of this in less than five months: two months at the end of the 1980 season, and then spring training and the first month of '81. I would guess that Wills, in those five months, did something wrong just about every day. (Oh, gotta mention this one: on May 1, just a few days before he got canned, Wills moved second baseman Julio Cruz to shortstop, saying, "I am doing it with the intention of it being permanent."[19] Twenty-four hours later, Cruz was back at second base, permanently.)

Many years later, Wes Stock, the pitching coach in 1981, said, "God, there wasn't much he didn't know. But he didn't deal with the personalities. They didn't communicate with Maury. Maury didn't communicate with them."[20]

When the Mariners hired Wills, somebody asked why it took so long for him to become a major-league manager. He said, "Many times I wondered why I didn't get an offer. I couldn't come up with anything reasonable."[21]

My thanks to Joshua Field for his help with this chapter.

kept Swift, Jackson, Burba, and Hampton, they would have dominated the American League West, and perhaps the whole league, from 1994 through 1997.

1. Maury Wills and Don Freeman, *How to Steal a Pennant* (New York: Putnam, 1976).

2. Steve Rudman, "Darrell Johnson, M's Scapegoat," *Seattle Post-Intelligencer*, Aug. 6, 1980, p. D4.

3. Jim Cour, "M's have a lot of talent, but it's confused'—Wills, *Seattle Times*, Aug. 6, 1980.

4. John Owen, "The First Verse for the Banjo Man," *Seattle Post-Intelligencer*, Aug. 13, 1980.

5. Tracy Ringolsby, "Maury Blasts 'Babied' M's," *Seattle Post-Intelligencer*, Sept. 4, 1980.

6. Maury Wills and Mike Celizic, *On the Run: The Never Dull and Often Shocking Life of Maury Wills* (New York: Carroll & Graf, 1992).

7. Jon Paul Morosi, *Seattle Post-Intelligencer*, Sept. 8, 2005.

8. Jim Cour, " 'Preparation' for Respectability is Wills' Credo," *Seattle Post-Intelligencer*, Jan. 28, 1981, p. D2.

9. Steve Rudman, "Will M's Promises be Broken?" *Seattle Post-Intelligencer*, April 19, 1981.

10. http://www.baseballlibrary.com/baseballlibrary/ballplayers/S/Seattle_Mariners.stm.

11. Steve Rudman, "Wills v. Hired Hands: Some See Eye-for-eye," *Seattle Post-Intelligencer*, April 1, 1981, p. F4.

12. Tracy Ringolsby, "Brand New Look for '81, But . . ." *Seattle Post-Intelligencer*, April 8, 1981.

13. Georg N. Meyers, "Has Maury Cheated Himself out of a Chance to Save Mariners?" *Seattle Times*, April 19, 1981.

14. Hy Zimmerman, "Wills Suspended, Fined $500," *Seattle Times*, April 28, 1981, p. D2.

15. Hy Zimmerman, "M's Owner: 'We'll Fix It,' " *Seattle Times*, May 3, 1981.

16. Wills and Celizic, *On the Run.*

17. Steve Rudman, "The Blunders of Maury Wills," *Seattle Post-Intelligencer*, May 7, 1981.

18. Wills and Celizic, *On the Run.*

19. Tracy Ringolsby, "Wills Shuffles Lineup in Search of Some Wins," *Seattle Post-Intelligencer*, May 2, 1981.

20. Jon Paul Morosi, "M's of 1980: The Original Bad Boys," *Seattle Post-Intelligencer*, Sep. 8, 2005.

21. Steve Rudman, "The Blunders of Maury Wills," *Seattle Post-Intelligencer*, May 7, 1981.

YANKEES TRADE 493 HOMERS

Frank Costanza: "What the hell did you trade Jay Buhner for? He had thirty home runs, over one hundred RBIs last year. He's got a rocket for an arm. You don't know what the hell you're doin'!"

George Steinbrenner: "Well, Buhner was a good prospect, no question about it. But my baseball people loved Ken Phelps's bat. They kept saying, 'Ken Phelps, Ken Phelps.'"

—*Seinfeld*, Episode 122

Because virtually everything said in every *Seinfeld* episode has been not only memorized but also internalized by every male American born between 1960 and 1980, a hefty percentage of baseball fans believe the Buhner trade was not only the Yankees' worst in recent memory, but perhaps their worst ever. Recently I asked a Yankees fan—actually, a fanatic—to name the franchise's worst trade of the 1980s, and he chose Jay Buhner for Ken Phelps.

Not even close.

On December 9, 1982, the New York Yankees consummated a trade with the Toronto Blue Jays. Coming to the Yankees: left-handed relief pitcher Dale Murray and middling first-base prospect Tom Dodd (whom the Yanks had traded to the Jays just seven months earlier). Coming to the Blue Jays: Fred McGriff, Mike Morgan, Dave Collins, and $400,000.

I don't know if this is the most lopsided deal in history. I suspect that it's not. Here's how it broke down afterward, though, and you'll have a hard time finding a bigger disparity in Win Shares, probably because few great players are traded before they even reach the major leagues.

	Seasons	Win Shares
ex-Yankees	46	519
ex-Blue Jays	4	3

Those four "seasons" are a stretch for the ex–Blue Jays. Dodd's one "season" consisted of thirteen at-bats with the Orioles in 1986. Dale Murray's three "seasons" include one in which he pitched three innings (and gave up five runs) and another in which he pitched twenty-four innings (and gave up fifteen runs). Murray's only real season, posttrade, was 1983. It's not at all apparent what the Yankees were expecting—at the time of the deal, Murray's career record was 50–44 with a 3.70 ERA, which was respectable enough—but we can assume they didn't get it, as Murray went 2–4 with a 4.40 ERA in forty games and ninety-four innings over the course of his tenure in pinstripes.

Dave Collins *alone* was more valuable after the deal than Dodd and Murray—hell, the $400,000 was more valuable than Dodd and Murray—and of course Collins would be the least of the three players the Yankees sent to the Blue Jays. The second most valuable was Mike Morgan, who pitched in nineteen seasons afterward and piled up 137 Win Shares. Granted, the Yankees have rarely shown much patience with young pitchers, and Morgan didn't pitch well in the majors until 1987. Still, one gets the distinct impression the Yankees didn't have any idea how good he would eventually become.

The real prize was Frederick Stanley McGriff. But can we fairly fault the Yankees for trading the man who would eventually hit nearly 500 home runs in the major leagues?

The Yankees drafted McGriff out of high school in 1981, and that summer he batted .148 with zero home runs in the Gulf Coast League. He was only seventeen.

In 1982, now eighteen, McGriff returned to the Gulf Coast League and did a little better: league-leading nine home runs, league-leading forty-one RBI, league-leading forty-eight walks (in sixty-two games). At which point the Yankees traded him.

Oddly enough, though, after the trade McGriff didn't look much like a future superstar while scaling the Blue Jays' organizational ladder. They kept moving him up, though, and his first season in the majors was probably the best of his professional career. And of course that was just the beginning.

That was in 1987, the same season Mike Morgan finally broke through with a good season for the Mariners. So to get anything impressive out of Morgan and McGriff, the Yankees would have had to wait five seasons. This of course is the problem with being the Yankees: you don't want to wait for one season, let alone five.

It's easy to fault the Yankees for trading McGriff and Morgan, but those guys probably didn't have much of a future in the organization anyway. McGriff, of course, would have been blocked at first base by Don Mattingly. What about DH, you ask? From 1987 through 1992, the Yankees' primary designated hitters were Ron Kittle (.318 OBP, .535 slugging percentage), Jack Clark (.381/.433), Steve Balboni (.296/.460), Balboni again (.291/.406), Kevin Maas (.333/.390), and Maas again (.305/.406). It's not likely that McGriff would actually have made a difference—the closest the Yankees got to first place in those seasons was three-and-a-half games, in 1988,

Trading Buhner

Obviously, the Buhner trade was pretty awful, too. But 1) Buhner never became anything like the player McGriff did, and 2) at least Phelps did *something* for the Yankees. On July 22, 1988, when Ken Phelps debuted with his new club, the Yankees were only two games out of first place (and the Yanks owned the best run differential in the division). Phelps was acquired to give the Yankees some punch from the left side of the plate, and that's exactly what he did: in a limited role with forty-five games and 107 at-bats, Phelps batted just .224 but drew a bunch of walks and hit ten home runs. The Yankees wound up in fifth place (in a top-heavy division), three-and-a-half games behind the first-place Red Sox. That wasn't Ken Phelps's fault, and if the Yankees had won a few more games this trade wouldn't look so bad at all (granted, Phelps was awful after 1988).

when Jack Clark actually did fairly well—but McGriff would, at the very least, have been great trade bait.

And who was the architect of this brilliant deal? None other than George Steinbrenner, who essentially served as his own general manager. December 9, 1982 just wasn't kind to Steinbrenner. That very same day, he signed free agent outfielder Steve Kemp to a five-year deal for $5.5 million, and Kemp still ranks as one of the biggest disasters in the history of modern free agency.

BRAVES GET (AND KEEP!) LEN BARKER

I feel on top of the world. I'm going from a last-place team to a team that is in first place. Everyone who knows me knows I've always wanted to pitch for a contender. This is perfect. And I've always pitched some of my best games in hot weather, so Atlanta should be fine.

—Len Barker, *The Sporting News* (September 12, 1983)

It's not particularly uncommon for baseball teams to make trades that don't pay off in the long run. It's not particularly uncommon for baseball teams to sign baseball players to long-term contracts that don't pay off (for the teams) in the long term. What's fairly rare is for a baseball team to do both, with the same player, in the space of just a few days.

Here's what the National League West standings looked like when August 28, 1983, dawned in the Americas:

1.	Braves	75–54	–
2.	Dodgers	73–53	½
3.	Astros	67–61	7½

The Braves were awfully unfortunate to own a lead so small. They'd outscored their opponents by 123 runs, while the Dodgers were only forty-six runs to the good. Nevertheless, the standings were what

they were. In late August it was anybody's race, and everybody was picking the Dodgers. On August 14 the Braves had led the Dodgers by six-and-a-half games, but then the Braves went through a rough stretch while the Dodgers were winning ten of twelve, dropping Atlanta's lead to just half a game. By which point the Braves were in full panic mode.

How do we know they were panicky? Because what they did next, only an incredibly panicky franchise would do. On August 28, the Braves agreed to send $150,000 *and* three players to the Indians in exchange for right-handed pitcher Len Barker. The identity of the three players was supposed to be a secret until after the season, because all three were major leaguers and the Braves would be keeping them until the season ended. Unfortunately, the word immediately leaked that the chosen three were pitcher Rick Behenna, third baseman Brook Jacoby, and (probably) center fielder Brett Butler.

This was a problem because Butler was 1) the

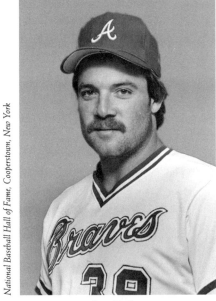

National Baseball Hall of Fame, Cooperstown, New York

Len Barker

Braves' everyday left fielder, and presumably didn't need the distraction of knowing his days with Atlanta were numbered, and 2) a very popular fellow with the local fans. Upon news of his inclusion in the trade, petitions began to circulate around Atlanta, asking the Braves to substitute somebody for Butler in the deal.

Butler set aside the distraction, and played well in September. The petitions did no good, though. The Indians wanted Butler, and after the season they got him.

How thrilled was Ted Turner to have Len Barker in the fold? So thrilled that within a few days after Turner locked up Barker for the last month of the 1983 season, he went to great lengths to lock up Barker for five more years, at a cost of $4 million-plus (which was, at that time, an immense amount of money).

Let me be very clear about this. At that moment, Len Barker was twenty-eight years old. In 1980, he had won nineteen games (with an ERA higher than league average). In 1982, he had won fifteen games (with an ERA slightly lower than league average). In no other season had Barker won more than eight games.

Did the trade and then the new contract work out for the Braves?

For the moment, let's explore a different question. Could the Braves reasonably have expected these moves to work out for them?

There was plenty of reason for skepticism. As Rick Hummel wrote in *The Sporting News*, "When the Dodgers got Honeycutt from Texas ahead of the Braves' desperate bid, Atlanta retaliated by acquiring Len Barker from Cleveland. But Barker has had bone chips in his elbow and this year he was 8–13, with an ERA over 5.00."[1]

That's right. The Braves were desperate because they couldn't get Rick Honeycutt (I guess you had to be there). According to Furman Bisher, here's what happened next:

> The knee jerk philosophy of Braves' management set in. Since the Dodgers had made a trade for a three-star pitcher, Ted Turner had to make one. Cleveland got wind of it and came running with an offer. The Braves could have Len Barker for Jacoby, Behenna and a third player, said to be Brett Butler.
>
> To a National Leaguer in Atlanta, Len Barker is no more than a mere name in the cast of the Cleveland Indians, a team of no stars. He did pitch a perfect game once, but so did Charley Robertson. He throws hard and strikes out a lot of batters, but in between he allows 4.24 runs—earned—per nine innings.
>
> But Turner, being a man of compulsion, had to make a deal. Reliable reports on his negotiations about wages with Barker produced this dialogue.
>
> Turner—"Ah, uh, what kind of salary do you have in mind?"
>
> Barker—"Four million dollars for five years."
>
> Turner—"Ah, uh, okay, you got it."[2]

What should Barker's history have told the Braves? Let's start with 1979, Barker's seventh season as a professional but the first in which he didn't spend at least part of the summer in the minor leagues. Here are some key stats, with the last column representing a sort of "adjusted ERA," prior to the Braves' acquisition of the big right-hander:

	Age	Innings	Ks	Walks	ERA+
1979	23	137	93	70	87
1980	24	246	187	92	98
1981	25	154	127	46	93
1982	26	245	187	88	105
1983	27*	150	105	52	83

* Barker turned twenty-eight on July 7.

"Stop me. Before I do it again."

Roughly fourteen months after Ted Turner threw a few million dollars at a pitcher who couldn't pitch, he did it again.

On December 7—and with some reluctance, I will try to avoid drawing an inappropriate parallel—of 1984, Bruce Sutter accepted an offer that would cost Turner $10 million, and pay Sutter slightly more than $44 million.

How does that work? Turner agreed to pay Sutter $800,000 per season for the next six seasons (1985–1990). Turner also purchased, for $5.2 million, an annuity that would pay Sutter, beginning in 1991, $1.4 million per annum for *thirty years*.[5]

Of course, $1.4 million today (let alone in 2020) doesn't buy nearly as many Lamborghinis as it did then. Still, Sutter did pretty well for himself.

Was this a krazy kooky kontract? Perhaps. But it certainly wasn't kooky like Len Barker's kontract was krazy. Sutter had struggled some in 1983, but bounced back in '84 with perhaps his finest season: 123 innings, 1.54 ERA, forty-five saves.

It's a funny thing, though . . . Whitey Herzog managed Sutter that season, and he must have figured his ace reliever would be gone after the season. Was it just happenstance that resulted in Sutter throwing more innings (by a hefty amount) than he'd ever thrown before?

Yeah, it probably was. According to both of Herzog's memoirs, he tried like hell to sign Sutter to a long-term contract extension, but Cardinals owner Gussie Busch wouldn't spend the money. Herzog even argued, "If he'd stayed with the Cardinals, Bruce would have never gotten hurt. He'd have had guys like us watching him throw. Instead, he took Ted Turner's millions, went to Atlanta where nobody knew him like we did, and blew out his arm."[6]

In October of Sutter's first season with the Braves, *The Sporting News* reported, "Pain in his right shoulder kept reliever Bruce Sutter from entering a game September 22 against San Diego. The problem has dogged Sutter since early summer. Two cortisone shots in the last week of August brought only temporary relief. 'I've never had a shoulder problem before,' Sutter said. 'There's no strength in it. One day I can throw fine; the next day, I can't get it to the catcher.' Understandably, the Braves are concerned."[7]

Gee, you think? Sutter recorded three saves in 1986, missed all of 1987, then saved fourteen games in 1988, posting a 4.76 ERA in his last season. For Ted Turner's $10 million, he got ten wins, forty saves, and a 4.55 ERA.

(One more note about this: at the time, it was said that Turner might well recoup his investment in increased attendance at, and television viewership of, Braves games. Perhaps. But attendance in Sutter's first [and only full] season with the Braves *dropped* twenty-two percent.)

After that season, Bill James came up with a complicated (some might say convoluted) method for rating starting pitchers, based on the pitchers' performance in both 1983 and 1982.

Among right-handed starters, Barker came in fifty-third.[3]

At the time, then, a reasonable amount of reasonable analysis would have led to the conclusion that 1) Barker wasn't all that likely to help the Braves finish ahead of the Dodgers, and 2) Barker wasn't worth a fourth of the amount listed on his new contract. Of course, analysis does have its limitations. What happened in real life? Because if Barker *did* pitch well for the Braves and they *did* win a division title in 1983, then one might reasonably argue that the trade "worked," regardless of what Jacoby and Butler did afterward.

Barker pitched reasonably well down the stretch in '83; he won just one of his six starts, but did post a 3.82 ERA. The Braves finished three games behind the Dodgers.

In 1984, the first year of Barker's new contract, he went 7–8 with a league-average ERA, and missed August and September with an elbow injury that required surgery. After the surgery, "All concerned gushed with optimism."[4] That's great, but in 1985 Barker went 2–9 with a 6.35 ERA, and missed much of the season with another elbow injury (which he blamed on starting the season in a four-man rotation). In 1986, at the end of spring training, the Braves released Barker even though they still owed him nearly two million dollars.

Meanwhile, Brook Jacoby would go on to enjoy a fine career, playing regularly for seven seasons and finishing with more than twelve hundred hits. Butler was the real loss, though. Playing center field, his natural position, he became a mid-level star with the Indians, and later the Giants and Dodgers. Meanwhile, back in Atlanta, center field was manned by Dion James and Albert Hall.

1. Rick Hummel, "Dodgers, Pirates Favored in Blistering N.L. Races," *Sporting News*, Sept. 12, 1983, p. 2.

2. Furman Bisher, "Braves Try Indian, Not Chief," *Sporting News*, Sept. 12, 1983, p. 9.

3. Bill James, *The Bill James Baseball Abstract 1984* (New York: Ballantine, 1984).

4. Gerry Fraley, "Oberkfell's Season Ends on Sour Note," *Sporting News*, Sept. 10, 1984, p. 24.

5. Gerry Fraley, "Sutter Goes for Turner's Pitch," *Sporting News*, Dec. 17, 1984, p. 54.

6. Whitey Herzog and Jonathan Pitts, *You're Missin' a Great Game* (Simon & Schuster, 1999).

7. Gerry Fraley, "As Usual, Ramirez Runs Out of Gas," *Sporting News*, Oct. 7, 1985, p. 16.

WHITE SOX UNLEASH HAWK

Harrelson begins his fifth season in the television booth as White Sox broadcaster, teaming with Tom Paciorek . . . His exuberant "YES" call has become familiar to Sox fans . . . Prior to his return to the air in 1990 for the Sox, Harrelson had previously worked in the broadcast booth for the Sox from 1982–85 . . . On 10/2/85 he left the booth and was named executive vice president for baseball operations . . . served as general manager for one season and then resigned his post to resume his broadcasting career . . .

Chicago White Sox Media Guide, 1994

Amazing, isn't it, how misleading a two-letter word like "to" can be? If you read the White Sox media guide—and Harrelson's entry today is little changed, more than a decade later—you might guess that he didn't *want* to serve as general manager any more, that perhaps he simply woke up one morning and decided that broadcasting was simply more fun than running a baseball team.

The truth was that Harrelson didn't have much choice. His disastrous reign as general manager lasted a few days short of one year, and in that short span he managed, among other things, to move a Hall of Fame catcher to left field and let a Hall of Fame manager get away.

Ken "Hawk" Harrelson was one of the more mercurial major-league players in an era—the 1960s and early '70s—loaded with mercurial players. An early product of Charlie Finley's incredibly productive farm system, Harrelson hit twenty-three home runs

in 1965, when he was twenty-three. But Harrelson got off to a lousy start in '66—in his autobiography, he blamed it on K.C.'s ballpark—and in June the A's traded him to the Senators for a pitcher who went 0–2 with a 9.00 ERA in the rest of his career. Less than a year later Harrelson was playing worse than ever—in his autobiography, he blamed it on a mutual hatred he shared with manager Gil Hodges—and the A's bought him back from the Senators.

"I couldn't have been happier," Harrelson wrote. In sixty-one games with Kansas City, he batted .305/.361/.471, outstanding numbers in that pitcher's year. Nevertheless, on August 25 the A's simply released Harrelson. There had been an incident—or not, depending on whom you believed—on a team flight, and Harrelson publicly criticized Finley's reaction. Finley demanded that Harrelson publicly retract his statements. Harrelson refused. So Finley released him. Just like that. For perhaps the first time in the history of the game, a premier player in the bloom of his career had been unconditionally released, thus making him a free agent.

The Red Sox were high bidders, with a package worth $150,000, covering the remainder of 1967 and all of '68. Harrelson took over in right field, barely hit his weight down the stretch, then went 1 for 13 in the World Series against the Cardinals.

In 1968, though, Harrelson earned his salary. In *the* Year of the Pitcher, he hit thirty-five home runs, led the American League with 109 RBI, and finished third in the MVP balloting. He was "the Hawk," a huge celebrity in Boston, known as much for his Nehru jackets and mod hairstyle as for his considerable athletic talents.

It didn't last long. Just a few games into the 1969 season, with the Red Sox giving up runs by the barrelful, Harrelson was traded to Cleveland as part of a package that netted Indians right-hander Sonny Siebert, then one of the better starters in the league. At first, Harrelson simply refused to leave, saying he would "quit baseball rather than leave Boston and his lucrative outside business ventures," supposedly worth $250,000 (a figure that was later doubled, probably as a further negotiating ploy). However, after a meeting with the Commissioner of Baseball, the President of the American League, and the President of the Cleveland Indians, Harrelson agreed to join the Tribe. He did all right with the Indians that season, but missed most of 1970 with a terrible leg injury suffered in spring training.* Harrelson came back in 1971 but didn't hit, and on May 29 he lost his job at first base to rookie Chris Chambliss. The Indians tried to trade him but couldn't, and when they were about to send him to the minor leagues, he retired instead, with the stated intention of joining the PGA tour. After a rain-out that prevented him from making one last pinch-hitting appearance at Fenway Park, Harrelson said, "My baseball career is over and my golf career begins tomorrow."

That went about as well as you might guess. Harrelson played golf for a few years, signed on as a Red Sox broadcaster, then hooked on with the White Sox crew in 1981. Which brings us to 1985.

Late in the '85 season, White Sox co-owners Jerry Reinsdorf and Eddie Einhorn had a question: why hadn't the Sox been able to win again after cruis-

---

* On March 19 in a game against the A's, Harrelson's spikes got caught in the dirt when he "launched a late slide into second base." He suffered a fractured fibula, torn ligaments, and a serious ankle injury. Harrelson didn't return to the lineup until September 6.

ing to an American League West title in 1983? Reinsdorf and Einhorn "solicited testimony from several persons," but only broadcaster Ken Harrelson offered a "blueprint" that would instill "aggressiveness" into the organization.[1]

And just like that, Roland Hemond was out as the club's general manager, and Harrelson—who of course had absolutely no experience managing anything—was in. According to *The Sporting News,*

> Harrelson said his first priority would be to try to re-sign Carlton Fisk before the power-hitting catcher declares himself a free agent. In addition, Harrelson said he would try to (1) trade Tom Seaver to one of the New York teams, (2) acquire a third baseman "with some pop," (3) bolster the bullpen, (4) draft high school players instead of college talent, and (5) reduce the number of scouts.

As it turned out, Harrelson's first priority was to hire a bunch of men he admired. Within a week after taking over, he hired Alvin Dark (his old manager in Kansas City) to oversee the franchise's farm system. He also hired Moe Drabowsky (an old teammate in Kansas City) to shepherd the White Sox relievers; essentially, the club would have two pitching coaches—Drabowsky joining manager Tony La Russa's buddy Dave Duncan, who would henceforth be responsible for only the starters—which was a first in the game's history. As you might imagine, La Russa wasn't thrilled, saying, "I can see the pluses, but I also can see a lot of potential problems."

Among Hawk Harrelson's weak spots as a general manager was his overwhelming fondness for his fellow ex-major leaguers. In addition to hiring Dark and Drabowsky, he also brought in Willie Horton as hitting coach, and fired the managers of all five farm teams and replaced them with ex-major leaguers. Explaining this "strategy," Harrelson voiced a common (and probably misguided) opinion: "If a kid is going bad, in the back of his mind he'll believe the guy who knows what's going on because that guy has been there."

All things being equal, maybe that's right; maybe you want the guy that's been there. But all things aren't equal, and a great number of ex-major leaguers don't have the intellect or the patience to effectively teach the game to smooth-faced youngsters. And in 1986, not one of Chicago's five farm clubs won more games than they lost.

As for the rest of his priorities, the note about Fisk isn't quite complete; in addition to re-signing Fisk, Harrelson planned to shift the All-Star catcher to left field, thus opening a slot in the lineup for young catcher Joel Skinner. Radical? Sure. But Harrelson said of Fisk, "He can run and has a heckuva arm. He's not going to be a Joe Rudi or Carl Yastrzemski. But with his pride, by June 1 he'll be an average left fielder."

White Sox broadcaster Jimmy Piersall demurred. "It took me at least twelve years to learn how to play the outfield, so you tell me how a catcher is going to learn it at age thirty-eight," Piersall said. "I think Ron Kittle can play it better, and he can't play it, either. Don't you think White Sox fans are ready for a real left fielder after Kittle, Steve Kemp, and Ralph Garr?"

Why was Harrelson so intent on getting Skinner into the lineup? For one thing, Skinner'd spent the better part of three seasons in the Pacific Coast League, where he was regarded as a fine defensive receiver and also managed to hit some balls out of the park. But Harrelson's primary motive was a noble one. At least to hear him tell it. "I happen to be a Joel Skinner fan," he said. "To sit him now would be to retard him. It wouldn't do the individual any good, and that's what is number one. The individual. I don't want to take a chance of killing a young man's career."

That's admirable, it really is. As a baseball fan, it breaks my heart to see some kid stuck in the minors because the parent club has somebody better at the position in the majors and won't make a deal.

That said, there are two reasons why you don't move Fisk to left field. One, Piersall was right: it's not easy to play the outfield when you've spent the last twenty years behind the plate. And two, it's a hell of a lot easier to find a left fielder who can hit than it is to find a catcher who can hit. If you've already *got* a catcher who can hit, you're generally better off leaving the catcher where he is.

There's one reason why you *do* move Fisk to left field: he would be thirty-eight in 1986, and catchers in their late thirties generally are just about finished. It wasn't that Fisk couldn't still play—he'd hit thirty-seven home runs in 1985—it was that Fisk probably wouldn't play much longer, and Harrelson wanted his next catcher in place when Fisk was finished (neither Harrelson nor anybody else could have possibly guessed that Fisk would still be an effective player at forty-three).

As Peter Gammons wrote in his *Sporting News* column, "Some critics will laugh at some things Harrelson tries, but there's nothing wrong with trying new things once in a while."

Particularly if they work.

Moving Fisk didn't work, in the same way that Custer's tactics at the Little Big Horn didn't work; the results were both immediate and disastrous. In April,

- Fisk played left field, and batted .194 with two home runs.
- Skinner caught, and batted .171 with zero home runs.
- White Sox pitchers went 7–12 with a 4.95 ERA.

On May 9, Fisk caught one inning, his first of the season. The next afternoon, he started behind the plate. And from that point forward, Fisk served as the regular catcher until September, when he was injured. Skinner continued to play occasionally, though, so the Joel Skinner Era didn't officially end until July 30, when he was one of three players traded to the Yankees for a package that included veteran catcher/hitter Ron Hassey.

In the end, though, Harrelson's mishandling of Fisk didn't really hurt the White Sox all that much. He never did get his bat going that season, but bounced back in 1987 and of course now he's in the Hall of Fame.

Harrelson's draft certainly didn't help the organization, though. For example, the White Sox's first-round pick, Northwestern left-hander Grady Hall, went straight to Class AAA, struggled, and then suffered an elbow injury the following spring. He apparently was close to reaching the majors again in 1990, but it didn't happen and his professional career ended in 1992.

But among the list of charges against Hawk Harrelson, the cases of Carlton Fisk and Grady Hall rank low compared to that of Tony La Russa.

La Russa took over as White Sox manager in 1979, and in 1983 he led the club to its best record (99–63) since 1920. The Sox declined severely in 1984 (74–88), then returned to respectability (85–77) in 1985. And on June 20, 1986, Harrelson fired La Russa.

Seventeen days later, when La Russa took the helm of the Oakland Athletics, the A's were in last place, eight games behind the White Sox. When the season ended, the A's were in third place, four games ahead of the fifth-place White Sox.

But by then Harrelson was gone. He'd resigned on September 26. Harrelson blamed his departure on poor public relations, some of his own making and some not. "I was hurt most by rumors from people who don't like me, people from inside the organization."[2]

Of Harrelson's tenure, Moss Klein wrote in *The Sporting News*, "The Chicago White Sox, to put it politely, were a mess this season, displaying the chaotic confusion usually reserved for the New York Yankees in those years when Owner George Steinbrenner gets especially edgy."[3]

Back when Harrelson played for the Senators, his roommate was big Frank Howard. The two quickly developed a standard greeting . . .

"Barry *who?*"

Even aside from first-round pick Grady Hall, Harrelson's only amateur draft was something of a disaster, with only four 1986 draftees reaching the majors, and only one of them (Scott Radinsky) making any sort of impact. And with all due respect to Radinsky, when the best player in your draft class is a career middle reliever, it probably wasn't a very good draft.

The White Sox draft in 1985 was worse, though. Oh, they did draft Bobby Thigpen (who would set, and at this writing still owns) the single-season saves record, and also Randy Velarde (though the Sox traded him to the Yankees for little value before he reached the majors). The problem wasn't with who the White Sox drafted in 1985; it's with who they didn't draft.

The White Sox owned the fifth pick that June. The first four players chosen were B. J. Surhoff, Will Clark, Bobby Witt, and Barry Larkin, who would eventually combine for sixty-nine seasons in the majors. Bobby Witt had the worst career among those four, and he won 142 games.

With the fifth pick, the White Sox selected . . . [drum roll, please] . . . catcher Kurt Brown, fresh out of Glendora High School. He never reached the majors.

With the sixth pick, the Pirates selected . . . Barry Bonds.

Five years later, Bonds was winning the first of his many National League MVP Awards, and Brown was batting .269 in the Southern League.

Howard: "So you're the fabulous Hawk, eh?"

Harrelson: "Yeah-uh."

Howard: "What makes you so fabulous?"

Harrelson: "Because I can do it all." [4]

But he couldn't. Not quite.

1. Joe Goddard, "Harrelson Handed Front Office Keys," *Sporting News*, Oct. 14, 1985, p. 29.

2. Dave Van Dyke, "Harrelson Resigns, Bowing to Anti-Hawk Forces," *Sporting News*, Oct. 6, 1986, p. 21.

3. Moss Klein, "Team Turmoil of '86 Is a Builder's Dream," *Sporting News*, Nov. 24, 1986, p. 45.

4. Ken Harrelson with Al Hirshberg, *Hawk* (New York: Viking, 1969).

COLLUSIONS I, II, . . . AND III
(A HARD LESSON LEARNED)

Peter Ueberroth: "I never did anything wrong."

Lou Hoynes: "Technically, you didn't. The clubs heard your words, but they also heard the music, and it was a martial music. They all fell into the beat."

—John Helyar, *Lords of the Realm* (1994)

Blunders can cost a team games. Big games. Blunders have changed the course of franchises. A few blunders have even resulted in *Curses*.

But this blunder is bigger than all those. This blunder is bigger than perhaps any other blunder in the game's long history; bigger, that is, than any blunder but the one that left so many wonderful ball players in the shadows for far too long (and that one's so big that it wouldn't fit in this big book).

Peter Ueberroth, Major League Baseball's sixth commissioner, got owners started down their ruinous path on October 22, 1985. After eleven straight years of supposed financial losses for the "industry," Ueberroth addressed the owners at the headquarters of Anheuser Busch (courtesy of Gussie Busch, one of the original hard-line owners).

At one point in what amounted to a stern lecture, Ueberroth said,

If I sat each one of you down in front of a red button and a black button and I said, "Push the red button and you'd win the World Series but lose $10 million. Push the black button and you would have a $4 million profit and you'd finish in the middle." You are so damned dumb. Most of you would push the red button. Look in the mirror and go out and spend big if you want, but don't go out there whining that someone made you do it.

In closing, Ueberroth told his employers, "I know and you know what's wrong. You are smart businessmen. You all agree we have a problem. Go solve it."[1]

A few weeks later at the general managers' meetings in Tarpon Springs, Florida, Ueberroth hammered home his point, saying, "It's not smart to sign long-term contracts. They force clubs to want to make similar signings," he said. "Don't be dumb. We have a five-year agreement with labor."[2]

What might have been lost on the Lords in the first meeting was made clear in the second: Keep player salaries down. However you have to.

Did even one owner stand up and ask the obvious questions, like "Is this legal?" and "Are we setting ourselves up for big problems down the line?" There's no evidence that one of them did. The owners were cowed by each other, and by Ueberroth's reputation. After all, this was the man who had, just a few years earlier, somehow turned the Olympics into a money machine. If he could do that with team handball and the modern pentathlon, what might he do with America's National Pastime?

So the owners fell in line, and began drafting internal memos to clarify Ueberroth's message. Contracts should typically run no more than three years for hitters, two years for pitchers. And some clubs simply swore off free agents altogether.[3]

Collusion was on. With the owners working in concert and with little deviation, the final tally for the 1985–1986 off-season read as follows: of the thirty-three free agents, twenty-nine went back to their old clubs (and the other four were not wanted by their old clubs). Among the prominent free agents, only Carlton Fisk "got so much as a nibble from another team. George Steinbrenner . . . admitted he made an offer for Fisk but it was withdrawn after he got a call from White Sox chairman Jerry Reinsdorf."[4] Salaries increased by five percent; a year earlier the increase had been eleven percent (and in fact, since free agency's advent in the 1970s, salaries have typically gone up roughly ten percent per year). In addition to Fisk, other notable free agents shut out included Kirk Gibson, Donnie Moore, the knuckleballing Niekro brothers, and Tommy John.[5]

By December, furious agents were calling union chief Don Fehr, asking what was going on. The union smelled collusion, and in early February 1986 they filed their first grievance (which came to be known as "Collusion I"). When asked if the owners were working together to limit salaries, Ueberroth responded, "They aren't capable of colluding. They couldn't agree on what to have for breakfast."[6]

Ueberroth was wrong, or lying (you choose). An idea—"Hey, let's not be so reckless every winter!"—had become a habit, enforced by tacit agreement. Instead of worrying about buying the best players they could afford (or not), now the owners worried about what their colleagues might think (not to mention the scary Olympics guy). In the winter of 1986–1987, a second group of free agents felt collusion's sting, and this included some fantastic players, including Jack Morris, Lance Parrish, Tim Raines, Andre Dawson, Bob Horner, Ron Guidry, Rich Gedman, Bob Boone, and Doyle Alexander. Out of this group, only four—Parrish, Dawson, Horner, and Ray

Knight—signed with new teams.[7] Dawson famously offered to sign a blank contract with the Cubs, and wound up taking a significant pay cut and a one-year contract.*

The fix was in, and it was working better than anyone could have predicted. The average free-agent salary for 1986–1987 had declined by sixteen percent, and roughly three-quarters of them had to settle for one-year contracts. With MLB reporting that revenues were actually up fifteen percent, the union suspected that collusion was still in play and filed a second grievance—Collusion II—on February 18, 1987.[8]

If nothing else, Ueberroth was persistent. Even though the union knew what was happening and continued to file grievances, Ueberroth kept hounding the owners. He wanted to know if they planned to offer contracts running more than three years. If so, he told them, "I want you to come and tell me eyeball-to-eyeball that you're going to do it."[9]

In September of '87, the note on the owners' perfidy—or rather, the first of their perfidies—came due. Arbitrator Thomas Roberts ruled, in Collusion I, that the owners were guilty as charged (damages would be assessed later, after Thomas conducted the hearings and collected the evidence that would allow him to get an accurate take on just how collusion had affected salaries).

Ueberroth and the owners didn't get the message. They continued to collude, but this time through the mechanism of a so-called "information bank." The idea was simple. If Team A makes an offer to Free Agent Z, the team reports all details to the Players Relations Committee (PRC). That was an information "deposit." Next, Teams B, C, and D, curious about Z's offers, could (and presumably would) call the PRC and make a "withdrawal" from the information bank. More collusion, of course. But in sheep's clothing.

Eleven players, including Paul Molitor, Jack Clark, and Dennis Martinez, felt the squeeze in this new twist. The Players Association filed a third grievance in January 1988 (Collusion III).

Early in 1988, the damages for Collusion I were finally announced—of the sixty-five free agents of 1985, only fourteen were still on major-league rosters—and seven players were awarded "new-look" free agency. They could, without forfeiting their existing contracts, solicit offers until March 1 from other teams. Out of that group, Kirk Gibson was regarded by many as the plum. He had one season remaining on a three-year, $4 million contract

---

* To his credit, Dawson hit forty-nine home runs in '87, after which he was rewarded with a lucrative new multiyear deal.

Los Angeles Dodgers

"Thank you, Mr. Ueberroth."

with the Tigers, but on January 29 he signed a new deal with the Dodgers: three years and $4.5 million.[10]

Collusion, then, did help one club: without Ueberroth and his willing accomplices, Gibson never would have hit that walk-off piece against Eckersley, and the Dodgers almost certainly wouldn't have won that World Series (because they wouldn't have reached it without Gibson, the National League's MVP that season).

The spanking by the arbitrators continued in October 1989 when George Nicolau presided over Collusion II and, just like Roberts, ruled that the owners had conspired to restrict movement of the players in question.[11]

This time, new-look status went to (among others) stars like Rich Gedman, Bob Boone, Brian Downing, Doyle Alexander, Ron Guidry, and Willie Randolph.

But setting players free was just a part of the process. Somebody also had to figure out how much *money* all that colluding had cost the players. Roberts ruled that the owners owed union members $10.5 million for 1986, and Nicolau came up with $38 million for 1987 and $64.5 million for 1988. In addition to these salary shortfalls, the owners would also have to compensate the players for ancillary losses related to multiyear contracts and various sorts of bonuses.[12]

Late in 1991, the players and the owners reached a settlement: the owners would surrender $280 million, with the money then distributed to affected players via a complicated (and often lengthy) process.[13]

So the blunder had run its course . . . or had it? The seeds of distrust, well rooted within the union even before Collusions I through III, grew to venomous heights. As Fay Vincent told the owners shortly after taking over as commissioner in 1989, "The single biggest reality you guys have to face up to is collusion. You stole $280 million from the players, and the players are unified to a man around that issue, because you got caught and many of you are still involved."[14] Certainly, every labor negotiation since has been freighted with memories of what the owners did (particularly considering that Bud Selig and Jerry Reinsdorf—two of collusion's most enthusiastic ringleaders—have remained in positions of power over the last two decades).

And there was still all that money. In 2005, this writer asked Vincent if the two rounds of expansion in the 1990s were motivated by the owners' desire to offset the financial losses they incurred as a result of Collusions I, II, and III. Vincent replied, "I remember one of the owners said, 'That's the single dumbest idea I've ever heard!' But what he was really saying was, 'We need the money to pay off the union because we colluded.' "[15]

—*Maury Brown*

1. Jerome Holtzman, *The Commissioners: Baseball's Midlife Crisis* (New York: Total Sports, 1998).

2. John Helyar, *Lords of the Realm: The Real History of Baseball* (New York: Villard, 1994).

3. Ibid.

4. Ibid.

5. Clifford Kachline, *Sporting News Official Baseball Guide: 1988* (St. Louis: Sporting News, 1988).

6. Holtzman, *Commissioners*.

7. Kachline, *Baseball Guide*.

8. Andrew Zimbalist, *May the Best Team Win: Baseball Economics and Public Policy* (Washington, D.C.: Brookings Institution Press, 2004).

9. Helyar, *Lords*.

10. Clifford Kachline, "Pitchers Reestablish Control in Historic 1988 Campaign," *Sporting News Official Baseball Guide: 1989* (St. Louis: Sporting News, 1989).

11. Kachline, "Pitchers."

12. Zimbalist, *May the Best Team Win*.

13. Ibid.

14. Fay Vincent, *The Last Commissioner: A Baseball Valentine* (New York: Simon & Schuster, 2002).

15. Maury Brown interview with Fay Vincent, http://www.businessofbaseball.com.

Curses. Foiled Again.

If not for Don Drysdale and Sandy Koufax, the Collusion rulings of the late 1980s and early '90s might never have happened.

In 1966, Don and Sandy announced that they would negotiate only as a team, and they—with the help of an agent, another first (or near-first)—both asked for three-year contracts that would pay $166,000 per season. It all added up to one *million dollars*, a number that caused bile to rise in the throats of team owners struggling to make the mortgage payments on their hunting lodges and island getaways.

Don and Sandy eventually caved, signing one-year contracts that paid them handsomely (if still far less than what they were worth to the Dodgers). But the owners never forgot. And in 1977, they requested that one sentence be added to the new Collective Bargaining Agreement:

> Players shall not act in concert with other players and clubs shall not act in concert with other clubs.

Marvin Miller agreed to the sentence, but added many years later, "I was only going to give in if it was a two-way street. They yielded instantly. It wasn't a big deal."

Except it was a big deal, a decade later. As usual, the owners had been outsmarted. As usual, the players had the better lawyers, and they won.

October 7, 1977

It wasn't nearly as famous (or decisive) as McNamara's snooze job, but Phillies manager Danny Ozark committed a similar crime in Game 3 of the 1977 National League Championship Series against the Dodgers. With the best-of-five series tied at one game apiece, the Phillies carried a 5–3 lead into the top of the ninth inning in Philadelphia.

But with two outs and nobody on base, forty-year-old Vic Davalillo reached on a drag bunt, and then Manny Mota—another pinch hitter, and nearly as old as Davalillo—drove a two-strike pitch to deep left field. As Carl Clark would write in the *Official Baseball Guide*, "Luzinski, oddly unreplaced by Jerry Martin, a more capable fielder, got his glove on it but could not hang on as he bulled into the wall."

Officially it was a double, with Davalillo scoring and Mota taking third on the play. And a few minutes later, after a bad call at first base, an errant pickoff throw, and a bouncing single up the middle, the Dodgers were ahead 6–5. Mike Garman pitched perfectly in the bottom of the ninth, and the Phillies were down two games to one. And the Series ended the next night when, with rain falling for the entire game, Tommy John pitched a complete game to beat the Phillies 4–1.

It should be noted that just as replacing Buckner with Stapleton wouldn't have guaranteed anything but (probably) a tie, replacing Luzinski with Martin wouldn't have guaranteed anything but (probably) a fifth game. Assuming Game 4 goes the same way, Game 5 would

	At-Bats	Batting	On-Base	Slugging
vs. LHP	1,232	.277	.361	.459
vs. RHP	2,182	.245	.322	.429

Again, fairly typical platoon splits. And looking at these numbers compared to Buckner's, Baylor has a fifty-point edge in on-base percentage and (nearly) a seventy-point edge in slugging percentage. Everything else being equal, you'd rather have Baylor batting against the lefty every time.

Essentially, Baylor was a loaded gun. So why didn't McNamara pull the trigger? Lack of imagination. Buckner was the everyday first baseman and finished with 102 RBI (thank *you*, Wade Boggs and Marty Barrett), and he'd been lifted for a pinch-hitter just once all season.[1] All of that is nice enough, but leaves aside the salient facts that 1) Buckner actually wasn't much good during the regular season, and 2) whether because of his terribly sore ankles or not, Buckner was lousy in October. Including the last three regular-season games, the seven ALCS games, and the World Series games up to the eighth inning of Game 6, Buckner's October stats included sixty-six at-bats, *one* walk, *one* extra-base hit (a double), and ten singles.

The reason for Buckner's postseason struggles wasn't any mystery. He was hurt. As Red Sox general manager Lou Gorman later wrote,

> Buckner had played the entire ALCS against the Angels and the World Series in intense pain. He had re-injured his right ankle, a recurrence of an old and serious injury that he had suffered seasons ago while playing for the Dodgers. He had torn away much of the muscle and tendons attached from his ankle to his foot. In the last few weeks of the regular season sliding into second base he re-aggravated the same ankle and foot, bone scraping against bone, ever so painfully.
>
> Prior to every playoff game and the World Series we had to freeze his ankle in ice, tape it, and then place him in hightop shoes. His mobility and range were severely restricted.

Buckner's ankle injury has generally been given as the reason for pulling him for defensive purposes, but that misses the point; Buckner shouldn't have been playing at all, and particularly not with a left-handed pitcher on the mound.

He simply was the wrong man for the job, and he lifted Orosco's first pitch into center field for an easy out. Rally aborted, Red Sox still clinging to one-run lead. And then of course, came the tenth inning (the Mets tied the game in the bottom of the eighth).

In Game 1 of the World Series, with the Red Sox protecting a 1–0 lead in the eighth inning, Dave Stapleton replaced Buckner at first base. In Game 2, with the Red Sox leading the Mets 8–3 in the eighth, Stapleton pinch-ran for Buckner, then remained in the game at first base. In Game 5, with the Red Sox nursing a 4–2 lead in the ninth, Stapleton replaced Buckner at first base. And in Game 6, with the Red Sox up 5–3 in the tenth? McNamara sat on his hands, Stapleton sat on the bench, and Buckner gained his infamy.

When asked, after the game, if he'd considered replacing Buckner with Stapleton in the tenth (or, for that matter, earlier), McNamara said, "No."

Asked to elaborate, McNamara said he replaced Buckner only when Buckner reached base. "Normally, when Bill Buckner is on base, we pinch run for him because he has bad ankles," McNamara said. "Besides, Buckner has very good hands."

Could McNamara really have forgotten that he *had* replaced Buckner with Stapleton purely for defensive reasons, in Games 1 and 5? I doubt it. McNamara knew he'd let sentiment get in the way of winning, *knew* he'd really screwed up, and after the game he was just trying to cover his ass.

According to Gorman, afterward he asked McNamara if he'd even thought about replacing Buckner with Stapleton in the fateful tenth. McNamara said, "I thought about it, but I felt Buckner deserved to be on the field when we won."

The players knew, too. As Dave Stapleton later told author Mike Sowell, "I think everybody knew it. Our manager knew it. He wouldn't admit it to this day, but he damn well knows that he messed up. And he very well could have cost us the World Series that year."[2]

have been played in Philadelphia. Steve Carlton would have started for the Phillies, and that season he was 17–3 with a 2.14 ERA at the Vet. But in baseball, there's no such thing as a sure thing.

---

1. http://www.retrosheet.org.

2. Mike Sowell, *One Pitch Away: The Players' Stories of the 1986 League Championships and World Series* (New York: Macmillan, 1995).

ROYALS SIGN DAVIS BROS.

The dream for me this Christmas was to get a Davis. We got two.
—Royals manager John Wathan

You have to give Ted Turner a great deal of credit. If it were *me* who'd been looking for a new general manager after the 1990 season, Royals GM John Schuerholz would have been somewhere near the bottom of my list of candidates. Hell, he wouldn't have been *on* the list. Not after what he'd done just a year earlier.

It's hard to remember now, and if you weren't there you might not believe it, but it really wasn't all that long ago that the Kansas City Royals were one of Major League Baseball's best-heeled franchises.

- In 1985, when the Royals won the World Series, their $11.8 million payroll ranked ninth in the majors (and they were within $600,000 of fourth).
- In 1988 and '89, the Royals sported the seventh-biggest payroll in the majors (and again,

there wasn't a whole lot separating them from fourth).

And here's the shocker, I think: in 1990, the Royals of Kansas City boasted *the* most expensive roster in the major leagues: $23.2 million, roughly a million bucks higher than those of the megamarket Red Sox and Mets.*

There are only a few long-ago news events that I can connect to my physical location. I remember exactly where I was when I heard that Reagan had been shot. Same thing with John Lennon . . . the Challenger Disaster . . . 9/11, of course. And oddly enough, I also remember exactly where I was on the afternoon of December 11, 1989, when I learned that the Royals had signed Mark Davis: I was sitting

---

* And it wasn't until 1995, after the strike, that the Royals' payroll fell (permanently, probably) below the MLB average.

in my car, waiting for my friend Mike Kopf outside of Allen Press in Lawrence, Kansas.

What I don't remember is whether or not I was excited by the news. But in those days I wasn't nearly as cynical/realistic about the Royals as I would become a few years later. And as the Royals were so thrilled to announce, now they would have *both Cy Young winners*.

That season, K.C. right-hander Bret Saberhagen had gone 23–6 and was easily the best pitcher in the majors. And over in the National League, left-hander Mark Davis took Cy Young honors.

Davis probably wasn't the best pitcher in his league that year—relievers almost never are—but he was pretty close. He took over as the Padres' closer early in 1988, and over the next two years he threw 191 innings, allowed 136 hits (including only eight home runs), and struck out 194 batters while posting a 1.93 ERA.*

So Davis was a terrific reliever when the Royals signed him to a four-year deal worth $13 million, giving him the richest per-year deal ever. No question about that. But did the Royals need another terrific reliever? The man Davis would be replacing as Royals closer, Jeff Montgomery, had—in his quietly unimpressive way—put together a *better* 1989 than Davis, with a 1.37 ERA in ninety-two innings. But the Royals couldn't help themselves. The prospect of having both Cy Young winners on the same pitching staff was simply more than they could resist.

Still, if the Royals made a mistake in signing Mark Davis, at least it was a mistake of excess. No, he didn't fill a particular need, but when you can get a great player, you write the check first and sort things out later. On the other hand, the December 7 signing of Storm Davis—three years, six million dollars—was a mistake by any definition.

Storm (no relation to Mark) had, just a few years earlier, ranked as one of the better young pitchers in the game. He was in the majors at twenty, and a world champion with the Orioles at twenty-one. Of course, he also pitched 200 innings when he was twenty-one, then 225 innings when he was twenty-two, and like most young pitchers he simply couldn't survive that sort of workload. By the time he was twenty-five, his second team (the Padres) had given up on him. Tony La Russa and Dave Duncan, then in Oakland, indulged their fondness for reclamation projects and gave Davis a shot. He responded with sixteen wins in 1988 and nineteen more in '89.

---

* This predated interleague play, of course, but the Royals got an up-close look at Davis in the 1989 All-Star Game, when he struck out Bo Jackson on three pitches (not that striking out Bo on three pitches was a particularly notable accomplishment).

Must . . . protect . . . shortstop . . .

Ask ten different Royals fans at what moment they knew their favorite team had jumped the shark, and you're likely to get the same answer each time: it was the moment they found out that the Royals placed a higher value on David Howard than Jeff Conine.

Howard was the quintessential good-field/no-hit middle infielder. In Howard's pro debut (1987) he batted .194. He bumped that up to .223 the following year, then .236, then .250 in double-A in 1990, when he even set career highs in home runs *(five)* and doubles *(ten!)*.

In 1991, manager Hal McRae became so frustrated with his team's defense that he benched starting shortstop Kurt Stillwell and promoted Howard from triple-A Omaha, where he was hitting a robust .122. McRae was telling his team, "I don't care whether you hit or not; you've got to make the plays in the field." Which Howard did, even as he hit .216/.267/.258. The following year, it was more of the same: .224/.271/.283.

Conine, meanwhile, had emerged from the fifty-eighth round of the draft; he was a pitcher at UCLA, but his pitching coach convinced the Royals that Conine could really hit. And he could: Conine reached Class AA in his third pro season (1990), batting .320 with fifteen homers and ninety-four walks, and was widely considered the Royals' top prospect.

He broke his wrist the following year and played only fifty-one minor-league games, struggling when he did play. But Conine returned to Omaha in 1992, and hit .302 with 20 homers in 110 games. That September he manned left field for the big club, and didn't embarrass himself.

That fall, the majors held their first expansion draft in sixteen years. The list of protected names—each team could protect fifteen players during the first round—was supposed to be a secret, but of course a great deal was leaked.

Howard's name was on the Royals' list, because he was "the only proven major league shortstop in the organization." [1]

Conine's was not, because the Royals were rolling around in first basemen (Wally Joyner, Bob Hamelin, Joe Vitiello) and the front office did not consider Conine a good fit in left field.

To the surprise of no one, Conine was drafted by the Marlins, with the twenty-second overall pick. He was one of the National League's top rookies in 1993, and one of the game's top left fielders from 1994 through 1996. He is, at this writing, still playing.

After the Expansion Draft, David Howard earned twenty-two Win Shares, and played in more than 100 games in just one season (1996, when he batted .219/.291/ .305). In his career with the Royals, Howard played 547 games, batted .229, and hit eight home runs.

Shake a tree, and a dozen gloves will fall out. Howard's glove was little better than those of a dozen utility infielders hanging on to that twenty-fifth roster slot. Conine's bat was the rare commod-

Those nineteen wins weren't nearly as impressive as they looked, though. In fact, you could make a compelling case that Storm had the most *unimpressive* nineteen-win season in major-league history.

For one thing, despite starting thirty-one games for the A's that year, Davis threw only 169 innings, less than five-and-one-half innings per start. No other pitcher has ever won so many games in so few innings.[*]

Then there's the fact that Davis wasn't all that effective in the innings he did pitch. His ERA in 1989 was 4.36. The *league* ERA was 3.88. The Athletics played their home games in a pitcher's park.

So how did Davis, pitching not all that often and not all that well, win nineteen games? It was simple, really. Pitchers don't win games. *Teams* win games. And the Athletics were, in 1989, the best team around. They had one of the best hitting attacks in the game, and when Davis started they were *the* best hitters; Davis had the highest run support of any starter in the majors.

And the A's bullpen was not only the best in baseball, but one of the best ever. Four relievers threw fifty or more innings for the A's in 1989, and their ERAs were 3.26, 2.35, 2.24, and 1.56. That 1.56 belongs to Dennis Eckersley, then in the midst of the greatest reliever peak of all time. Combine league-leading run support with a bullpen that (almost) never blows a lead, and it's surprisingly easy to rack up the W's.

And the W's were all the Royals saw. As pitching coach Frank Funk said when asked about Davis's ERA with Oakland, "We don't want pitchers with good ERA's. We want pitchers with wins."

That's an astonishing statement. It's the equivalent of the CEO of a publicly held corporation announcing to the world, "We don't care about making a profit. We care about raising our stock price." The Royals confused the ends with the means. They were obsessed with the *product*—Davis's record—while ignoring the *process*—the fact that Davis owed all those wins more to his teammates' performance than to his own.

After Davis signed with Kansas City, the process hardly changed. After accounting for league and park effects, Davis's ERA in his last season with the A's was fifteen percent below average. In his two years with the Royals, his ERA's were nineteen percent and then sixteen percent below average. But the product went to pot: his record was 10–19 as a Royal, and by the end of his contract he was pitching garbage relief.

But where Storm's decline was eminently predictable (and was predicted by virtually every objective analyst around), Mark's fall from grace was as

---

[*] No one has come close; the fewest innings by another nineteen-game-winner is 199, by Bob Grim in 1954.

surprising as it was rapid. Everything went according to plan in his first few appearances: three-and-one-third innings, three saves, zero hits, zero baserunners, zero runs.

On April 21 in Toronto, it all came apart.

With the Royals already trailing by three runs, Davis gave up a couple of hits and a couple of walks, with one run scoring. Less than twenty-four hours later, Davis gave up one hit and two more walks (though nobody scored). And in his next appearance, five days later against the Rangers, Davis walked two *more* batters and gave up four hits, with four runs scoring as he blew a 5–3 lead. There would be two more walks on May 3, two more on May 6, and on May 7 Davis recorded his last save for a while.

At that point, the Royals had a choice: they could stick with their $13 Million Man, or they could exile him to middle relief and give the job back to Jeff Montgomery. We can't get inside Davis's head and neither could the Royals, really. But they decided that the possibility that a demotion would destroy his confidence wasn't outweighed by the possibility that he'd continue to destroy everybody else's confidence if he kept blowing late-inning leads. Montgomery got his job back, and served admirably as the Royals' closer for most of the 1990s.

Mark, meanwhile, finished that season having allowed fifty-two walks and seventy-one hits in sixty-nine innings. His 5.11 ERA remains, fifteen years later, the highest ever for a pitcher in the season after winning a Cy Young Award. He never recovered, and the Royals buried him deep in the bullpen before finally dumping him on the Braves during the third year of his four-year deal. And the Royals, who had won ninety-two games the year before they signed Mark and Storm, haven't so much as sniffed the postseason since.

And finally, the punch line for this rather unhappy joke . . .

Oddly enough, the failure of the Davis Bros. might wind up putting John Schuerholz in the Hall of Fame. Somebody had to be held responsible for the debacle that was the Royals' 1990 season, and who better than the architect? Schuerholz wasn't exactly *fired* after the Royals finished 75–86 with the highest payroll in the major leagues. But owner Ewing Kauffman wasn't exactly begging Schuerholz to return, either. So when Ted Turner came calling, it was with Kauffman's blessing. And if Schuerholz had spent the 1990s in Kansas City rather than Atlanta, his Hall of Fame chances would be roughly the same as David Howard's.

—R.N. *(with a great deal of help from Rany Jazayerli)*

ity, and the fact that the Royals convinced themselves to keep the dime-a-dozen glove guy over their most potent young hitter was an indelible sign that the team was about to fall on some very hard times.—*Rany Jazayerli*

---

1. Jeffrey Flanagan, "Royals' List Not Hard to Deduce," *Kansas City Star*, Nov. 10, 1992.

MISSED IT BY *THAT* MUCH

(Part 2)

All his life he had been schooled that nothing was worse than to finish second. But crushing fears are no longer so crushing once they are experienced.

Jack Newfield, *Robert Kennedy* (1969)

Nothing is as obnoxious as other people's luck.

F. Scott Fitzgerald

Continuing our discussion of teams that finished just one game out of first place, and how they might have finished in first place if only they'd been a little smarter about things.

1962 Los Angeles Dodgers (first place: S.F. Giants)

Elsewhere in this book, I spend a great deal of time on the best-of-three playoff series between the Dodgers and the Giants, but no time at all on what happened earlier in the season. And when you look at the Dodgers' statistics, what jumps at you is Larry Burright, a part-time second baseman who batted .205/.264/.317 in 249 at-bats.

Burright was essentially veteran Jim Gilliam's caddy. Gilliam, considered past his prime with the glove, would often start a game at second base, then shift to third in the later innings, with Burright tak-

ing over at second. But Burright also started sixty-nine games at second base, completing fifty-four of those. And in retrospect, he shouldn't have played nearly as much as he did. It's just hard to believe that his glove could have balanced his bat, and that the Dodgers wouldn't have been better off just letting Gilliam play second base nearly every day. It's true that Burright, in 1961, had batted .291 with Atlanta, in the Southern Association, but that was just the Southern Association, and probably a fluke anyway. He'd batted .257 with Atlanta in 1960, and in '63 would bat .224 with Buffalo and .220 with the Mets.

1964 Philadelphia Phillies and Cincinnati Reds (Cardinals)

It's the Phillies who are remembered as the great losers, of course, because they blew the big September lead. But the Reds also wound up just one game behind the pennant-winning Cardinals, so they're also worth a peek.

Well, I found my scapegoat. It's whoever (Bill DeWitt? Managers Fred Hutchinson and Dick Sisler?) thought giving Chico Ruiz 336 plate appearances was a good idea. Ruiz, a twenty-five-year-old rookie, batted .244/.269/.318, which might be excused as a sick fluke, except that those numbers are dead even with Ruiz's eventual career totals (somehow he managed to hang around until the early '70s). It would be one thing if Ruiz were a Gold Glove–quality shortstop. But the Reds had Leo Cardenas at shortstop, and he played literally every game. So Ruiz played in seventy-seven games, all of them at second base or third, and all that playing time cost the Reds the pennant.

1964 Chicago White Sox (Yankees)

If not for Veeck's post-1959 World Series trades (see "Bill Veeck Trades the Farm," page 102), the White Sox would have won pennants in both 1964 and '67. But even with the trades, the Sox finished just one game out of first place in '64. Could they have won with the talent on hand? Of course. Should they have won?

In *Minnie and The Mick: The Go-Go White Sox Challenge the Fabled Yankee Dynasty, 1951 to 1964*, Bob Vanderberg writes about the oh-so-close finish, "If only they had kept Nellie Fox around for one more year, moaned those who had seen too many crucial errors at second base by the inexperienced Buford."

That's not it, though. Don Buford made sixteen errors that season: thirteen at second base, and three at third. Of those sixteen errors, only two—the first, on April 16, and the last, on September 18—could reasonably be described as "crucial." Of the other fourteen, eight came in games the White Sox won, three did not contribute to runs being scored, and three led to one unearned run in games the Sox lost by at least three or four runs.

So yes, Buford's errors cost the White Sox a couple of games. But Nellie Fox, in 115 games at second base with the Houston Colt .45s, made thirteen errors that season. Isn't it likely that his errors would have cost the White Sox a couple of games, too? Actually, I checked; Fox's errors led directly to three Houston losses.

Fox was a great second baseman, in his prime. But in 1964 he was thirty-six years old and wasn't the player he'd been. Buford was twenty-seven. And though he'd eventually shift to third base and then the outfield, there's little if any evidence that the White Sox would have been better off with Fox in '64.

1967 Detroit Tigers and Minnesota Twins (Red Sox)

Tigers outfielder Mickey Stanley was not a particularly good hitter, but there's no way management could have seen *this* coming. As a part-timer in 1966, Stanley batted .289 with mid-range power. As a full-timer in 1968, Stanley batted .259 with mid-range power (which was fairly impressive in '68). But in 1967, when the Tigers really needed him, Stanley batted .210/.273/.312 in 145 games (but only 367 plate appearances).

Hey, it wasn't anybody's fault. If Stanley was reasonably healthy, he deserved to play. I'm not sure the same can be said about Ray Oyler. He is, of course, famous for his famously terrible hitting. Oyler batted .186 as a rookie in 1965, then .171 in '66. Yes, his defense at shortstop was fantastic. But even though Oyler upped his average in '67 to .207, he simply didn't deserve the 424 plate appearances that he got. The Tigers did figure this out in '68, as he played less often and the Tigers won the pennant by twelve games.

As you're no doubt aware, 1967 was not exactly a hitter's season; the American League batted .236/.300/.351, and as a team the Twins were just .240/.305/.369. Still, the club truly distinguished itself at two positions. Twins shortstops batted .196/.243/.275; that was mostly Zoilo Versalles. Twins catchers were even worse. A lot worse. As a group, the quartet was so impressive that they deserve to be listed in all their glory.

	Games	At-Bats	Bat	OBP	Slug
Jerry Zimmerman	104	234	.167	.243	.192
Russ Nixon	74	170	.235	.304	.300
Earl Battey	48	109	.165	.254	.211
Hank Izquierdo	16	26	.269	.296	.346

Zimmerman just couldn't hit. No secret there. Even for him, though, .167 was pretty terrible. Nixon was better, and entered that season with a .274 batting average. But he wasn't much of a catcher, which is why he'd never been able to establish himself as more than a part-timer. Battey was supposed to be the Twins' starter in '67; he'd been an All-Star in four of the previous five seasons. Granted, Battey had slipped some in 1966—perhaps due a neck injury he'd suffered in the '65 World Series—but there was no reason to think he would completely collapse in '67. But he did, and never played in the majors again.

Versalles's decline was just as surprising. He'd been the American League's MVP in 1965, which was a fluke. But he'd also been decent enough in 1964 and '66, and in '67 he was still only twenty-seven. Could anybody have guessed this career .257 hitter would slump to .200 over the course of 160 games? (Apparently the Dodgers couldn't have; they gave him a job in '68 and he batted .196.)

Another weak spot for the Twins: starter Mudcat Grant, who went 5–6 with a 4.72 ERA. But just the season before, he'd won thirteen games, 3.25 ERA. As it turned out, Mudcat was just about finished, but he'd certainly earned his 95 innings in '67. And everybody else on the staff with any sort of meaningful role pitched well.

If I'm going to fault the Twins, it's for playing Ted Uhlaender in center field as often as they did. Uhlaender's stats—.285 on-base, .381 slugging— were right in line with the rest of his career. He wasn't awful, but his defense wasn't quite good enough to balance his on-base percentage. In retrospect, Cesar Tovar, who played all over the field that season, probably should have been the regular center fielder. But then again, if Tovar had played center every day, Rich Rollins would have been the everyday third baseman, and Rollins wasn't any more productive at the plate than Uhlaender (the Twins did have Graig Nettles in the minors, but he was only twenty-two and wouldn't establish himself in the majors until 1970).

1971 Los Angeles Dodgers (Giants)

We've not found nearly as many cut-and-dried blunders during this exercise as I thought we would. Here's one, though. In 1971, the Dodgers gave Steve Garvey sixty starts (and fifty-two complete games) at third base. He was pretty crummy in the field (and would be even worse in '72), and didn't compensate at the plate, batting just .227.

The Dodgers had a problem: too many first basemen (Garvey, Dick Allen, Wes Parker) and corner outfielders (Willie Crawford, Bill Buckner, Willie Davis, Manny Mota), and not enough third basemen (vacant). So Garvey played a lot of third base, even though his shoulder injury didn't allow him to really play the position, and Allen played a lot of third base, even though his ability didn't allow him to really play the position.

Let's assume the Dodgers didn't have any competent third basemen in their farm system. Were there really so few good third basemen in *baseball*

Los Angeles Dodgers

Dick Allen and Steve Garvey: between the two of them, there
must have been one third baseman.

that the Dodgers couldn't have traded for one of them? It wasn't Garvey's
and Allen's faults that they couldn't play third; this was a failure of management.

1972 Boston Red Sox (Tigers)

As I've written elsewhere in the book, if the Red Sox hadn't traded Sparky
Lyle for Danny Cater shortly before the season, they would have finished
ahead of the Tigers.

What I didn't write in that essay is that with Cater struggling, the Red
Sox gave Bob Burda eleven starts at first base in late June and early July. Including those games and some brief appearances afterward, Burda went hit-
less in his last twenty-six at-bats. Leaving aside the ill-advised trade for
Cater, the decision to make Burda the everyday first baseman, however
briefly, might have been enough to cost the Red Sox the pennant.

1978 Boston Red Sox (Yankees)

See "The Ballad of Zim the Gerbil" (page 181).

Transcendental Graphics

Rodney Scott

1980 Montreal Expos (Phillies)

Would the Expos still be in Montreal if they'd enjoyed some postseason success? We'll never know, but certainly their chances would have been better. And they came so close, so many times . . .

In 1994, the Expos had the best record in the National League—and a huge lead over the second-place Braves—when the strike hit. In 1981, they won the second half of the split season in the National League East (by just a half-game), then lost a close Division Series by the thinnest of margins (to the Dodgers, who won the World Series). In 1980, they finished one game behind the Phillies (who won the World Series). In 1979, they finished two games behind the Pirates (who won the World Series).

The Expos were managed by Dick Williams, who in most respects was a better manager than half the guys in the Hall of Fame. Williams did, unfortunately, have one fatal weakness. In his memoirs, Williams wrote about his Expos, "Moving around the horn, the next important piece in our contending years' teams was second baseman Rodney Scott, one of my all-time favorites, whom we acquired from the Chicago Cubs mostly because he could do things like steal third base nine times in one season with the pitcher holding the ball."

That's great. Unfortunately, we don't have comprehensive information about stealing third base while the pitcher was holding the ball. We do have comprehensive information strongly suggesting that Rodney Scott was terribly miscast as an everyday player.

Year	Batted	Games	OBP	Slug	Runs
1979	2nd	151	.319	.294	69
1980	2nd	154	.307	.293	84
1981	2nd	95	.308	.250	43

So here you've got a player with (essentially) a .310 on-base percentage and absolutely no power, batting in the No. 2 slot for a contending team, season after season after season. The Expos might have won division titles in both '79 and '80 simply by moving Scott to the eighth spot in the order. And with all due respect to Scott (who probably doesn't deserve this abuse), the Expos *would* have won division titles in both seasons if only they'd had some semblance of a hitter at second base in those seasons. And in 1981, when they did reach the postseason? Scott started all five games against the Dodgers, reached base four times, and didn't score. So maybe it was three division titles that he—or rather, that Dick Williams—cost the franchise.

1980 Los Angeles Dodgers (Astros)

The Dodgers and Astros finished the season with ninety-two wins apiece, after the Dodgers swept a three-game set from the Astros on the season's last weekend. But the Astros won the one-game playoff for the pennant, and the Dodgers went home.

It's not hard to figure out why. Manager Tommy Lasorda had three catchers at his disposal, and the one who played the most was the one who did the least.

	Games	PA	OBP	Slug
Steve Yeager	96	248	.274	.273
Joe Ferguson	77	214	.371	.436
Mike Scioscia	54	152	.313	.328

A few points in defense of Lasorda: 1) Yeager wasn't usually (quite) this bad; 2) Ferguson wasn't usually (quite) this good, and 3) Scioscia was just a baby, didn't turn twenty-two until after the season.

Rebuttal: 1) Yeager had batted .193 in 1978 and .216 (albeit with some power) in 1979; 2) Ferguson was a good enough hitter that he'd played a couple of hundred games in the outfield, over the years, and 3) Scioscia was young, but the year before he'd batted .336 in the Pacific Coast League.

Yeager was a fine defensive player. But there's simply no way his skills behind the plate made him more "playable" than either Ferguson or Scioscia. And if those two had split time all season, the Dodgers would have won the division by three or four games.

1982 Los Angeles Dodgers (Braves)

Two years later, Scioscia was nominally the regular, backed up by Yeager, and Yeager actually hit better than Scioscia, who was awful (.219/.302/.296). But I can't exactly criticize Lasorda for playing Scioscia too much; it was just one of those fluky things.

The Dodgers would have been better if they'd given some of Steve Garvey's at-bats to rookie Mike Marshall—at twenty-two, already a better hitter than Garvey, who was thirty-three but played older—but considering Garvey's reputation (not to mention his salary), that simply wasn't going to happen.

Scioscia and Garvey were the only weak spots in the lineup. The Dodgers' top three starters—Jerry Reuss, Fernando Valenzuela, and Bob Welch—were all pretty good, as were their top relievers (actually, Steve Howe was fantastic). The bottom of the Dodger rotation wasn't real good, mostly because of Burt Hooton, who went 4–7 with a 4.03 ERA in twenty-one starts. But Hooton had pitched brilliantly in 1981 (11–6, 2.28), besides which he'd been an organizational mainstay since 1975.

I'm sure that somebody—the general manager, the manager, a parking-lot attendant—made a mistake in '82 that cost the Dodgers a game or two. But it's not obvious to me what that mistake might have been.

1982 Baltimore Orioles (Brewers)

This was the last season of Earl Weaver's first tenure, and most of the hitting production was supplied by Eddie Murray and Gary Roenicke/John Lowenstein, Weaver's super-platoon in left field. Oh, and a rookie named Ripken did some swell things.

Meanwhile, center fielder Al Bumbry (.262/.315/.338) and right fielder Dan Ford (.235/.281/.371) were both terrible drags on the lineup.

But both Ford and Bumbry had been productive enough in 1981, and anyway the Orioles didn't have replacements on hand for either of them (John Shelby was considered Bumbry's eventual successor in center field, but Shelby simply couldn't hit, as he would later prove in great detail).

But whose bright idea was it to let Glenn Gulliver step to the plate 185 times? Weaver loved Gulliver because Gulliver was a walks machine. In 1981, playing for Detroit's farm club in the American Association, Gulliver drew eighty-seven walks in 121 games. He showed some power, too. But the Tigers already had a third baseman. Not a *good* third baseman—it was Tom Brookens, who in his twelve-season career was not a league-average hitter even once—but he was theirs and they liked him. So shortly before Opening Day in 1982, the Tigers sold Glenn Gulliver to the Orioles, and Weaver used Gulliver at third base for most of the second half of the season, after Cal Ripken shifted from third to shortstop.

Gulliver did draw plenty of walks for Weaver—thirty-seven in only fifty games—but he also managed to bat just .200, with seven doubles and one homer. Gulliver's .363 on-base percentage played well in the No. 2 slot, but the rest of his stats just didn't merit an everyday job. On the other hand, Gulliver had earned his shot; before his promotion to the Orioles in mid-July, he'd batted .295 with a dozen homers (and *ninety* walks!) in half a season with triple-A Rochester.

It just didn't work out. But I can't find anything that Weaver did that I wouldn't have done, if all I knew was what he knew.

1985 California Angels (Royals)

Ah, the '85 Angels. I'll always love them because they didn't play quite well enough to finish ahead of my beloved Royals (and for those of you too young to remember, until 1994 the Angels and Royals both played in the American League West).

At the time, I paid very little attention to anything about the Angels, aside from the score of their latest game. Looking at them now, though, one thing is obvious: they were exceptionally fortunate to come as close to the Royals as they did. Yes, the Angels were a pretty good team; they'd prove that in '86 by very nearly reaching the World Series. But in 1985 the Angels were 30–13 in one-run games, and of course that was due mostly to luck (in '86, they would go 27–16, also an outstanding figure). So it's easier to find reasons the Angels should have lost than to find reasons they should have won. And looking at the roster, composed mostly of players on the wrong side of thirty and a pretty lousy bench, it's hard to find much that Gene Mauch might have done better.

1988 Detroit Tigers (Red Sox)

Like the '85 Angels, the '88 Tigers were lucky to be anywhere near first place. They outscored their opponents by forty-five runs; the Red Sox outscored theirs by 124 runs. In fact, the Tigers' run differential was just fourth-best in the division (worse than that of the Blue Jays and Brewers, too).

Still, with all that luck the Tigers really could have finished ahead of the Red Sox. And if they hadn't populated the roster with the desiccated corpses of so many once-good players, they might have. Among those playing key roles: Darrell Evans (age 41), who batted .208; Tom Brookens (34), who was his typical uninspiring self; Gary Pettis (30), who did his usual solid job in center field while posting sub-.300 on-base and slugging percentages; Larry Herndon (34), who'd enjoyed a fine comeback (in a part-time role) in '87 but slumped terribly in '88, his final season; Ray Knight (35), in the process of finishing off *his* career; Fred Lynn (36), who came to the Tigers in a late-August trade—apparently the roster wasn't *quite* old enough yet—and batted .222 in twenty-seven games.

I've stacked the deck here, of course. Some of Detroit's other oldsters played well enough, particularly longtime Tigers Chet Lemon and Dave Bergman. But this was an old team, and if not for Trammell and Whitaker they'd have finished fifth.

You can't really blame manager Sparky Anderson, though. He was stuck with what he had, and there certainly wasn't any help from within the organization. The Tigers' top farm club, the Toledo Mud Hens, finished with the worst record in the International League, and there literally was not a single Mud Hen with performance that merited promotion.

If there's anybody to blame, it was management. The Tigers had edged the Blue Jays for the division title in 1987, and in the following off-season the only significant move the Tigers made was a non-move: they didn't make a real effort to retain free agent Kirk Gibson (who led the Dodgers to the World Series in '88). Nor did they make any effort to get younger. Or better.

1991 Los Angeles Dodgers (Braves)

The Dodgers' pitching was fantastic; they led the league in ERA by a wide margin, and would have done that even if Dodger Stadium were a neutral ballpark. Four pitchers started more than thirty games, and all four were good (Ramon Martinez, Bob Ojeda) or great (Tim Belcher, Mike Morgan). As usual, Tom Lasorda didn't give all the saves to one pitcher, and got good work from half a dozen relievers.

The hitters were pretty good, too. Eddie Murray was something of a disappointment, but just the season before he'd been the second-best hitter in the league, so you could hardly begrudge him his 156 games.

The real problem was the utter lack of production the Dodgers got from shortstop Alfredo Griffin, who batted .243/.286/.271 in 109 games. We might cut the Dodgers some slack, except they had to have known *exactly* what they were getting with Griffin. He'd been their shortstop since 1988, and in his first three seasons his OBP's had been well below .300. Those 1991 numbers represented *exactly* the hitter that Griffin was at that point in his career (when younger, he'd showed a tad more power, if not patience).

Sometimes the Dodgers let twenty-two-year-old Jose Offerman play shortstop, and in 113 at-bats he batted .195 with two extra-base hits (doubles, both). What should the Dodgers have done? First, general manager Fred Claire shouldn't have traded for Griffin after the '87 season. Second, Claire shouldn't have signed him to a lucrative three-year contract after the '88 season. And third, once Claire realized how bad he was—Claire did realize this, didn't he?—the Dodgers should have replaced Griffin with somebody who could get on base more than twice a week.

1993 San Francisco Giants (Braves)

I call this one The Last Great Pennant Race, by which I mean the last meaningful pennant race between two great teams.

The Braves won 104 games and the Giants won 103, and in every season since then, if two teams in the same division won that many games, both would earn tickets to the World Series Derby, the "loser" grabbing the Wild Card slot. Not in 1993, though. In 1993, the Braves were still in the National League "West" and "Wild Card" was still something they had only in the football league.

On the morning of August 23, the Giants owned a seven-and-one-half-games lead over the Braves. But then the Giants started losing while the Braves kept winning. After the Giants lost their eighth straight on September 15, they were actually three-and-a-half games out of first place; they'd dropped ten games in the standings in little more than three weeks.

But then, like so many other teams that have blown big leads, the Giants fought their way back into the race, winning fourteen of their next sixteen games. Over that same span, the Braves won ten of fifteen, leaving the two clubs tied with one day left in the season. The Braves finished at home. Against the Rockies. With Glavine on the mound. It was generally assumed they would win. The Giants finished on the road. Against the Dodgers. And they didn't have Tom Glavine.

Who did they have? The Giants' best starters that season were Bill Swift and John Burkett, but they'd already beaten the Dodgers in the first two games of the (four-game) series. Trevor Wilson and Bud Black were pretty good, but both were injured. By the end of the season, there were so many injuries that the Giants were using a four-man rotation: Swift, Burkett, Bryan Hickerson, and rookie Salomon Torres. Hickerson had started (and been quickly knocked out of) Saturday's victory. So it would be Torres starting the Giants' biggest regular-season game since 1962.*

It didn't go well. In Atlanta, Glavine and his mates beat the Rockies, 5–3. That game ended just a few minutes before the game in Los Angeles began; the Giants knew if they lost, their season was over. Which it was, and quickly. Torres didn't escape the fourth inning, and after five the Giants trailed 5–1. Manager Dusty Baker's decision to start Torres was essentially irrelevant, though, as Dodger starter Kevin Gross gave up just one run while pitching a complete game.

No, if I've got a beef with Baker, it's for wasting 572 plate appearances on Darren Lewis, who played center field with great skill but was easily the worst hitter in the lineup, and one of the worst-hitting regulars in the league. On the other hand, Baker's only viable alternative was Dave Martinez, and in 1994, Lewis actually out hit Martinez. I just think the Giants would have been slightly better off—remember, they won 103 games anyway—if Baker had, instead of falling in love with Darren Lewis, merely fallen in like.

1995 California Angels (Mariners)

As you probably remember, the Angels sported an eleven-game lead in the middle of August, then suffered *two* nine-game losing streaks and were three games out of the lead in late September. But then they won five straight to

---

* According to one ex-Giant to whom I spoke, the players' choice was Dave Burba, a young reliever with a 5.32 ERA in his five starts that season.

finish the schedule in a tie before losing to the M's in a one-game playoff for the West title.

The Angels obviously could have won, and probably would have if shortstop Gary DiSarcina hadn't missed the last two months with a thumb injury.

But the Angels' collapse cannot be blamed solely on bad luck.

For example, catcher Jorge Fabregas absolutely killed the Angels. Actually, the Angels used essentially three catchers in '95, and two of them were just terrible.

	Games	PA	OBP	Slug
Greg Myers	85	294	.304	.418
Jorge Fabregas	73	248	.298	.304
Andy Allanson	35	91	.244	.317

Or how about the Angels' second basemen?

	Games	PA	OBP	Slug
Damion Easley	114	405	.288	.300
Rex Hudler	84	241	.310	.417

And in case you're wondering, these were not platoons. Fabregas and Myers both batted lefty. Easley and Hudler both batted righty. Myers did spend roughly six weeks on the disabled list (spread among three different stints), but Hudler was active all season. Both should have played more than they did.

And then there's Mitch Williams. Shortly after he gave up the World Series–ending home run in 1993, the Phillies traded him to the Astros. In 1994, Williams went 1–4 with a 7.65 ERA, walking twenty-four batters in twenty-one innings.

So whose bright idea in Anaheim was it to sign Williams as a free agent? Predictably enough, in eleven innings he walked twenty-one batters, lost two of his three decisions, and drew his release in June.

The man who didn't play Myers or Hudler enough was manager Marcel Lachemann. The man who signed Mitch Williams was general manager Bill Bavasi (who, as g.m. of the Mariners ten years later, signed Adrian Beltre, which might be fodder for some future version of this book).

2000 Cleveland Indians (Mariners)

The M's finished a half-game behind the A's in the West, and the Indians finished a whole game behind the M's in the Wild Card standings. The A's played only 161 games, because if they'd played No. 162 and lost it, the result would have been a tie for the West title and the Indians still would have been left out. On the other hand, if the Indians had won just one more game, the A's would have been forced to play one more, and if they'd lost there would have been a three-way tie for two postseason berths (there was a similar situation in play in 2005, with the Yankees, Red Sox, and Indians). And if the A's had won, the Indians and M's would have played for the wild card.

Which is a long-winded way of saying that if the Indians had won ninety-one games rather than ninety, they'd have been very much alive in the postseason derby. And when trying to figure out why they didn't win ninety-one, the glaring reason is a quartet of starting pitchers who started eleven games apiece and combined for a 6.69 ERA (at 3–3 and 5.67, Steve Woodard was the *best* of them). But you know what? All those guys should have pitched better than they did, and if only one of them had been just decent, the Indians would have been fine.

No, I think the real problem here is outfielder Jolbert Cabrera, who somehow wangled nearly 200 plate appearances. That might have been all right if he'd been playing Gold Glove–quality defense in center field. But in addition to starting twenty-one games in center—Kenny Lofton spent some time on the DL—Cabrera also started four games in left, four in right, four at second base, and two at shortstop. He just played too much, and nobody in Cleveland should have been surprised when he put up a .290 on-base percentage and a .314 slugging percentage, because those numbers are exactly what his minor-league performance suggested.

2003 Houston Astros (Cubs)

Tough darts for the Astros, whose run differential (+128) was significantly better than the Cubs' (+41). These sorts of things do happen, though, which is why you can't just sit around and assume that you'll win because, dagnabit, you really are better.

Maybe it was arrogance, then, that led management to sit on its collective hands during June and July and August, when trades could have been made. In all those months, the Astros made exactly one notable move: in late July, they acquired reliever Dan Miceli from the Yankees (and Miceli, who'd already pitched for three teams that season, gave the Astros thirty good innings). Nothing was done to bolster a terribly ineffectual bench, and Brad Ausmus was permitted to continue making oodles of outs in his merry way.

The players didn't lose this one; the front office did.

2004 Oakland Athletics (Angels)

Eric Karros came cheap: only one million dollars (and if the rumors were true, a wealthy friend of Karros's subsidized his salary). Then again, while he might not have cost the A's much money, he did cost them a great deal of production: in 103 at-bats, Karros batted .194 before finally drawing his release in early August. Meanwhile, Dan Johnson—like Karros, a right-handed-hitting first baseman—was down in Sacramento, terrorizing Pacific Coast League pitchers all summer long. Granted, Johnson was not considered a Grade A prospect. But in 2005 we saw what Johnson could do when given a chance. And if he'd been promoted to the big club in the middle of 2004—he never was promoted, not even in September—the A's would most likely have won another game or two, and finished ahead of the Angels.

2005 Philadelphia Phillies (Astros)

Don't get me started . . . oh, all right. The Phillies failed to make the postseason—they finished one game behind the Astros in the Wild Card race—because of one big mistake they made in 2005, and one big mistake they'd made a few years earlier.

In 2005, they wasted 242 plate appearances on Jim Thome, who batted .207 before he finally—mercifully—landed on the DL with a back injury. Finally, they were forced to give Ryan Howard a shot, and he earned Rookie of the Year honors despite playing in only eighty-eight games.

A few years earlier, they'd signed third baseman David Bell to a long-term contract, which eventually had the unique effect of, one way or the other, keeping both Chase Utley and Placido Polanco out of the lineup. For a while, Utley remained in the minors so Bell and Polanco could play; then in 2005, Polanco was traded so Bell and Utley could play. And *after* the Phillies traded him—but before they finished one game out of the playoffs—Polanco batted .338 in eighty-six games with the Tigers.

---

1. Dick Williams and Bill Plaschke, *No More Mr. Nice Guy* (San Diego: Harcourt Brace Jovanovich, 1990).

BAGWELL FOR ANDERSEN

You never know exactly how good a young player will be, but with some luck (for Bagwell) Lou Gorman will hear about the Bagwell trade until the day he dies. It could be one of those deals, like Lou Brock for Ernie Broglio, Nolan Ryan for Jim Fregosi and Frank Robinson for Milt Pappas, that haunts the man who made it.

—Bill James, *The Baseball Book 1991*

On August 30, 1990, with the Boston Red Sox holding a six-and-a-half game lead over the second-place Blue Jays in the American League East, Red Sox general manager Lou Gorman traded minor-league first baseman Jeff Bagwell to the Houston Astros for relief pitcher Larry Andersen. Andersen pitched twenty-two innings for the Red Sox. Bagwell went to the Hall of Fame for the Astros.

In Gorman's autobiography, he offers a spirited defense of the trade. For one thing, "reports indicated that Bagwell would have to move from third base to first base, because his basic fielding skills were not suited for playing third base." Also, "none of the reports projected that he would have above-average major league power." And finally, "We could not . . . hold onto our lead in the division unless I could find a way to strengthen our bullpen."

I called Bob Watson and made the trade, Bagwell for Andersen. Andersen would strengthen our bullpen and help us win the Eastern Division title, and we'd go on to face the A's. Andersen worked mostly as a setup man, pitching in 22 innings, walking only three and striking out 25 with a 1.23 ERA. He was exactly what we needed to bolster the pen at a critical juncture in our run at the division title.[1]

Uh, okay. Remember, the Red Sox owned a six-and-a-half-game lead when Gorman got Andersen. I don't care how well you pitch—and Andersen did pitch well—it's very difficult for a relief pitcher to make a real difference to a team with a big lead and just one month to play. True, the Red Sox wound up winning the division by just two games; they *could* have blown it.

But they didn't *not* blow it because of Andersen. After the trade, the Red Sox won eight games by three or fewer runs. In four of those games, Andersen did not pitch. In two of them, he pitched both briefly and ineffectively. So the case for Andersen's difference-making really comes down to two games. On September 7, he pitched three innings of scoreless relief in a game the Red Sox eventually won with a run in the bottom of the eleventh. And on September 21, he earned a save—his first and last with the Red Sox—with two scoreless innings in a 3–0 game.

The Red Sox wound up getting just one month of Larry Andersen in exchange for Jeff Bagwell's career, but that's not what Gorman expected.

> There were some questions about whether Andersen would become a free agent as a result of the collusion ruling against baseball ownership. There were supposedly twelve or thirteen players who could be declared free agents as a result of some legalities resulting from the original collusion case. I called our player relations committee in the commissioner's office in New York to determine Andersen's status. The committee indicated to me that they were certain that Andersen would not be one of those players given his free agency. I was confident therefore, that if we traded for him, we'd have him in our bullpen for the foreseeable future.[2]

Okay, fair enough; Gorman got some bad information from the boys in New York. (Considering that Andersen would soon turn thirty-eight, it's not clear what Gorman means by "foreseeable future," but we'll let that one slide.)

Even if we assume that Bagwell couldn't have played third base in the majors, though, there's this thing in the American League called "Designated Hitter." Let's assume for the moment that if Bagwell hadn't been traded, he'd have spent most of 1991 tearing up the International League. The Red Sox would have retained his rights from 1992 through 1997. In each of those seasons the Sox had Mo Vaughn—a lousy fielder, by the way—at first base, while the DH slot was held by Jack Clark, Andre Dawson, Jose Canseco, and Reggie Jefferson. Canseco was pretty good, but Bagwell was just as good and would have been a lot cheaper. (Clark, Dawson, and Jefferson were not pretty good.)

And I haven't even mentioned the corner outfield slots; Bagwell was an athletic sort of fellow, and probably could have done all right in right or (especially) left field. Considering that Bob Zupcic and Lee Tinsley got plenty of playing time in this period, I suspect the skipper could have found a spot in the lineup for the .400 OBP guy with power.

The real problem with Gorman's defense—which runs for more than three pages—is that he tries to fool the jury into thinking that the choice was Bagwell for Andersen or nothing.

According to Garry Brown in the *Springfield Republican*, "The Astros asked for Mo Vaughn. They asked for Scott Cooper. Phil Plantier. Kevin Morton. David Owen. Gorman held his ground. He said no to every name until Jeff Bagwell's came up."

Cooper was slated to eventually replace Wade Boggs at third base. Phil Plantier batted .300 with twenty-seven home runs in the Carolina League that summer. Kevin Morton and David Owen were solid pitching prospects.

Morton was the twenty-ninth player taken in the 1989 draft. That summer he'd blown through three levels of the Red Sox farm system, then spent 1990 with Bagwell in New Britain. Thirty pitchers qualified for the Eastern League ERA title that season. Morton's was twenty-fifth. On the other hand, he was barely twenty-two and his 131 strikeouts were good for second in the league. Dave Owen, a seventh-round draft pick in 1988, also spent most of the 1990 season with New Britain, and went 7–9 with a 2.93 ERA. Like Morton, he certainly qualified as a prospect.

But these guys were *pitchers*. Didn't Gorman know *there's no such thing as a pitching prospect? TNSTAAPP. Tinztap.*

More to the point, did Gorman have any idea how good Bagwell was? Could Gorman possibly have guessed that Jeff Bagwell would someday become a fantastic player? Yes, he could have.

In the *STATS 1991 Major League Handbook*—published shortly after the 1990 season—Bill James published projections for 413 major-league hitters. Among the National Leaguers, Tony Gwynn's .317 was the highest projected batting average. But there was another set of projections: fifteen minor-leaguers included under the heading, "These Guys Can Play Too And Might Get A Shot." And among those fifteen minor leaguers was Jeff Bagwell, with a .318 batting average. Better than Tony Gwynn's.

Nobody meant to predict that Bagwell would win a batting title in 1991, and if Bill had noticed, he would have knocked Bagwell down a few points, just to avoid the *appearance* of such a prediction. But the underlying *causes* of the nonprediction were simple: the Eastern League was a pitcher's league, and New Britain's Willow Brook Park was a pitcher's ballpark. Bagwell was twenty-two in 1990, and he'd batted .333 with thirty-four doubles (tops in the league) and seventy-three walks (fourth in the league).

Gorman simply didn't know how good Bagwell was. Near the end of spring training in 1991, with Bagwell having won the job as Houston's regu-

Two Stars for an Old Man?

Does Curt Schilling and Brady Anderson for Mike Boddicker sound like a good deal to you? It did to Lou Gorman, who sent Schilling and Anderson to the Orioles for Boddicker on July 29, 1988. In terms of career value, it has to rank as one of the worst trades of the era. After the deal, Boddicker earned 51 Win Shares; Anderson, 212 Win Shares; and Schilling, 228 Win Shares (not to mention the postseason heroics).

Nevertheless, it *was* a good deal for Gorman and the Red Sox. Schilling, who by his own admission didn't really know what the hell he was doing early in his career, didn't become a good major-leaguer until 1992. Likewise, Brady Anderson struggled terribly for the Orioles until 1992, when seemingly overnight he turned into a good hitter. Prior to '92, in three-and-a-half seasons with the O's he'd batted .218 and slugged .307. In retrospect, the Orioles were amazingly patient with Anderson. But he wasn't even decent until his fifth major-league season.

And Boddicker? After joining the Red Sox in 1988, he went 7–3 with a 2.63 ERA, and the Red Sox won the American League East by a single game over the Tigers (and two other clubs finished only two off the pace). In 1990, he went 17–8 with a 3.36 ERA, and the Red Sox won the American League East by two games over the Blue Jays. The trade for Boddicker worked *exactly* as trades like that are supposed to work.

lar first baseman, Gorman said he would be "greatly astonished" if Bagwell hit .300 in the majors.[3] He just didn't know.

In 1997, Kevin Morton pitched professionally for the last time, going 2–1 with a 6.84 ERA for the Mexico City Tigers. He retired with a winning record (6–5) in the major leagues, but a losing record (34–57) in the minor leagues. Also in 1997, Jeff Bagwell played in 162 games for the Astros, scored 109 runs, drove home 135, and finished third in the Most Valuable Player voting.

1. Lou Gorman, *One Pitch from Glory: A Decade of Running the Red Sox* (Champaign, Ill.: Sports Publishing, 2005).

2. Ibid.

3. Phil O'Neil, *Worcester Telegram & Gazette*, Oct. 31, 1991.

RUNNELLS SHIFTS WALLACH

With Dan Duquette in place as the new general manager for 1992, the players had a more sympathetic ear for their complaints against Runnells. One particularly criticized move was the manager's insistence that the veteran Tim Wallach, a Gold Glove winner and one of the most popular players in the history of the franchise, switch from third base to first base.
—Donald Dewey and Nicholas Acocella, *Total Ballclubs* (2005)

People remember three things about Expos manager Tom Runnells: 1) he switched Tim Wallach to first base, 2) he was an idiot for switching Wallach to first base, and 2) he got fired for switching Wallach to first base.

Runnells probably didn't have a long and happy future as a manager, but it didn't have much to do with Tim Wallach.

Tom Runnels took over as manager of the Expos in early June 1991, replacing the popular Buck Rodgers. The Expos went 51–61 under Runnels the rest of the way, and played their last twenty-six games on the road after a concrete beam fell off Olympic Stadium.

Runnels fancied himself as the stern disciplinarian, just what the doctor ordered for these spoiled kids making the big coin. As owner Claude Brochu later wrote, "With the players, it was a disaster. Runnells' arrival at spring training dressed in military garb and driving an army jeep, to impress his charges and show them who was boss, was hardly a stroke of genius. The players didn't find it the least bit funny."[1]

Runnels had another problem: he had a young player who'd earned a job but didn't have a position.

Bret Barberie was a hot prospect coming out of high school, but spurned a professional contract and went to USC. The Expos drafted him in 1988, in the seventh round, and he blew through the minors in two-and-a-half seasons. He debuted in the majors on June 16, 1991—two weeks into Runnells's tenure—was sent back to the minors a month later, returned in early August . . . and batted .371 over the last two months of the season. Clearly, Barberie belonged in the lineup in 1992.

But Barberie's best position was second base, and the Expos had Delino DeShields at second base. Barberie had played some shortstop, but he really didn't have the range for shortstop. The Expos had Tim

Jumping the Gun

When the Expos traded Delino DeShields to the Dodgers and received Pedro Martinez, shortly after the 1993 season, the local writers pitched a collective fit. In Claude Brochu's book, he catalogued the outrage.

- "Deal is rotten to the core. Expos' one big deal to balance books will sicken fans."
- "There's no puzzle why the Expos made the deal. Too many decisions are made to balance the books."
- "For a matter of money, the Expos sacrifice Delino DeShields and obtained Pedro Martinez."
- "Trading Delino DeShields to the Los Angeles Dodgers shows, once again, that the Expo executives are thinking only about reducing their payroll."
- "So begins the fire sale; where will it end?"

Five writers, five identical reactions, all of them (as things turned out) misguided. Martinez pitched well (11–5, 3.42) in 1994, the Expos owned a six-game lead over the Braves in mid-August . . . and if the players hadn't chosen that moment to strike, the Expos might still be in Montreal. DeShields? He had a few more good seasons. Martinez? He'll be in the Hall of Fame someday. Later, with the Red Sox, Dan Duquette would take a lot of heat for letting Roger Clemens get away; for signing Manny Ramirez to a megadeal; for any number of other foolish moves. But as long as people are singing the Ballad of the Duke, there should be room for DeShields-for-Martinez.

Wallach at third base. And you don't take a kid who's 5'11" and 180 pounds and put him at first base unless you don't have a choice (oh, and the Expos had Larry Walker, Marquis Grissom, and Moises Alou in the outfield).

But Wallach was ten years older than Barberie, and was coming off a season in which he batted .225/.292/.334. True, he'd been outstanding in 1990, batting .296 with twenty home runs and winning a Gold Glove. But Wallach was thirty-three and it certainly looked like his good years were mostly (and perhaps completely) behind him.

So Runnells—presumably with the approval of general manager Dan Duquette—did the smart thing: he shifted Wallach to first base and handed third base to Barberie, who looked like he'd become a solid major-league regular and quite possibly a star.

It just didn't work. Barberie batted .229 in April; Wallach, .224.

Was that Runnells' fault? Hardly.

Runnells got fired because he lost control of the team. According to Montreal baseball writer Jeff Blair, the low point of the Expos' 1992 season came in a game the Expos actually won: "Seldom has a winning team looked as dispirited as Montreal did following a 6–5 comeback victory over the Reds on May 20. Most of the 9,651 fans left in the middle of a five-run Cincinnati seventh, booing Manager Tom Runnells and chanting for his firing. Two days later, Runnells was fired."[2]

It was a comeback *victory* and as thrilling as they get, with the Expos scoring four runs in the bottom of the ninth. But with nobody in the ballpark to see it, Runnells's demise was probably inevitable (and it probably didn't help that he'd been hired by Duquette's predecessor, Dave Dombrowski).

Runnells got fired because a) his players didn't much like him, 2) nobody else liked him much, either, and iii) there was some real talent on the roster but the team wasn't winning. When Runnells got canned, the Expos were 17–20. Under new manager Felipe Alou, they went 70–55 and finished in second place—but both Wallach and Barberie struggled all season long. After the season, the Expos foisted Wallach off on the Dodgers, and Barberie never really did pan out.

---

1. Claude R. Brochu, *My Turn at Bat: The Sad Saga of the Expos* (Toronto: ECW Press, 1992).

2. *The Sporting News Baseball Guide: 1993 Edition* (St. Louis: Sporting News, 1993).

THE BUCK STAYS THERE

One man gathers what another man spills.

—"St. Stephen," The Grateful Dead

On June 16, 1995, the St. Louis Cardinals fired Joe Torre, their manager. So on October 8, an unemployed Torre sat in his Cincinnati home and watched Buck Showalter manage the Yankees in Game 5 of their Division Series against the Mariners. And as Torre said in 2005, "Little did I know that game was going to impact my situation."[1]

Whatever Torre was thinking—*Should I revise my resume? Is ESPN happy with Joe Morgan? Hey, what's for dinner?*—when the Mariners came to bat in the bottom of the eighth inning, trailing 4–2, he certainly could not have imagined that Showalter's imminent miscues would (in a roundabout sort of way) punch his own ticket to Cooperstown.

Yankee starter David Cone was visibly fatigued. He'd already thrown 119 pitches in seven innings, and had tossed eight innings five days earlier in the Yankees' Game 1 victory. Due up for the Mariners were Joey Cora (who had homered earlier), Ken Griffey (who had hit four home runs in the series, including two long shots off Cone in Game 1), and Edgar Martinez (who at that point was four for six against Cone in the series, including a double two innings earlier).

The Yankees—only two innings away from their first ALCS since 1981—had both their closer, John Wetteland, and a rookie setup man named Mariano Rivera available in the bullpen. Although Wetteland had pitched poorly in two of his three appearances in the series, he'd been excellent during the regular season: thirty-one saves, 2.93 ERA, and nearly ten strikeouts per nine innings. Rivera, who'd struggled in ten starts but fared better after shifting to the bullpen, had dominated the Mariners in his two Division Series outings, striking out seven men and allowing only two hits in four-and-two-thirds scoreless innings.

And yet there was Cone, trotting out of the dugout to pitch the eighth. Perhaps the Yankees'

"What, Me Regret?"

Showalter's bullpen bungling has all the hallmarks of the quintessential blunder: not only was the disaster eminently predictable (and thus preventable), but events actually unfolded precisely as one would have expected them to under the circumstances. To compound his mistake, even after the fact Showalter refused to admit the obvious. "That's his game," Showalter said. "David Cone is one of those people you trust and one of the people who got us there. He deserves the chance there to finish it."[2]

Likewise, Cone would not second-guess himself for throwing a full-count forkball to Doug Strange with a tired arm and the tying run on third. "I'd thrown a hundred and forty-six pitches in the game up to that point, and I had nothing left, but I was still sure that was the right call."[3] Indeed, according to the notoriously competitive Cone, he would have kept pitching even beyond the eighth inning; "I'd have thrown *two* hundred and forty-seven to win that game," he insisted.[4] Judging from how Showalter managed the game, Cone should be glad he wasn't asked to do exactly that.—*D.M.*

bullpen phone was broken. Perhaps Showalter was playing a hunch. Whatever the reason, Showalter sent Cone to the mound . . . *without bothering to warm up Rivera or Wetteland.* As Joey Cora stepped to the plate, Randy Johnson—the Mariners' Game 3 starter (and winner)—began to loosen up in Seattle's bullpen, thus raising both the volume in the Kingdome and the stakes for Showalter's gambit.

Cora flew out to right on Cone's 124th pitch of the night, bringing Griffey to bat. With Cone's 126th pitch, exactly one-half of the Yankees' lead soared over the right-field wall. As unfazed as Nero, Showalter stuck with his ace—*still* refusing to warm up a reliever—and was rewarded when Cone needed only one pitch to retire Edgar Martinez on a ground ball.

Four outs to go.

Cone, with his 132nd pitch, walked Tino Martinez.

Next up: right-handed-hitting Jay Buhner, who'd hit forty home runs that season. Had Showalter had Rivera getting loose at the start of the inning, or even after Griffey's loud wake-up call, he'd have been ready to face Buhner. Now, though, the best that Showalter could do was finally order Rivera to commence warming up . . . and then watch as Buhner singled to center.

Cone, with his 141st pitch, walked pinch-hitter Alex Diaz (who'd posted a .286 on-base percentage during the season). Cone had now walked two of the last three batters after previously going the entire game without a walk. It was a desperate cry for help.

Showalter wasn't listening. Surveying the field, he saw, or should have seen, 1) the bases loaded with Mariners, 2) pinch-hitter Doug Strange at the plate, 3) Randy Johnson ready to pitch the ninth inning, and 4) an exhausted David Cone on the mound. On the other hand, the Yankees needed only one out to escape the inning with the lead, and Rivera was ready to pitch.

The skipper didn't budge.

Letting Cone face Tino Martinez had been questionable. Letting Cone face Buhner and Diaz had been foolhardy. Staying with Cone after 141 pitches, instead of bringing in Rivera to face Doug Strange . . . well, that was just . . . *odd.*

Doug Strange had walked ten times all season.

Cone, with his 147th pitch, walked Doug Strange.

Doug Strange trotted to first base. Alex Rodriguez trotted home to tie the game. The Kingdome exploded. David Cone slumped, hands on his knees. And Buck Showalter finally (*finally*) summoned Mariano Rivera from the bullpen. Rivera's subsequent performance only underscored Showalter's folly, as he blew Mike Blowers away on three pitches.

The Yankees lost in the eleventh; a few weeks later, Showalter turned down George Steinbrenner's final contract offer . . . the same offer accepted, shortly thereafter, by Joe Torre. Over the next ten seasons, managing the squad that Showalter had helped build, Torre won nine division titles, six American League pennants, and four World Series. And he couldn't have done it without his abiding faith in the same two men that Showalter ignored that night in Seattle. In 1996, John Wetteland saved all four of the Yankees' World Series wins, and Rivera eventually would establish himself as the greatest postseason reliever in baseball history.

Someday Joe Torre's going to be in Cooperstown, giving his Hall of Fame acceptance speech. And when he's thanking all the people who helped him get there, he should be sure and leave some room for Buck Showalter.

—*David Mlodinoff*

1. Joe Torre interviewed by Alan Schwarz, September 2005.

2. Jack Curry "Showalter Is Still Dwelling on the Past, Not His Future," *New York Times*, Oct. 11, 1995, p. B9.

3. Roger Angell, *A Pitcher's Story: Innings with David Cone* (New York: Warner Books, 2001), p. 12.

4. Ibid., p. 54.

DEVIL RAYS SET THE TONE

We couldn't be more pleased with the way the expansion draft went. We think we have a great combination of young players and experienced players. We're going to try to be as competitive as we can, as quick as we can, and never lose sight of our long-term goals.

—Chuck LaMar[1]

News Item—November 8, 1997: With the fifth pick in the 1997 Expansion Draft, the Tampa Bay Devil Rays select Astros outfielder Bob Abreu. Moments later, the Devil Rays trade Abreu to the Philadelphia Phillies for shortstop Kevin Stocker.

In his *1997 Minor League Scouting Notebook,* my friend John Sickels rated Bob Abreu the twenty-third-best prospect in professional baseball, right between Chad Hermansen (who was a bust) and Mike Cameron (you know about him, probably). In his comment about Abreu, Sickels wrote, "He will strike out and be prone to slumps, but should have a productive career, with some star-quality seasons."

Yeah. Some.

But I'm not trying to rip John. Looking at Abreu's age and his minor-league track record, there was little reason to think he'd become the player he became. I'm just trying to put his career into context.

Anyway, that season the star-quality train was de-

railed. Abreu opened the season in right field, didn't hit much, and in late May he suffered a broken hamate bone in his right hand. Abreu returned to active duty in July, but was sent to New Orleans soon afterward and didn't hit there, either.

So when the Astros had to come up with a list of fifteen players to protect during the first round of the expansion draft that November, Abreu was not on the list.

The Devil Rays led off the draft, followed by the Diamondbacks, and here's how the first four picks went:

T.B.—Tony Saunders, lhp (Florida)
Ariz.—Brian Anderson, lhp (Cleveland)
T.B.—Quinton McCracken, of (Colorado)
Ariz.—Jeff Suppan, rhp (Boston)

Based on what we know now, you'd have to say, advantage Diamondbacks. Until, that is, the next pick, when the Devil Rays selected Bob Kelly Abreu, who would wind up putting together the greatest post-expansion draft career in the history of expansion drafts.

Some significant portion of that career would not come with the Devil Rays, though. Prior to the draft, the Rays already had made a tentative deal with the Phillies: they would draft Abreu, and immediately trade him to Philadelphia for Kevin Stocker, a twenty-seven-year-old shortstop who'd put up decent numbers in his five-year career.

Could Devil Rays general manager Chuck LaMar have guessed that Stocker would go in the tank immediately after joining the new franchise, batting .208 in 112 games? Hardly. Could LaMar have guessed that Abreu would quickly become one of the top right fielders in the major leagues? No, not really. But should he have known that Abreu might become a star and Stocker almost certainly would not? Should he have known that it's almost impossible to win without stars? Yes, and yes. On what was essentially the first meaningful day in franchise history, LaMar made a terrible decision that served as an ill omen for what would follow . . .

News Item—May 7, 1999: Devil Rays lead Indians 10–2 in the sixth inning but wind up losing, 20–11.

News Item—March 29, 2004: Devil Rays owner Vince Naimoli says, upon getting general manager Chuck LaMar's signature on a contract extension that will pay him through 2006, "I'm very pleased. We've always had a plan here to build a championship club and Chuck LaMar has been our chief architect."

News Item—June 21, 2005: Devil Rays lead Yankees 10–2 in the fifth inning, but wind up losing, 20–11.

News Item—July 17, 2005: Chuck LaMar tells the *St. Petersburg Times*, "There's no question I'm a better GM than when I took this job, and I think we're a better organization. People are tired of losing, and I understand that. I've been the GM the whole time, and we're tired of losing. Everyone's tired of hearing my rhetoric about what's going to happen in the future, and I understand that completely. I wish I had some of the decisions we made early in those 10 years back. But you can't. You just hope you learn from them and go on. We think we have . . . We don't need to go into a lot of detail over what a struggle the last five [years] have been. But I believe as strongly now as I ever have that there will be a winning team in Tampa Bay in the future."

The One That Got Away (Twice)

Why didn't the Astros protect Bobby Abreu in the Expansion Draft? According to *The Sporting News*, "G.M. Gerry Hunsicker soured on Abreu and when Derek Bell returned to right field after opening the season in center, there was no position for Abreu."

In 1998 and '99, the Astros paid Derek Bell nearly nine million dollars, and in return he gave them 284 games and twenty-six Win Shares. In those same two seasons, the Phillies paid Bobby Abreu nearly $600,000, and in return he gave them fifty-two Win Shares.

The Astros traded Bell after his horrible '99 season, and even without Abreu they featured an outstanding outfield over the next couple of seasons. But that's only because they spent a lot of money to sign free agent Moises Alou; if they'd kept Abreu, they'd have had an outfield that was both outstanding *and* exceptionally cheap: Abreu, Richard Hidalgo, and Lance Berkman. And of course the money spent on Alou could have been used elsewhere.

It's fair to castigate the Devil Rays for trading Bobby Abreu before he'd played a game for them. But it's just as fair to nail the Astros for giving Abreu away in the first place.

News Item—October 6, 2005: Charles Steinberg takes over from Vince Naimoli as principal owner of the Tampa Bay Devil Rays. Steinberg's first order of business: fire Chuck LaMar. Lamar's parting words: "The only thing that kept this organization from being recognized as one of the finest in baseball is wins and losses at the major league level."

1. Bill Koenig, "Deals Help Devil Rays Grow Up," *USA Today Baseball Weekly*, Nov. 20–25, 1997.

ROCKIES THROW MONEY AT PROBLEM (LOTS OF MONEY)

Dan O'Dowd might tell you his job is like designing and building an expensive airliner, then piloting it with a remote control.

. . . Guiding the most active front office in the majors, O'Dowd made some redirections during the 2000 season. He completed seven more trades, touching 22 players . . . Trades, though, might not prove to be O'Dowd's most important moves. This past December, free agency secured reservations from two solid passengers: pitchers Mike Hampton and Denny Neagle. And it's no accident that two of the market's top three pitchers chose to sign with a GM who has an office at Coors Field.

Colorado Rockies Information Guide, 2001

On December 4, 2000, the Colorado Rockies agreed to pay $51 million for five seasons of Denny Neagle's services. Five days later, they upped the ante by signing Mike Hampton for eight seasons . . . and *$121 million.* Just two years before Hampton inked his deal, the Red Sox signed Pedro Martinez to a seven-year, $90 million contract. Martinez was twenty-six and had just won the Cy Young Award. Hampton was twenty-eight when he got his deal, and not Pedro Martinez.

Now, we might wonder why a young and fairly successful pitcher like Mike Hampton would want to spend half his time in Coors Field. According to Hampton, "This was a place I could move my family to without having to take my kid out of school every three months. Colorado was the place for my family."

Sandy Alderson, then a vice president at Major League Baseball, responded in his typical no-bullshit way: "Announce the deal. It was a lot of money. Case closed. I don't want to hear about the Wheat Ridge school system."[1]

It was a lot of money. According to Bob Nightengale, the next-best offer was seven years and $105 million. The Cardinals, Mets, and Cubs all made serious offers. Hampton supposedly ruled out New York because he didn't want to live in New York. He supposedly ruled out the Cubs "because it could be years before they'd be serious contenders." And the Cardinals . . . well, their offer didn't even top $100 million.[2]

So we can guess what really motivated Hampton. But why would general manager Dan O'Dowd and the Rockies invest such huge amounts of money in two pitchers of considerable-but-less-than-heroic qualities? Essentially, O'Dowd became irrationally infatuated with a "plan" that was both untested and internally inconsistent. From O'Dowd's biography in the 2001 media guide (and you don't often read things like this in a media guide):

Conservative but dotted with *exciting risks*, the plan has three branches. First, it calls for a team of more athletic, defensively sound players, with an offense focused on quality at-bats and on-base percentage. The pitching staff should consistently throw strikes, with low walks/nine innings ratios, essentially a group of hurlers who don't defeat themselves. Second, the plan involves long-term strategic planning that *fixes costs while creating greater decision-making flexibility.* Finally . . . it ties every part of the organization into one focused goal: winning both on and off the field.

Italics mine *(all mine)*. And I wonder if the writer considered the wisdom of referencing *exciting risks* in an essay featuring commercial aviation as a running metaphor. The real problem, though, is with this supposed three-branched plan itself, which sounds less like a plan than some sort of marketing gimmick. Everybody wants athletic, defensively sound players: everybody wants an offense focused on quality at-bats, and does anybody look for hurlers who *do* defeat themselves? As for fixing costs while creating greater decision-making flexibility, those often are two competing imperatives, and O'Dowd proved much better at the first of them than the second. And the second is more important.

The Rockies signed Hampton and Neagle for a total of thirteen player-seasons; they wound up with five. Here's what happened over the next three seasons:

	W-L ERA	Innings	ERA+
Hampton '01	14-13 5.41	203	96
Neagle '01	9-8 5.38	171	97
Hampton '02	7-15 6.15	179	80
Neagle '02	8-11 5.26	164	93
Hampton '03	w/Braves	–	–
Neagle '03	2-4 7.90	35	60

What happened to Hampton? Prior to signing with the Rockies, Hampton had started four games at Coors Field, going 4–0 with a 5.72 ERA.[3] Of course 5.72 isn't good, but for Coors Field it wasn't bad, either. And in his two seasons with the Rockies, Hampton posted a 5.73 ERA at Coors. That wasn't the problem. The problem was that his ERA on the road over those two seasons was 5.77.[4]

On November 16, 2002, the Mike Hampton branch of the plan was officially pruned. Whatever his faults, Dan O'Dowd is a wizard at "moving bad money," and he got together with Marlins general manager Larry Beinfest—who had some bad money of his own—for a blockbuster deal. The Rockies sent Hampton and Juan Pierre to the Marlins for a quartet of players, including Preston Wilson and Charles Johnson. The Marlins would be on the hook for most of Hampton's contract (and two days later they traded Hampton to the Braves), and the Rockies would be on the hook for the $44 million still owed to Wilson and Johnson.

It was a great deal for the Rockies, considering that Wilson and Johnson were, though terribly overpaid, at least moderately useful. The Rockies weren't completely off the hook with Hampton, though. They still owed him a deferred signing bonus ($19 million, with interest) and $6 million to buy out a 2009 contract option, and they paid $6.5 million to help pay his salaries from 2003 through 2005. Overall, the Rockies wound up spending—or rather, will eventually wind up spending—roughly $52 million for two seasons and twenty-one wins: $2.5 million per win.

There wouldn't be any trading Neagle, though; while the Braves—who wound up with Hampton—thought Hampton still had something in the tank, apparently nobody held such illusions regarding Neagle, who missed most of 2003 and all of '04 with various injuries.

And on December 3, 2004—almost exactly four years after he signed his deal with the Rockies—Neagle was pulled over in a Denver suburb for speeding. There was a woman in the car with him who wasn't his wife, and this woman told the police that she'd been paid forty dollars to perform a sex act (one that's relatively easy to perform in a moving vehicle). A year earlier, Neagle had pled guilty to drunk driving.

On December 6, the Rockies terminated Neagle's contract, citing section 7(b)(1) of the Uniform Player Contract, which states a team can terminate a contract if a player shall "fail, refuse or neglect to conform his personal conduct to the standards of good citizenship and good sportsmanship or to keep himself in first-class physical condition." Presumably it was Neagle's citizenship, rather than his sportsmanship, with which the Rockies found fault.

Actually, it was his contract they didn't like. At that point, the Rockies still owed Neagle $19 million: $10 million for 2005 and a $9.5 million buyout of the club's 2006 option. I understand that salaries in the entertainment industry can seem hard to understand (if not downright ridiculous to people who actually work for a living), but I still can't help thinking about how much money that is, particularly when every single penny would be utterly wasted.

Win-Win

Believe it or not, despite committing more than $170 million to Denny Neagle and Mike Hampton, Dan O'Dowd wasn't quite finished. As *Baseball Weekly* noted, "With Hampton and Denny Neagle signing heavily backloaded contracts, general manager Dan O'Dowd hopes to use some of the saving to redo the contract of NL batting champ Todd Helton." [5]

Saving.

And roughly three months after consummating two of the worst deals in major-league history, O'Dowd convinced Todd Helton to sign a nine-year contract extension that would lock up Helton through the 2011 season.

2011.

And for the privilege of keeping Helton for all those seasons, the Rockies agreed to pay him $141.5 million. Sure, that might seem like a lot of years and a lot of money. But Helton did make one concession. If the Rockies want to keep him for an extra season—2012, when he'll turn thirty-nine—it's *their* option. He can't do a single thing about it. All the Rockies have to do is pay Helton another $23 million, and he's all theirs for one more glorious season. A *bonus* season.

Maybe that's what they meant by "decision-making flexibility."

Well, almost every penny. Neagle and his people filed a grievance, of course. And faced with almost certain defeat before an arbitrator, the Rockies agreed to give Neagle $16 million to go away, finally. So for $43.5 million—$51.5 million, less the $3.5 million from that settlement, less $4.5 million in insurance money they collected on Neagle's 2004 arm injury—the Rockies wound up with nineteen wins, twenty-three losses, and a 5.57 ERA. Or to put it another way, the Rockies paid Neagle $2.3 million per win.

What's worse, though, is what else they *might* have gotten for that $43.5 million, whether in the way of pitching, hitting, better lawn care, whatever.

Improbably enough, Dan O'Dowd, the man who engineered the signings of Hampton and Neagle, is still, as I write this, piloting the big plane in Denver. I've spent some time with O'Dowd, and I can confidently report that he's a bright, friendly, and open-minded sort of fellow. And considering that O'Dowd hasn't been fired after five straight sub-.500 finishes and two super-mega-catastrophes like Hampton and Neagle, he must be one hell of a good talker, too.

---

1. Bob Nightengale, "Inside Pitch," *USA Today Baseball Weekly*, Dec. 13–19, 2000.

2. Bob Nightengale, "Hampton Opts to take the Rockie Road," *USA Today Baseball Weekly*, Dec. 13–19, 2000.

3. *USA Today Baseball Weekly*, Dec. 13–19, 2000.

4. Jim Callis, http://www.baseballamerica.com, Nov. 16, 2002.

5. *USA Today Baseball Weekly*, December 13–19, 2000.

CUBS HIRE DUSTY BAKER

I remember my old general manager Al Campanis telling me that a player doesn't reach his peak until he's somewhere between thirty-two or thirty-six and beyond, and it depends on how his legs are and his desire and if he keeps his weight down and his waistline down.

—Dusty Baker (2005)

"Thirty-six *and beyond.*"

Well, that explains a lot. It's not that Dusty Baker has anything against young players. It's just that Matt Murton, Ronny Cedeño, and Jason Dubois (and Hee Seop Choi and Juan Cruz and Mark Bellhorn, etc.) needed another ten years of seasoning. One wonders, in light of this new data on the theoretical peak of baseball players, how the Cubs could have let free agent Jeromy Burnitz get away last winter. He was only thirty-seven! Great seasons may lie just . . . *beyond!*

In 2003, Baker's first year as Cubs manager, Lenny Harris batted 146 times and hit .183, which, if you follow baseball, you know is not very good. But as the soulless, pasty-white stats geeks who live in their mothers' basements with their computers for best friends are always telling us, batting average ain't everything. Harris's on-base percentage plus slugging percentage was 484, roughly sixty-three percent of the league average. This is about as bad as

major-league ballplayers are allowed to play before they're retired in the interest of, if nothing else, their own safety. Willie Harris of the White Sox posted a slightly lower OPS in a similar number of plate appearances that season, but then, he was only twenty-five, and thus still a decade or so away from his peak.

That same season, Shawn Estes, the Cubs' fifth starter—well, it's probably more appropriate to say he was their *last* starter, because if the Cubs had suddenly decided on a thirty-seven-man rotation, he'd have been No. 37—posted a 5.74 ERA in twenty-eight starts. No pitcher in the league who pitched as many innings was as bad.

All of this happened in the middle of a pennant race. Even though Baker started Estes every five days and used Lenny Harris as his main bat off the bench (and even, for a while, as his starting third baseman), the Cubs won eighty-eight games and the Central Division title, edging the Astros by a single game.

It shouldn't have been nearly that close. Dusty

Dusty's Rookies

Dusty Baker has never managed a Rookie of the Year Award winner. Well, Todd Hollandsworth, Eric Karros, and Nomar Garciaparra, but you know what we mean: no player has ever won the award *while being managed by Baker*. In fact, no one has ever come close.

In 1994, Dusty's second year with the Giants, William Van Landingham (who?) received nine points in Rookie voting, good for seventh place. In 2002, Dusty's last year with the Giants, Ryan Jensen came in sixth place with four points. That's it. That's the list. Ten years in San Francisco and three years with the Cubs have yielded exactly thirteen points in Rookie of the Year voting.

Since 1993, eleven Braves (almost one per season) have received at least one point in the balloting, including Rafael Furcal (who won in 2000), Chipper Jones (who came in second in 1995), Greg McMichael (second, 1993), Ryan Klesko (third, 1994), Andruw Jones (fifth, 1997), and Jeff Francoeur (third, 2005).

Joe Torre has managed five players who placed fourth or better in Rookie of the Year voting, and that's only counting his tenure with the Yankees. Ten other players received Rookie of the Year votes with the Mets, Braves, and Cardinals while under Torre's tutelage.

Tony La Russa managed Albert Pujols (first), Rick Ankiel (second), and Matt Morris (third). Felipe Alou managed Brad Wilkerson (second), Moises Alou (second), Brad Fullmer (fifth), Vlad Guerrero (sixth), Cliff Floyd (fifth), and Wil Cordero and Kirk Rueter (they tied for seventh in

Baker had better options than Lenny Harris and Shawn Estes. It's just that those other options were younger or had some other disqualifying defect . . . for example, the ability and desire to take pitches for balls.

"[Mark Bellhorn] has been programmed, before we got him, by the A's," Baker observed early in the season. "Their philosophy is taking a lot of pitches and getting deep in the count. Most times, I notice guys who come from the American League to the National League weren't used to being aggressive and took a lot of pitches. It's going to take time to change your mind-set." *Programmed*, mind you. Not taught, or encouraged, but rather brainwashed by the soulless automatons in Oakland. (They probably used computers to do it, too. Bastards.)

Throughout the season, an unspoken tension seemed to exist between Baker and general manager Jim Hendry, at least when it came to matters of personnel. Time and again, Hendry would promote or trade for a player, only to have him languish on the bench. Rather than order Baker to play Choi or Bellhorn, Hendry seemed to adopt a strategy of moving players Dusty didn't favor, and bringing in ones he did, whenever possible. Thus, Randall Simon, Jose Hernandez, and Tony Womack were acquired, and Bellhorn was jettisoned (this pattern repeated itself in 2005, when Jason Dubois was traded to Cleveland). Choi, who barely played in September '03 and was left off the roster for both of the Cubs' postseason series, was sent to the Marlins in November, in a challenge trade for Derrek Lee. That deal obviously worked out, but most such transactions, made not so much to improve the team but to indulge the manager's predilections, did not. In this way, Baker had de facto control over the roster.

After a heartbreaking loss in the 2003 NLCS, it was hoped that Derrek Lee, newly acquired free agents Todd Walker and Greg Maddux, and a full season from Aramis Ramirez would spur the Cubs to greater glory in 2004. And with the departures of Choi, Eric Karros, and Bellhorn, the starting roster was basically set, leaving Baker with fewer opportunities for mischief. Nevertheless, it's hard to understand why Tom Goodwin was allowed to step up to the plate 184 times in 2004. He was thirty-five and absolutely punchless (.200/.254/.276) in what would turn out to be his last season. It seems like a lot of ballplayers end their careers as Cubs. Rey Ordoñez also played his last season with the Cubs in '04. He was worse than Goodwin.

Jose Macias, a crummy ballplayer in his own right, batted almost 400 times in 2004 and 2005. That's a lot of chances for a batter with a sub-.300 OBP. Could Dusty have used, say, Jerry Hairston in his place? I suppose he could have, but Hairston is four years younger than Macias, and besides, Dusty doesn't like Jerry Hairston. On July 20, 2005, with Hairston sporting a nifty .369 OBP, Dusty remarked, "Hairston is doing pretty good. We still want him to stay out of hitting the ball in the air. We want him to be more aggressive running on the bases too. But he's getting better." This grudging tribute remains, by a considerable margin, the nicest thing Baker has ever said about Jerry Hairston.

Does Dusty know the difference between a good ballplayer and a bad one? His handling of Todd Hollandsworth would suggest that he does not. Hollandsworth, or "Holly," as Dusty invariably calls him, is a fine fourth outfielder, and had a nice season in limited duty with the Cubs in '04. But after losing Moises Alou to free agency, Baker, resisting all entreaties to play Jason Dubois (who'd smacked fifty-seven extra-base hits with Iowa the previous year), stretched Hollandsworth into a regular role in '05, one for which he'd spent many years proving he was ill-suited. Around the time Dubois was thrown overboard, Matt Murton, a superior outfield prospect obtained from the Red Sox in the Nomar Garciaparra deal, was 1) promoted to the majors and 2) essentially ignored by his manager. Despite Murton's hitting .337/.396/.505 at three levels in 2005, it wasn't until Jim Hendry sent Hollandsworth to Atlanta at the trade deadline that Murton was given the chance to play that he'd already earned.

So Baker doesn't like young players (always making their "young player mistakes"), he holds weird grudges against guys named "Jerry," and he disdains players who draw walks (Barry Bonds notwithstanding). Does he have any virtues as a manager?

Perhaps. But these are serious weaknesses to overcome. Pity the poor G.M. who hires Dusty as his manager. His odd penchant for Proven Veterans™ adds a complicating element to the job. Instead of simply hiring or promoting players who might help your team, Dusty's general managers must also wonder . . . Will Dusty play Jason Dubois or Mark Bellhorn or Ronny Cedeño? Or will he bench them in favor of older, lesser players like Todd Hollandsworth or Neifi Pérez, whom Dusty viewed in 2005 as some sort of savior: "I hear a lot of people say, 'Hey, put Cedeño in.' What am I supposed to do, push Neifi out now? This guy has *saved* us."

But who will save Cub fans from Dusty?

—Jason Brannon and R.N.

1993). Lou Pinella managed Freddy Garcia (second), Jonny Gomes (third), and Rocco Baldelli (third).

What does all this mean? Don't bet on Adam Greenberg being the National League's Rookie of the Year in 2006.—*J.B.*

LITTLE KILLS SOX

Red Sox seasons die the deaths of spaghetti western cowboys: never graceful, but rather writhing, painful and melodramatic. This ending, at the hands of Boone and the Yankees, was true to form. Five outs from the World Series with a three-run lead, no one on base and their best starting pitcher on the mound, the Red Sox lost the lead without ever using their bullpen. Nobody but the Sox could lose a game so spectacularly.

Tom Verducci, *Sports Illustrated*

If you don't mind, I'll dispense with an extensive setup. Sufficing: *Yankees, Red Sox. American League Championship Series. Game 7. Roger Clemens, Pedro Martinez. Yankee Stadium.* Ready? Let's go . . .

In the fourth inning, the Red Sox knocked Clemens out of the game. Jason Giambi led off the bottom of the fifth with a home run, but otherwise Martinez was cruising.

After a "rather easy" sixth inning, though, Martinez sat on the bench and said to assistant trainer Chris Correnti, "Chris, I'm a little fatigued."[1]

No wonder. It had been a long season, Martinez wasn't the stoutest of pitchers, and the mental pressure must have been immense. And the Yankee lineup allowed little chance for coasting.

The seventh inning wasn't remotely easy. Giambi homered again, making the score 4–2. Enrique Wilson and Karim Garcia singled. Martinez escaped the seventh by striking out Alfonso Soriano, but it took him six pitches (which might have been Soriano's

season high). He'd thrown twenty-one pitches in the seventh, and exactly one hundred in the game.

From 2001 through 2003, Pedro Martinez was essentially unhittable through his first 105 pitches: .200 batting average, .253 on-base percentage, .301 slugging percentage. And he was even tougher on pitches 92–105 than pitches 1–15.

But after 105 pitches, his performance seemed to suffer (and yes, I know 105 is arbitrary, but it's a nice round number and it's what we've got). While Martinez rarely was allowed to face more than a few batters after reaching 105 pitches—only thirty-eight hitters concluded their plate appearances on a pitch numbered so high—the difference was fairly dramatic. Those thirty-eight plate appearances resulted in a .291 batting average and a .392 on-base percentage.

In 2003, Boston's bullpen had been a disaster, the biggest story in town for most of the season. Red

Sox relievers posted a 4.83 ERA, third-worst in the league. Statistically, the most impressive member of the Red Sox bullpen was Byung-Hyun Kim, who saved sixteen games during the regular season. But Kim became progressively more irrelevant as the season progressed. He pitched to only three batters in Boston's division series against the A's, and the Red Sox, no doubt remembering his meltdown against the Yankees in the 2001 World Series, didn't even bother including Kim on their ALCS roster.

On the other hand, Alan Embree, Mike Timlin, and Scott Williamson—all of whom had pitched decently enough in the regular season—had been outstanding in the postseason. Against the Yankees, they'd combined to pitch eleven-plus innings and allow just five hits and one run—and they'd been even better against the A's in the division series. Here are the postseason numbers, through the seventh inning of Game 7, for those three relievers:

	IP	Hits	K's	ERA
Timlin	8⅓	1	10	0.00
W'll'ms'n	8	3	6	1.13
Embree	6⅓	4	1	1.42
Totals	22⅔	8	17	0.79

Perhaps all the talk about the Red Sox bullpen during the season had poisoned Grady Little's mind, but it shouldn't have; the guys who did most of the damage that summer were Ramiro Mendoza (6.75 ERA), Todd Jones (5.52), and a bunch of lesser lights not even on the postseason roster. Little had no reason for an acute lack of confidence in Embree, Timlin, and Williamson. The trio had been effective in all ten postseason games in which one or more of them had been employed. So why not eleven?

In the top of the eighth, David Ortiz homered to restore Boston's three-run lead.

In the bottom of the eighth, Pedro Martinez took the mound. He retired Nick Johnson on a pop-up, but it took him seven pitches. Martinez got two quick strikes on Derek Jeter, but Jeter drove the next pitch over right fielder Trot Nixon's head for a double. The Red Sox were still ahead by three runs and they still had the league's best pitcher on the mound. But said pitcher had thrown 110 pitches in an incredibly stressful game.

On Fox, the following exchange took place after the count on Bernie Williams went to 2–1, Martinez having then thrown 113 pitches:

October 14, 2003

In 1986, Bill Buckner let a ball go through his legs, and fans point to that moment as the downfall of the Red Sox. However, twice in the same game, Buckner batted with runners on base and two outs, and ended the inning. Boston's No. 3 hitter batted with men on every time he was up in that game, and did not drive in a run. He hit just .188 in the World Series. Yes, Bill Buckner was to blame for that series, but it was his offense, not his error, that caused all the pain.

In Chicago, nearly seventeen years later, a ball was popped into the night sky. It drifted foul down the left-field line. Moises Alou kept his eye on the ball as he headed for the wall in foul territory. Steve Bartman, sitting in the front row, also kept his eye on the ball. Alou saw an out. Bartman saw a souvenir. The souvenir hunter's hand got there first—he had the benefit of elevation—and a potential out vanished. Soon, the Cubs' 3–0 lead melted away, the win became a loss, and a World Series berth disappeared.

Steve Bartman became the focus of the fans' ire and the media's attention. Dusty Baker became the beneficiary of Bartman's larceny.

Mark Prior, pitching a shutout, had started the eighth inning. He hadn't quite thrown one hundred pitches yet, and the Marlins had managed only three hits in the first seven innings. Still, it was late in the game, and after an out and a double the following note was recorded: "Fox just pointed out that there is no action in the Cubs

Grady Little and Pedro Martinez, 2003 ALCS Game 7.

Joe Buck: With Matsui the left-handed-hitting outfielder on deck, Alan Embree the lefty is getting ready in the bullpen for the Red Sox.

Tim McCarver: And you get the feeling that he will be the pitcher who gets Matsui, one way or the other.

Au contraire, mon frère. Au contraire . . .
Two pitches later, Williams drove a single to center field, scoring Jeter.

Buck: Grady Little out of the dugout . . . With 115 pitches on the night, Grady Little is going to stick with his starter.

McCarver: He gave Martinez the chance to say yay or nay. He said yes.

Three pitches later, Hideki Matsui drove an 0–2 pitch down the line for an automatic double.

McCarver: The way I see this, this is the most blatant situation for a second-guess in this series: whether to bring Embree in to pitch to Matsui or not. If you're not going to bring him in against Matsui, where are you gonna make that move?

Pedro Martinez's 123rd pitch was a fastball in Jorge Posada's kitchen. Posada lofted a flare into short center field, almost perfectly centered between Johnny Damon, Nomar Garciaparra, and Todd Walker. The ball dropped, and both runners scored.

And finally, with the game tied, Grady Little made a move. Three innings later, Aaron Boone hit a knuckleball a long ways. The (supposed) Curse endured.

When Embree and Timlin finally did pitch in Game 7, with the horse already out of the barn and over the hill, they again pitched well (Williamson never did pitch, but that's a particular sort of blunder—losing a close game without ever using your best pitcher—that we'll discuss elsewhere).

Why didn't Little use Embree against Matsui, with one run in and one runner on base? Or Timlin against Posada, with runners on second and third, still only one out? Why wait to employ his bullpen until the game was tied?

According to Tom Verducci in *Sports Illustrated*, "Little would later tell club officials that, as well as the trio had pitched, he did not trust them to keep their nerves under control in such a pressurized spot. He trusted no one more than Martinez."

I would trust Martinez, too—*if he were in condition to pitch.* But by the accounts of almost everybody watching, participating in, or listening to the game, Martinez was no longer Martinez. He didn't belong in the game after Bernie Williams plated Jeter.

In the locker room afterward, Little said to Martinez, "Petey, I might not be here anymore."

"Why?" Martinez asked. "It's not your fault. It's up to the players. Any other situation I get the outs, and you're a hero."

True enough. And when Grady Little got fired, there were people who thought it unfair. Sure, he'd made a mistake. But everybody makes mistakes. What a lot of people didn't understand, though, was that Little didn't just make a mistake. *He didn't do as he was told.* A manager is an employee, and like almost any employee he must answer to his employers. As an organization, the Red Sox devoted a great deal of their resources to preparation, and management had gone to unusual lengths to make sure Little knew that Pedro wasn't *Pedro* after throwing 105 or 110 pitches. He knew it, and ignored it.

Of course, it could have worked out. If Posada's pop fly had dropped into a Red Sox glove—as it easily could have—the Red Sox would likely have won, and Little would likely still be managing the Red Sox today. But at the

bullpen. I think that's a mistake this late in the game. You have to be ready for anything."

Prior goes 3–2 on Luis Castillo before Kyle Farnsworth starts throwing in the bullpen. On the next pitch, Steve Bartman enters baseball lore. No big deal, though: Prior just needs to get the out.

Prior throws ball four. Still, nobody in the bullpen is ready.

Then! A single by Ivan Rodriguez. An error by shortstop Alex Gonzalez. It's 3–1. Bartman is gone, escorted from his seat to protect his safety. Derrek Lee steps to the plate. Farnsworth is still getting loose. Lee doubles, and it's 3–3. Farnsworth is finally ready to pitch. It's too late. The Marlins are on a roll, and score five more runs to salt away the game.

What really makes this managerial gaffe inexcusable is that Dusty did not learn from his own mistake. Just a year earlier, in Game 7 of the 2002 World Series, with Baker managing the Giants, Livan Hernandez struggled in the first inning, but escaped thanks to David Eckstein's baserunning blunder. It was Game 7; there was no reason to save anyone. Dusty did not have the bullpen going in the second inning, and Hernandez gave up three runs. That was enough, and the Giants lost the game and the Series.—*David Pinto* single most important moment of his career, Little didn't make the decision he should have made, didn't make the decision he'd been *told* to make.

It got him fired. And he had to wait two years for another job.

---

1. Tom Verducci, "5 Outs Away," *Sports Illustrated*, Oct. 11, 2004.

MO GETS MO' REST

. . . But that's the way I've always managed. I'm more concerned about winning the game than trying to cover my butt.

Joe Torre, *Chasing the Dream*

As you might remember, the New York Yankees were heavily favored to beat the Florida Marlins in the 2003 World Series. The Yankees won 101 games during the regular season, outscoring their opponents by 161 runs. The Marlins won ninety-one games, outscoring their opponents by fifty-nine runs. The Yankees spent roughly $150 million on their players in 2003; the Marlins, something like a third of that. And of course, the Yankees were *the Yankees* while the Marlins were just . . . well, the decidedly non-italicized Marlins. Faced with the pinstripes and the superstars and the *mystique*, the upstarts might just fall to the turf and assume a sort of collective fetal position.

And for about four days, it looked like that's exactly what might happen. In Game 1, the Yankees managed to score only two runs despite getting fourteen men on base, and the Marlins eked out a 3–2 win. Games 2 and 3, though, went according to

form, with first Andy Pettitte and then Mike Mussina pitching the Yankees to 6–1 wins.

Game 4 pitted Roger Clemens (17–9, 3.91) against Carl Pavano (12–13, 4.30). Pavano pitched the big game of his life, and when Nick Johnson pinch-hit for Clemens in the top of the eighth, the Marlins were up 3–1. Johnson made out, as did Soriano and Jeter. The Yankees still trailed, and Joe Torre needed a new pitcher to face the heart of the Marlins' lineup.

Torre chose Jeff Nelson, who blanked the Marlins in the bottom of the eighth.

In the top of the ninth, Ruben Sierra's two-out triple tied the game.

Torre could have stuck with Nelson in the bottom of the ninth, but instead he summoned Jose Contreras, who shut out Florida that inning and again in the tenth.

In the top of the eleventh, the Yankees loaded the

bases with nobody out, but couldn't score. In the bottom of the eleventh, Torre replaced Contreras with Jeff Weaver, who hadn't pitched against the Red Sox in the League Championship Series, nor against the Twins in the Division Series . . . in fact, Weaver hadn't thrown an official pitch in nearly a month. And that was just three batters, on September 24.

One wonders why Weaver was even on the roster, considering that his ERA with the Yankees that season was 5.99. Anyway, Weaver did all right in the eleventh, the Yankees didn't score in the twelfth, and Alex Gonzalez led off the bottom of the twelfth with a walk-off home run to even the Series at two games apiece.

What one *really* wonders is how Joe Torre could manage to lose an incredibly close game without ever using Mariano Rivera, his best pitcher. Every October, some nitwit manager does this, and every year it makes me crazy. Yes, Torre was holding Rivera until the Yankees got a lead. Until there was a *save situation* (he wrote, disdain dripping from his fingers).

Except the Yankees never got a lead, and so there never was a save situation. And they never got a lead, in part, because Torre was holding Mariano Rivera until the Yankees got a lead. It was a Catch-42.

Or maybe Torre felt like he needed to conserve Rivera because Rivera pitched two innings in Game 3 and might well be needed for Game 5. To which I would respond, "Then why did you let Rivera pitch a second inning in Game 3 when you had a five-run lead? Wasn't *that* the time to baptize Wild Man Weaver in the postseason waters?"

Prior to Game 3—in which he threw only twenty-three pitches—Rivera hadn't pitched in four days. I know exactly why Torre didn't use Rivera in Game 4. He didn't use Rivera because he was afraid. He was afraid that if he used Rivera for a couple of innings before the Yankees took a lead, he'd have to use Contreras or Weaver or Chris Hammond in the "save situation." Which is problematic for most managers (not just Torre), because a) they believe that many pitchers are psychologically incapable of finishing games, and b) they're afraid of the second-guessing that would ensue if they burned their closer in a non-save situation, then saw a subsequent reliever fail to preserve a lead.

Look, Jeff Weaver (or Chris Hammond or whoever) might have lost Game 4 eventually. We have absolutely no way of knowing. But isn't it obvious that in a close game, you want to delay using your worst pitcher for as long as you possibly can? Yes, if Rivera pitched while the game was still tied, there was an excellent chance that Weaver or Hammond would eventually have been asked to protect a lead. But what's more difficult? Protecting a tie, or a lead that might be one run or (quite possibly) some larger number?

Amorphous psychological considerations aside, it's pretty obvious that protecting a tie is more difficult than protecting anything else.

I'm not sure the Culture of the Save is really so terrible. It makes the manager's job easier because he doesn't have to think too hard, and it probably makes the reliever's job easier because he knows exactly what his job is. Also, a set role for the ace reliever has the (probably) positive effect of limiting his workload.

But the equation changes in October. Once you're in the World Series, you don't have to worry about Mariano Rivera's workload—and Torre, to his great and everlasting credit, often has used Rivera for two innings in postseason games—and it's the manager's responsibility to think harder than he does from April through September.

The Yankees lost Game 5, and then they lost Game 6 when Josh Beckett pitched a shutout. There was no Game 7, but if Joe Torre hadn't been trying to cover his butt, or slavishly conforming to mindless convention, there might have been.

APPENDIX: BLUNDERS BY TEAM (VICTIMS AND BENEFICIARIES)

Angels: 147, 152, 194, 242, 245

Astros: 193, 194, 247, 249, 259

Athletics: 74, 80, 84, 95, 151, 155, 179, 186, 248

Blue Jays: 127, 158, 196, 208

Braves: 196, 198

Brewers: 18, 39, 73, 77, 78, 81, 82, 127, 132, 154, 169

Cardinals: 18, 39, 73, 77, 78, 81, 82, 127, 132, 154, 169

Cubs: 31, 45, 73, 77, 78, 81, 82, 127, 132, 154, 169

Devil Rays: 168, 268

Diamondbacks: 71

Dodgers: 40, 47, 57, 70, 77, 82, 89, 91, 111, 120, 156, 224, 225, 228, 234, 237, 240, 241, 243, 254

Expos: 126, 193, 239, 253

Giants: 24, 31, 70, 76, 78, 93, 111, 192, 199, 244

Indians: 32, 34, 65, 74, 79, 121, 123, 134, 174, 192, 199, 200, 211, 247

Mariners: 152, 202, 255

Marlins: 156, 232, 273

Mets: 146, 151, 196, 226

Orioles (née Browns): 34, 60, 120, 137, 139, 141, 193, 197, 241, 251

Padres: 198

Phillies: 129, 154, 158, 169, 195, 228, 234, 248

Pirates: 11, 21, 31, 96, 123, 200

Rangers (née Senators): 124, 151, 154, 161

Red Sox: 5, 37, 47, 65, 77, 165, 181, 194, 226, 238, 249, 268

Reds: 76, 81, 126, 139, 192, 193, 234

Rockies: 261

Royals: 146, 150, 196, 230

Tigers: 24, 32, 35, 80, 134, 162, 236, 243

White Sox: 1, 33, 80, 102, 127, 152, 154, 176, 215, 235

Yankees: 5, 18, 34, 37, 42, 52, 57, 77, 81, 84, 155, 158, 165, 183, 208, 255, 268, 273

Twins (née Senators): 11, 22, 35, 79, 153, 194, 236

THANKING MY PEOPLES

I've certainly made my share of blunders over the years. But I must not have made *too* many, otherwise I wouldn't have so many fine humans (and one canine) on my side. What follows is a partial accounting. . . .

First, the contributors, all of whom brought something to the party that I could not: Mark Armour, Jim Baker, Jason Brannon, Maury Brown, Rany Jazayerli, Mike Kopf, Richard Lally, David Mlodinoff, David Pinto, Keith Scherer, and Don Zminda. In addition to penning actual essays, most of these guys also contributed ideas that wound up within these pages, and Jason helped a great deal with research. Allen Barra, Rich Burk, and Rob Nelson also contributed ideas that wound up in the book (or should have).

Joey Berlin, Calvin Bohn, Jim Callis, Joshua Field, Bill James, Joshua Prager, Alan Schwarz, Lee Sinins, Glenn Stout, and Dave Treder all responded to my various calls for help, and always with good humor and fair speed. Hosannas also to David Smith and all the other good people of Retrosheet, any baseball author's best friend. Bobby Plapinger, who's been feeding my always expansive and sometimes expensive hunger for baseball books for nearly twenty years—has it really been that long, Bobby?—remains as accommodating as ever when I simply must have this or that obscure tome before the weekend. And special thanks are reserved for Bill Deane, my main man in Cooperstown.

For their help in acquiring the photos herein, thanks to the Los Angeles Dodgers and Mark Langill; the National Baseball Hall of Fame and Pat Kelly; Mike Webber, Mary Brace, and Mark Rucker.

This is my fifth book and, as usual, my editors at ESPN.com accommodated my moonlighting in good cheer. This time around, their number includes David Kull, Matt Szefc, Eric Ortiz, and Marty Bernoski.

My agent remains Jay Mandel of the William Morris Agency. When Jay first agreed to represent me, seven years ago, he was rustling up talent in a small literary agency, and I was just an Internet columnist trying to convince people that Nolan Ryan really wasn't *all that* (hey, that's how we talked in the '90s). Now Jay's got a big office with a window in a tall building, and an assistant, and I'm just an Internet columnist trying to convince people. . . . Anyway, what success I've enjoyed in the Super Exciting World of Book Publishing can mostly be blamed on Jay, and today I'm just as grateful for Jay's support and enthusiasm as I was seven years ago.

My editor remains Brant Rumble. This is my third book with Brant, there's a fourth in the pipeline, and I am absolutely convinced that there's no other editor in the world with whom I'd be as happy. Brant's my point man at Fireside, but this book wouldn't be in your hands without the good work of Anna deVries, Mark Gompertz, Trish Todd, Chris Lloreda,

Debbie Model, Megan Clancy, Sarah Bellgraph, Lisa Healy, Joy O'Meara, Marcia Burch, and publicist Jamie McDonald. And I'd like to offer a special measure of gratitude to copy editor Tom Pitoniak, who—with his annoying red pencil—not only made this book better, but also taught me some lessons I hope I remember.

As always, I'm grateful to Bob Valvano, Brian Kenny, Bob Haynie, Bill Hayes, Kevin Kugler, Norm Wamer, Max Kellerman, and Kevin Cremin for doing what they do and allowing me to occasionally participate. I'm grateful to David Fine for being the necessary fourth and to David Schoenfield, John Sickels, and Eddie Epstein for much more than will fit here.

Something else that won't fit: my feelings for Kristien, Micah, and Terra. They all deserve more attention than they get—well, not Terra—but somehow they manage to survive without me for the few months that I'm chained to whichever book I'm writing at the moment. Officially, I haven't yet dedicated a book to Kristien or Micah. But in my heart, all my books are dedicated to them.

And finally, this book is for you. Thanks for reading.

INDEX

Add these books from Rob Neyer to your baseball library.

Rob Neyer's
BIG BOOK OF BASEBALL LINEUPS

A COMPLETE GUIDE TO THE BEST, WORST,
AND MOST MEMORABLE PLAYERS TO
EVER GRACE THE MAJOR LEAGUES

ROB NEYER

ESPN BASEBALL ANALYST AND COAUTHOR OF *BASEBALL DYNASTIES*

"Rob Neyer is the best of the new generation of sportswriters. He knows baseball history like a child
knows his piggy bank. He knows how to pick it up and shake it and make what he needs fall out."
—BILL JAMES

THE
NEYER/JAMES
GUIDE TO PITCHERS

AN HISTORICAL COMPENDIUM
OF PITCHING, PITCHERS, AND PITCHES

BILL JAMES AND ROB NEYER

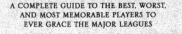

0-7432-4174-6

0-7432-6158-5

*Available now wherever books are sold
or at www.simonsays.com.*

FIRESIDE
A Division of Simon & Schuster
A VIACOM COMPANY